OUTSTANDING PRAISE FOR
CITIZEN KOCH

"It's quintessential Koch. If you like him, you'll find the book very readable and enjoyable; if you don't, you'll probably find it irritating."

—New York *Daily News*

"Here he reminisces about his pre- and post-political life. Gabby, caustic, funny, a self-described liberal with sanity, Koch has a blustering public persona backed by astute, subway-stop politicking."

—*Booklist*

"Thanks no doubt to Mr. Paisner, the Koch voice is here. Most substantially, his book catches important changes in the attitudes of New York liberals between the 60s and 90s."

—*The New York Times Book Review*

"Patriots will be heartened to learn that the former mayor of New York City hasn't lost his edge."

—*Publishers Weekly*

"Pungent and zestful."

—*Library Journal*

"While earlier books have rehashed political battles, this one . . . deals with personal moments. Testy as ever, with some juicy dish and a few good spite stories you can cheer."

—*Kirkus Reviews*

"A real eye-opener. More personal than his previous tomes, the book describes his childhood, his lonely, boring years in Washington as a congressman and the problems he encountered with his bachelorhood as a mayoral candidate in New York. The outspoken Koch pulls no punches when writing about his foes or opponents. As usual, he speaks his mind and lets his hair down—what's left of it."

—*North Jersey Herald & News*

"It's a rich account of names, obligations, valuing kindnesses, and getting even, and it's gossipy, politically sensitive and full of the push-pull that can evoke both a smile and a cringe while taking the city's pulse."

—*Staten Island Advance*

"Certainly he's extremely forthcoming . . . he's honest, too . . . as fresh and exciting as some of Koch's earlier works—MAYOR and POLITICS, for example. A good read."

—*Minneapolis Star Tribune*

"A far-ranging, entertaining autobiography."

—*Mobile Press-Register*

ED UNBUTTONED . . .

Son of immigrant parents, he worked as a hat-check boy in a Newark dancehall during the Depression, served as a humble infantry sergeant in World War II, then entered New York University Law School with no more than a high school diploma. After a promising career as a young attorney, Edward I. Koch took on the bruising arena of New York City politics—launching one of the most remarkable epochs in urban American life.

This is Ed Koch at his most pugnacious—and at his most personal. Here are recollections, both gracious and gritty, from his nine years as U.S. Congressman and three terms as New York's Mayor, his vivid encounters with major figures from the worlds of politics and show business, the eventful years after his departure from City Hall, as well as a candid account of his greatest crisis—when he was forced to contemplate suicide during the corruption scandals that clouded his third term.

**CITIZEN
KOCH**

Previous Books by Edward I. Koch

CITIZEN KOCH

An Autobiography

Edward I. Koch
with Daniel Paisner

ST. MARTIN'S PAPERBACKS

CITIZEN KOCH

Copyright © 1992 by Edward I. Koch with Daniel Paisner.

Cover photograph copyright © Benno Friedman.

Library of Congress Catalog Card Number: 92-18669

ISBN: 0-312-95098-5

Printed in the United States of America

St. Martin's Press hardcover edition/September 1992
St. Martin's Paperbacks edition/October 1993

10 9 8 7 6 5 4 3 2 1

To my mother and father, Joyce and Louis Koch,
who gave me life; and to the people of
New York City, who gave me the best years
of my life, and ultimately my liberty.

Contents

Acknowledgments

THIS BOOK WAS WRITTEN in collaboration with Daniel Paisner, whom I met after an introduction from the William Morris Agency. Robert Gottlieb, my literary agent there, submitted to me a list of people to consider working with on the project, and Dan was the first on the list. After our initial meeting, I didn't bother to look any further. I read Dan's most recent collaborative effort, which he wrote with television journalist Geraldo Rivera (and which was then climbing the best-seller lists and making headlines), and I confided to Dan that I couldn't possibly compete with many of Rivera's by then much-reported feats. He agreed to work with me anyway. I hope I haven't disappointed him.

I was further assisted by the insights of my closest friend, Allen Schwartz, and of my longtime friend and adviser Dan Wolf, who also edits my daily output of speeches, newspaper columns, and movie reviews.

The effort was also helped immeasurably by my staff assistant, Rosemarie Connors-McCallion, who is herself a talented writer and great researcher, and by my two wonderful secretaries, Mary Garrigan, who came to my Congressional office in Washington back in 1975 and has stayed with me ever since; and Mary Lehner, who is only twenty-four years old but whose common sense and phenomenal memory promise a brilliant career.

I am also grateful to my sister, Pat, and my brother, Harold, who read over relevant portions of the manuscript, and recalled for me incidents that I had omitted, and pointed out errors in what I had remembered.

Also, I want to acknowledge the contributions of Robert Pack, who helped to formulate many of my early ideas for this book, and Karen Chasin Kavanagh, who good-naturedly transcribed the long hours of interviews with Dan Paisner that formed the core of this book.

Lastly, I want to thank Tom Dunne and the entire publishing team at St. Martin's Press, for believing in this project, and for working to make it as successful as we all hope it will be.

Introduction

INDULGE ME FOR A MOMENT. I want to start out with a story. I like to tell stories, which will become abundantly evident as you stay with me through these pages. This is one of my recent favorites, and it fits at the beginning of this volume more than it does anywhere else. The story begins at the end, which is also a kind of beginning, as you'll see.

I moved out of Gracie Mansion at two o'clock in the morning, New Year's Day, 1990. I had lived there, as New York City's mayor, for twelve years, and a new tenant was moving in that day. I didn't want it to appear that I was reluctant to let go, but I thought I would treasure the last moment. I knew I wouldn't be coming back, even if invited. (In the nearly three years since I left, no invitation has been extended, and none appears to be forthcoming.)

What stays with me most about my leave-taking is not the last of the traditional New Year's Eve parties that immediately preceded it, nor the hectic uncertainty of dislocation that came immediately after, although each yielded its particular memories, pleasant and otherwise. No, what stays with me is a rather benign encounter on the streets of Greenwich Village the following week, during a trip to the supermarket. But I'll get to that. First, the story needs a little background, to savor it at its best.

The New Year's party was a fairly intimate and informal

gathering of about a hundred close personal friends and city commissioners, and my family, if you can imagine such an assemblage as anything resembling intimate and informal. I have been told that an invitation to one of these year-enders was seen as something of a hot ticket in my time, and I suspect it was, but I always saw the parties merely as a chance to relax, unwind, and celebrate with good friends and family, and to make good on some of the lingering political and social obligations that had invariably accumulated in the passing year.

This last party was bittersweet. I was not only leaving office, after serving twelve years as mayor of the most glorious and exciting city on this earth, but I was also leaving what had become my home, the beautiful and historic Gracie Mansion, a home where I had been pampered by an attentive staff who saw to my every waking need. I worried, in a small, private way, about the adjustments ahead. Consider, if you will, that for the previous twelve years virtually everything was taken care of for me, domestically speaking. I hadn't cooked or cleaned, or taken my own clothes to the cleaner or the laundry. I hadn't even made my own coffee. I was rusty to the point where the thought of a simple household chore—changing a fuse, or making a shopping list—was enough to give me pause. The mansion's household and security staff, which numbered about ten, was so attuned to my likes and dislikes that I sometimes wanted to run away from their constant concern and physical presence and be by myself. My retreat would be my bedroom, where I could be by myself with a good book, or an episode of "Masterpiece Theater" on the VCR. I appreciated the affection all these people had for me, and how easy they tried to make my life, but I sometimes felt as if the oxygen level had dropped and I was suffocating.

Even so, I wanted to linger at the mansion until the last possible minute. I was closing the door forever on a special period in my life. I didn't remain there until the eleventh hour (actually, the fourteenth) because I had any regrets about my three terms as mayor; I had none. I didn't remain there because I wanted to use the time to undo some aspect of my administration, or to finally do something I had not yet gotten around to; there was nothing to change, and nothing left to do. It was the end of an era for me, and I simply wanted to dwell on its final moment. The party was a kind of coda, or exclamation point, to one of the most important and exhilarating periods in my life, and in the lives of many of those around me. I like to think the moment signified the end of a special chapter for the city as well. My life wasn't over; I was entering, with some trepidation, into my third career.

Better, I was about to begin my third act.

By two in the morning, though, the party had clearly ended. It was time to go. I was the last to leave, along with Lee and Victor Botnick, two close friends who had served in my administration. Lee and Victor first met when they worked for me in Congress, so I felt as responsible for them in general as they did for me on this night in particular. The three of us went to my new Village apartment on lower Fifth Avenue. I was heading home; Lee and Victor were helping me to adjust. Believe me, I needed the assist. Oh, I knew where we were going, it's just that I didn't quite know what to do with myself when we got there. I couldn't believe the gizmos and gadgets that had been invented in the past twelve years, all of them, it seemed, not simply designed to make life easier but also to test me. I didn't know how to set up the coffee maker at night so a fresh-brewed pot would be waiting for me when I woke up the next morning; I didn't know this was an option. And the VCR? What a devilish little machine. I have now resigned myself to the constant flicker of its digital clock flashing, 12:00, 12:00, 12:00 . . . , which seems to be the preferred method of timekeeping in most Jewish households. At the mansion, there was always someone around to adjust the clock for me.

I am what my mother would have called a "gelamte," which is Yiddish for "cripple" and basically describes someone like me who finds it impossible to do with machines what even a child can do with ease. I understand there is now a machine you can point to the digital clock on the VCR, to set it or at least turn it off. If there isn't such a machine, someone should invent one.

Anyway, Lee and Victor helped me settle in for the night, and that was that. I was on my own. For the first time in a long while. If I called out in the middle of the night there would be no one to answer; that hadn't been true for twelve years. It was a little strange, that first week. Friends would call to see how I was doing, or if I needed anything. Some worried that I would be depressed, but I was fine. A little bit edgy, maybe, but fine. A few relatives and friends even worried that I would go into a real, clinical depression, that I would suffer some sort of letdown, leading just a normal life, without the hourly anxiety, without worrying about the budget, or the press, or the welfare of 7.5 million people. I knew that would not happen. I was fine. I had a stocked refrigerator and a new life to explore. I went to dinner with friends and to the movies. I caught up on some reading. I watched my "Masterpiece Theater" tapes. Some of my friends and family refused to believe I was as calm as I appeared, but I was. I realize it is not uncommon for someone leaving a high-profile public office to suffer from depression, but I slid into this next phase of my life with only a few difficult moments.

One of those moments came that very first week. Actually, to call it a difficult moment isn't entirely accurate. There wasn't anything difficult about it. It happened on a Saturday, as I recall, after one week in my new apartment. My supplies were running low. I had to go to the store, something I hadn't done (save for some campaign appearances that involved no actual shopping) since 1977. I walked up Fifth Avenue to Ninth Street, heading for Balducci's on Sixth Avenue. The people I passed, my new neighbors, were extravagantly gracious; their comments were like music: "It's great to have you back." "Welcome home." "You look terrific." "Don't blame me, I voted for you."

I have since gotten used to the post-mayoralty warmth and good feelings that often find me when I step out on the street (and I will always appreciate them), but back then it was a surprising comfort and a revelation. (The repeated cries of "Don't blame me, I voted for you," and such, led to a running joke: apparently, I lost the election after receiving 94 percent of the votes cast.) In the more than two years since I left office, rarely have I met anyone who hasn't claimed to have voted for me. At first, people would say, "I miss you," to which I would often reply (usually good-naturedly), "But you threw me out!"

"Not me!" they'd respond, emphatically.

"If not you, then who?" I'd shoot back, and then everyone would laugh.

By the second year of the Dinkins administration, as public attention began to focus on the next mayoral election, these man-on-the-street exchanges underwent a subtle shift. "I hope you'll run again," the people began to say, to which I would now reply, "No, the people threw me out. And the people must be punished!" Again, these exchanges were always good-humored, but underneath it all, I'm sure, I was playfully vengeful at having been denied a fourth term.

Okay. So there I was, basking in this affectionate glow, making my way to Balducci's to buy groceries. It was a lovely winter day. The sun was shining. I felt terrific. The weight of the city was off my shoulders. My own weight was soon to fall too, by design. I had just started the Ultra Slim Fast diet (getting paid to promote it while I enjoyed its benefits), which would help me to lose forty pounds in the next five months. Now I tell everyone I look like a Greek god. My belly is flat at last and I feel terrific.

When I left office, before the diet, I also looked like a god: a Jewish god. On this day, though, I felt terrific. As I approached the store, I noticed a slightly disheveled guy sitting on his bicycle; he was in his late twenties or early thirties. He wasn't a vagrant, but he was soiled, unkempt, and clearly hostile. I can still see his face. Our eyes met as I passed. He looked at me venomously.

"You were a terrible mayor," this stranger said to me, in a hateful voice.

I looked back. "Fuck you," I said, and then I went into Balducci's.

And that was that.

You have to understand, there had been many times throughout my tenure as mayor when I thought to respond to someone in just this way. But I never did. I never dared. The press would have slaughtered me. It's just not something a public official can do, without being condemned by the editorial writers and columnists. I happen to think there's nothing wrong with telling someone off like this—we've all done it—and I don't think the general public would have been angered by it. In fact, it has been my experience that people respond to genuine, unrehearsed flashes of emotion with applause.

I had, on occasion, used my middle finger to convey this very thought, after making sure there wasn't a photographer around to record the gesture. But, much as I would have liked, I had never before uttered these words in such a public way, not since I had been elected mayor. I made the most of the opportunity. I really drew it out as I said it: "F-u-c-k y-o-u!"

Let me tell you, it felt wonderful. I admit it unabashedly. It was as if twelve years of armor-plated restraint rolled right off my back. The bottled-up frustrations of a lifelong public servant were unloosed in an instant. I was liberated, back to where I was and who I was, and naturally so.

End of story. Beginning of book.

I went into the store and went about my shopping. I like to imagine that this jerk was shocked into some new understanding about me and what I stood for. I also like to think that, had they known of this exchange, everyone walking on Sixth Avenue between Ninth and Tenth Streets would have erupted into cheers and thumbs-up, proud of yesterday's mayor for resuming his commonsense spirit.

I came to see the exchange as a kind of awakening. Better, it stood as a dividing line between my time in office and my return to private life. For the first time since I lost the Democratic primary election to David Dinkins the previous fall, I recognized precisely how my life would change once I left office, how my world would be made over yet again. This business with the stranger on the bike told me my life was once again mine. I suppose I knew this, on some intellectual level, but I didn't feel it in my heart until that moment.

I later related this story to reporters for *New York* magazine and the now-defunct publication *7 Days*, and when their stories hit the stands in the same week, people began to respond. I don't know why, but for the first few months after I left office, people would come up to me and ask me to tell them "the fuck-you story," as it came to be known. This happened so many times, I began to feel like George in *Of Mice and Men*: Tell me about the rabbits, George. Tell me about the fuck-you story, Mayor. Whenever propriety allowed, and it almost always did, I tried to comply, and no one ever appeared offended. Most seemed to take a vicarious thrill in hearing me respond in just the way they would have in similar situations.

I tell the story again here because it nicely illustrates what this book is about: me, out of office and on my own. I have always been a very private public person. I had a public, political personality, which I maintained for nearly thirty years. These days, now that I am working in the private sector, my personality is somewhat muted, but not a whole lot different from what it had to be as mayor. I am a far less outgoing person in my private life. Hard as it may be for some people to believe, I am shy and retiring, which contrasts mightily with the brash and gregarious manner I displayed as mayor. The two faces are not false, put-on, or inconsistent; they simply represent different aspects of me.

This book represents more of my private side. In it, I write about my family, my growing up, my years in the service, and my evolution as a young attorney. I have never written about this early period in my life, and I haven't talked about it in any kind of meaningful way, either. I always thought the substantive issues confronting the city were far more relevant than my personal history, and whenever possible I tried to steer interviewers from my background to my foreground. I still feel that way, to a degree, but now that I have left public office, I realize that a fuller portrait might shed new and interesting light on my policies and performance as an elected official, and help to put my freely given and sometimes controversial opinions into a kind of context.

I also chronicle my first tentative steps into New York City politics, and detail some of the more private and personal moments from my five terms as a United States Congressman and three terms as mayor.

Last, and perhaps most significant, the book recounts my shifting of gears in the nearly three years since I left Gracie Mansion that New Year's morning, and it allows me the platform to sound off on the events that continue to shape my world, and yours.

I hope you enjoy it.

1

Newark

MANY PEOPLE THINK I HAVE a good memory. I do not. I have an average memory. What I have, and what I am good at, is the ability to convince people that I remember them. As a politician, if I planned to attend an important fund-raiser or event, I made it a point to learn the names of those involved, particularly if I had met them previously. I actually studied guest lists, press lists, whatever advance information I had available, and briefed myself on who would be there, what was relevant to talk about. Always, it was extra effort well spent. After all, I met thousands of people in the course of a few months, and I couldn't possibly have been expected to remember everyone's name. But a well-placed "Good to see you again, Frank" always made a big difference.

(I no longer pretend to know someone's name if I don't. I learned this the hard way, when someone said to me, "Do you remember me?" To be polite, I said, "Of course." To be difficult, he said, "What's my name?" Ever since, in response to the first question, I have always said, "Give me a little hint.")

I confess this now as an indication of the ground rules for this book. I do not intend to make up details and conversations I cannot remember. As I reach back for childhood memories, I return with a blurrier bundle of pictures than I would like. So much is lost with the years, and that's a shame. And so many of the people who would be able to replenish those memories are also gone, and that is also a shame. The texture is lost, the details. I recall images more than specific scenes; periods more than specific moments; relationships more than specific exchanges. I think I am not too different from most people in this regard. Of course, most people never set out to write their autobiographies, so it never becomes a problem; those who do, reproducing childhood conversations and other details, are surely making up much of what they say they recall. In my case, though, I find that the moments I do remember take on a deeper meaning, and a greater truth. The memories are made richer, more resonant, by the simple act of calling them to mind.

So, let me share some of them with you.

My father, Louis Koch, and my mother, Yetta Silpe, were Polish-Jewish immigrants. I always specify Polish-Jewish because most Poles, including Lech Walesa, have never thought of Jews as being Polish. When they want to be nice, they talk of the Polish nation and the Jewish nation. When they don't want to be nice, it's the Poles and the Jew Christ-killers.

My parents came from a part of Poland that is now in Ukraine. Back then it was in the Austro-Hungarian Empire. Mama would always refer to the Kaiser as "the good Kaiser Franz Joseph." I remember asking her, "Mama, why do you call him the good Kaiser Franz Joseph?" And she said, "Sonny, because he didn't kill the Jews." I wondered, would he be just plain "Kaiser" if he *had*? Her answer has stayed with me, I think, for the way she matter-of-factly praised this man, as if the mere act of not killing Jews was something special. To Mama, this was an act of generosity for which she was eternally grateful, and for which "the good" was forever appended to the front end of his name when uttered in our household. It has stayed with me also because of a recent biography on Franz Joseph, in which it was confirmed that he did indeed issue an edict that there was to be no Jew-bashing in his dominions. I read the relevant passage and thought of my mother, and her profound understanding of what it has meant for so many to be Jews in a hostile environment. Her pride, and her battles against anti-Semitism, became mine, as you will see.

Poland was a place to suffer, if you were a Jew—another learned truth from my growing up. My father suffered. As a child, he worked as a peddler, with his father. They traveled to the countryside on horse and wagon with goods manufactured in the city, which they sold to Polish peasants or bartered for agricultural goods. It was penny-ante stuff, traded for small change or something to eat. My father, the peddler boy, had a miserable childhood, by his own recounting. He worked hard, with few pleasures in life and not much to look forward to. I once asked him what he did for fun as a small boy, and he answered, "We would go inside to get warm."

He came to America in the early part of this century, at the age of fourteen; he traveled alone, his passage secured by his older brother who had come before him in the traditional exodus of Eastern European Jews to this country: the older brother sent money to pay for his younger sibling's steerage, as my father later did for his younger brother. There was a strong link between my father and his village that the years never erased. Until his death, in fact, he kept in touch with the "landsleut" from the old country, through a "verein," an organization of those who had come from the village of Uscieszko.

Once in New York, and reunited with some of his family, my father found work as a pantsmaker, and later as a waiter. He did not last long in any one job.

Unlike my father, my mother had no strong feelings for the land and the people she too had left behind, also at the age of fourteen. She wanted to forget where she had come from. Mama and my father had very little in common beyond their harsh Polish backgrounds.

My mother suffered, too, in her own way. She had no formal education. No one did in her circle of friends and relatives. Most of her suffering, as I recall, came when she was a young woman, already emigrated to American shores. She was quite beautiful, as our treasured photographs from her girlhood confirm. She was brought here by an older brother, Louis Silpe. He put her to work in a store that he owned and treated her like a servant. He wanted her to be a baby-sitter for his children, and to work in the store and in his home. She moved out on her own while still a teenager. Mama, strong-willed and independent even at that early age, would have none of that; she put herself through design school and became a blouse designer (and quite a good one, as I was told by others). Later on, during the Depression years, we were all dependent on Uncle Louie, as I'll explain.

Uncle Louie was our richest relative, which perhaps is why we did not care for him as much as Mama's other brother, Max, whom we liked a great deal. His family and ours were always close, our lives very much intertwined. In fact, he lived with us until he married. When he did, to a wonderful woman named Shirley, he simply moved to the building next door. We saw each other every day. Uncle Max was a bootlegger, and he did very well. Most bootleggers did very well in those days. It was a tough way to make a living, but Uncle Max was a tough guy. He was gentle with his family, but he was tough. I have a lingering image of a bathtub in his apartment filled with gin. He even made gin in our apartment when he lived with us. My brother, Harold, helped him with his deliveries. Uncle Max also had a gun. I remember that very clearly.

Uncle Louie was a big, gruff man, who treated us, his poor relations, without visible affection. Uncle Max was liked by everybody. No one thought of him as a criminal; in my family, and even in the community, he was admired and envied. Mama's brothers were very much opposed to her marriage. They didn't like my father. They thought he was not good enough for her. I don't know what their standards were. Perhaps no one was good enough for Max and Louie's sister. (I think I felt that way about my sister,

Pat, now happily married to my wonderful brother-in-law Alvin, with three intelligent, sensitive, and gifted sons—Shmuel, Jonathan, and Jared.)

Uncle Max and Uncle Louie were wrong in their assessment of my father, for different reasons, but they were prescient regarding my parents' prospects for a successful marriage. My mother and father were not well suited to each other. It pains me now to consider how mismatched they were, but both of them in their heart of hearts would agree if they were still alive. My mother was the smarter of the two, by far. My father was the nicer of the two, by far. They led tortured lives together. I hope they loved each other, but I don't think they did. Who can ever know how two people really feel about each other? In my youth, unhappily married couples stayed together for the sake of the children, and because of the shame of divorce, at least among Jewish families. Today, of course, there is a different ethic, but back then my parents intended to endure each other until their children were grown. When we were grown, and out of the house (finally, in my case, at the age of thirty-two), they endured each other some more. They were too settled, as they saw it, to make new and separate lives, or to explore their spiritual or emotional longings. This last strikes me as strange now. At sixty-seven, I feel vital and young; my mother, who died at the age of sixty-two, seemed old at the time of her death.

I suspect I inherited my integrity and character from my mother, and my personality and sense of humor from my father. Both of them were extremely strong-willed, and there I think I benefited from each of them. My mother was a proud and honest woman. And she was one of the most intelligent and insightful people I have ever known. My father was also very decent and honest, but he was a limited man intellectually. He had an occasionally irrational temper, which on rare occasions he displayed to his children. I remember one time when I went to a neighborhood carnival and arrived home later than the agreed hour, which caused both my parents great anxiety about my safety. We were living in Newark at the time. It wasn't the most elaborate of carnivals. A carnival, for us, meant maybe a few horses, maybe a couple of camels, sideshows, and, best of all, wonderful things to eat. I sneaked under the tent, like many kids in the neighborhood, in order to get in free. This was tremendously exciting for a small boy, and as the night wore on I lost track of the time. I came home late, maybe about ten o'clock at night.

My father was enraged. My mother was furious, too, but she approached the problem more rationally. My father responded with pure emotion: he hit me. Nowadays, of course, neighbors might call the appropriate child welfare agencies about such behavior, but back then it was not at all unusual for a father to discipline his children in this way. Even by today's standards, though, my father's behavior was certainly not child abuse. I wasn't surprised by it, and I still don't see anything egregious about it. This was my father's way.

There was one other time he hit me that I can recall specifically. It was on the morning of my bar mitzvah. My father was worried we'd be late, as I remember; we were expected at our synagogue, B'nai Jeshrum, in Newark. Actually, we weren't late at all, but my father was an extremely punctual man. I am, too, but with a difference. He liked to arrive at an affair ahead of time. I like to arrive on time. As mayor, and before and since, I would warn my hosts that if they wanted me to arrive at an affair at eight o'clock, they should say so, and not put seven-thirty on the invitation.

On that morning, we were all moving at a pace that would have brought us to the temple not quite as early as my father would have liked (maybe we would have arrived ten minutes ahead, instead of his usual half-hour). He decided I was dawdling in getting dressed, and so he slapped me.

I have met Jews of my age who can still recall the portion of the Torah that they read on their bar mitzvah day. I can't. But the slap I remember, without animosity. My father was a good man and did the best he knew.

I also inherited some of my father's temper, in a small way. But my anger is always controlled and takes the form of icy indifference—I make sure the offending party knows how I feel. Still, I hold grudges, the way my father did. He used to get angry at some relative or other and vow never to speak to them again, even long after the reason for the fallout had dissipated. We were always asking him for the story behind his not speaking to so-and-so, and he would always respond, "I don't remember why, but I'll never talk to him again." I have some of that in me. To be honest, I have a lot of that in me. I have modified President Kennedy's adage "Forgive your enemies but never forget their names" to one of my own: "I rarely forgive, and I never forget."

My parents did their best for their children. They also tried to make their marriage work. This wasn't easy. Part of my mother's frustration with my father was that he never learned to write English, and never wanted to change his life-style. Whatever it was that my mother hoped to do—move to a better neighborhood, take a vacation, buy nicer furniture—my father would resist. Mama wanted to shake her Polish roots and become an American, in every respect. She changed her name, something which was not lightly done in those days the way it is today. She thought "Joyce" sounded more American than "Yetta." Maybe it did. She worked hard to lose her Jewish accent and eventually succeeded. Polish was never spoken in our household, Yiddish sometimes, but never to the children.

Her accent distressed Mama a great deal. She eventually hired a tutor to help her eliminate it and to teach her to read and write in English. The trouble was, she hired a man who could only write English phonetically, so that's how Mama learned. She paid the tutor twenty-five cents an hour, which I think was the minimum wage. For the rest of her life, all her letters, and the entries she made in the diaries she sometimes kept, were written phonetically. Nevertheless, she was a wonderful, lyrical writer; it came naturally to her. But she never did learn to spell. When my sister Pat and I have occasion to read her diary now, with her references to "breakfist" and the "Missisppy" River, we smile with pride at the memory of our young mother—so eager to learn, and yet unaware that she had hired a tutor who couldn't spell.

Mama always wanted better, for herself and for her family. She wanted my father to improve his station in life, so he became a furrier. She always wanted us to move to a better neighborhood, and we always did, as soon as our fortunes allowed. My father would have been content to live out his days wherever we were, but my mother kept planning, willing to take chances.

The first apartment that I recall clearly was in the Bronx: 1680 Crotona Park East. I used to play in Crotona Park. I was never very athletic, even as a small boy. I was the student. My brother, who is four years my senior, was much better coordinated. He was the athlete. And he was the one who had lots of friends, both boys and girls.

In those days I could accurately have been described as a mama's boy. I loved being with my mother, and I think she loved being with me. She doted on me in a special way, different from with her other children. She kept me in short pants longer than she should have, and she kept my hair long—I had blond curls—also longer than she should have. She thought I was very smart, so she tried to smuggle me into the first grade a year early. Because my birthday is in December, I was not yet five years old when it came time to register for the new school year. My mother saw no reason for me not to get an early start and sent me to school anyway. I went to a few weeks of classes before I was found out and expelled. It was a very traumatic experience, to start school and then to be removed so suddenly. I liked school and didn't want to leave, but when my true age was discovered I had to give it up. We were sure a neighbor turned us in. The neighbor had to be

Jewish. Why? Because all of our neighbors were Jewish. In those days, our whole world was Jewish.

The only friend I can recall from this period was a little girl named Doris Schiffman, who was the daughter of my Aunt Shirley's sister. We used to play in Crotona Park all day long; it had wonderful, jutting rock hills with caves and crevices for hiding and seeking, and we filled our days climbing the rocks and playing doctor.

As it turned out, I did not remember that first Bronx apartment as well as I thought. It took a mayoral homecoming visit to set me straight. Our old building is still standing; it is now a low-income co-op occupied by black families. Years ago, when we were there, the residents were low-income Jews, struggling to get by. I returned to the neighborhood a few years ago, when I was being interviewed by Barbara Walters for ABC News, and as I stood outside with Barbara and the cameras, people opened their windows and shouted greetings down to the street. It was quite a wonderful scene.

"Hello, Mayor," they shouted from the windows.

"Hello," I shouted back from the gate at the front of the building. "I used to live here."

"No, you didn't," someone yelled back. "You lived next door."

Oh.

And so I stood corrected, while the ABC News cameras recorded the exchange for posterity, and I laughed to myself that everybody there knew more about me than I did. I hadn't even remembered which building we used to live in. This doesn't speak too highly of my abilities as an autobiographer. At least in this instance, I was close. (The building I thought was ours was where Uncle Max and his family lived.)

I often joke that we moved from one slum to another in those days, but perhaps that is stretching the point. I use the term to describe these neighborhoods of my youth in a joking way. We never really lived in a slum. On the other hand, my father's mother did. My grandmother was a gentle woman who resided on the top floor of a four-story walk-up on Hester Street on the Lower East Side. It was an old-law tenement, which meant there were shared bathrooms out in the hall. Because the roof leaked, umbrellas were pitched over the toilet my grandmother used. It was an awful building. But my poor grandmother was so heavy she could never leave her apartment: the three flights of stairs were too much for her. She must have weighed 250 pounds.

My father, the loving son, would visit her every Friday, to bring her food and, most important, to bathe her. I went with him. She may have had to share the bathroom with her neighbors, but her bathtub was private. The only problem was it was in her kitchen. It was a big tub, and she had to use a little stepladder to climb in. For the sake of modesty, my grandmother never took off her white slip (or shift, as they called it), and my father soaped her through the garment.

I cherished Fridays for the present my grandmother always prepared for our visit: rendered chicken fat, or *grivenes*. It would be in the stove, warm and waiting, and I would race up those stairs, burst into the apartment, and follow my nose to the kitchen. Let me tell you something: in memory, *grivenes* is far tastier than Godiva chocolates. If anybody tells you differently, they've never tasted *grivenes*. Of course it's more unhealthy than chocolate, but I don't know anybody who ever died from it. My grandmother's tasted heavenly. My father made the trek to the Lower East Side each week out of love and filial duty, but I went for the rendered chicken fat.

Mama's embrace of all things American did not extend to religion. My parents would never be like the assimilated German Jews who looked down on us; we never had contact with any German Jews, but somehow we knew this. Neither of my parents was very religious, mind you, but being Jewish was something that was important to them. It was a part of who they were, and a part of who I would become. Each observed in their own way; on balance, our household was run in the Conservative Jewish tradition. My father went to the synagogue whenever his busy work schedule allowed; my mother went only on the High Holidays. (Today, I too go only on the High Holidays.) We kept a kosher home until the Second World War. Outside the house, my father was semi-kosher, which simply meant he didn't eat pork or shellfish. Years later, my mother took particular delight in bringing bacon into the house, which we all considered a great delicacy. Part of its appeal, I am sure, was that it was a forbidden food and it drove my father crazy, but Mama brought it into the house just the same. I don't know if she even liked bacon that much. I think she brought home the bacon simply for the chance to torture Papa, although she did keep a separate frying pan for it.

As a boy, I thought the whole world was Jewish. All our friends were Jewish, everyone in the neighborhood was Jewish. The section of the park where we played was entirely Jewish. My world ticked to the beat of the Sabbath and the Jewish holidays. It was more than a religion, it was a way of life, a way of looking at the world. It invested me with an unshakable sense of who I was. I am, today, a proud Jew, although I am not observant. I sometimes think I will be punished for my failure to observe all the rituals and traditions. But I like Chinese food too much to give it up in this world. Maybe in the next.

During the 1920s, my father began to enjoy some short-lived successes as a furrier. He opened up his own shop, in partnership with his brother Bernie. They called themselves Koch Brothers. Bernie was a cutter and a much more skilled technician than my father; Papa was the sewing machine operator.

The Koch brothers prospered, for a while, albeit on a small scale. They ran into trouble with the union not long after they opened for business. The fur union was a Communist one led by a man named Ben Gold, who had a reputation as one of the city's most radical labor leaders. Ben Gold was that and more. Union thugs used to appear at my father's shop to threaten Papa's nonunion workers, and Papa. Predictably, and regrettably, the confrontations turned violent. Nonunion workers were beaten; my father's machines and loft were destroyed; for a time it was uncertain if the business would ever recover. I used to listen to my father's descriptions of the union's disgraceful conduct and share his rage. His business was nearly ruined. His people were hurt. The livelihood and well-being of his family were threatened. After one threat, Papa had my Uncle Max come by to walk him home; he felt safer with Uncle Max because Max had a gun. These incidents, as I heard them told and retold throughout my young life, did not make me antiunion, but they did shape my thinking on the need to control union excesses, in business and in government. As an adult, especially as a politician, I was reminded by this years-ago and close-to-home brutality that we cannot let people get their way through violence.

Papa might have stayed in business despite the union, but the Depression shut him down. Furs were a luxury people could no longer afford, so the business went into bankruptcy. By 1931, we were living in Newark, and our family was once again dependent on my Uncle Louie, as I'll explain. We lived in a two-bedroom apartment at 90 Spruce Street, with Uncle Bernie and his family. The rent was forty-five dollars a month, split between the two families. There were eight of us living in that apartment. My parents took one bedroom; Uncle Bernie and Aunt Mollie took the other, which they shared with their daughter Estelle.

Harold and I slept in a double, pull-out cot in the dining room; we pushed the table and chairs to the wall every night after dinner. The one substantial piece of furniture we didn't move was our old Emerson radio. That radio dominated the room. It had a beautiful cabinet, supported by long, carved legs. Harold and I used to lie under it for hours, playing tick-tack-toe on the underside of the cabinet with a piece of chalk. If I close my eyes I can still see our childish scratchings against the wood. We used to listen to the radio chapters as we played—"Jack Armstrong, All-American Boy," or "Little Orphan Annie." On Sundays we listened to "The Shadow." A program called "The Witch's Tale," which, as I recall, did not stay on the air long, was our favorite. We'd listen late at night to the spooky, eerie sound effects and enjoy the fright.

That old Emerson was the extent of our living room. In those days, people didn't have living rooms. At least no one we knew did. But we all had dining rooms, which were the centers of Jewish family life. After all, it made absolutely no sense to give over an entire room just to sitting. What excess! So we had the two bedrooms, the dining room, a bathroom, and a kitchen. It was cramped, but we managed. I thought everyone lived that way.

Really, it wasn't too bad. I look now at all the protections and reforms we have put into the system for families living in low-income housing projects provided by the government—no more than two kids can sleep in the same room, and they have to be of the same sex—and I think to myself, this is ridiculous. We're overprotecting people. I don't remember that Spruce Street apartment as any kind of hardship.

After a year, we were in our own apartment, in the same building. We needed the room for my new baby sister, Pat. Back then she was called Paulina. When she got to be about twelve she decided she hated the name and had it changed, continuing the family tradition that began with Mama.

I was seven years old at the time of our move from the Bronx, and it seemed as if my world had been reinvented: a new sister, a new apartment, a new extended family living under the same roof, a new neighborhood. It must have seemed that way to my father, too. He was broke, out of the fur business, and forced to work for his brother-in-law. Uncle Louie owned a dance hall in Newark, called Kruger's Auditorium, and he leased the hatcheck concession to my parents. The concession never brought in what we needed to get by; sometimes my father worked a second job, usually as a day laborer for a Manhattan furrier. There were even periods when he worked at third jobs. When I think of my father and the work that defined him during those years I recall his checking coats until two-thirty in the morning on weekends, or midnight during the week; and being up at four-thirty in the morning, ready to take the train from Newark to his day job in New York, or to get a head start on the other job seekers. He worked hard all his life, and he passed that ethic on to me. From my father I also learned how to get by on very little sleep; to this day, I get up at five-thirty each morning (my father was tougher than I am).

Kruger's Auditorium, a catering and dance hall on Belmont Avenue in Newark, used to be owned by Kruger's Brewery, and has long since been demolished. Throughout the 1930s, though, it was a popular nightspot and a favorite venue for parties. Everyone in the neighborhood —Jews, Poles, blacks—hired the hall for their big functions, and local organizations booked it for their major events. The place was busy several nights each week (especially weekends), and my parents were tenants in the hatcheck concession, although we all considered the terms of Uncle Louie's lease somewhat onerous. He paid my parents eight dollars a night for the privilege of sitting in a small cloakroom for six hours, checking coats. My parents paid him an annual rent for the concession. The most unconscionable thing was that my uncle charged patrons a quarter each to check their hats and coats, and he kept the entire amount. We were left hoping people would leave a ten-cent tip in addition to the house charge.

My brother and I helped out most weekend nights, and on some weeknights too, as we got older. It was a demeaning experience, the four of us cramped into that tight space, hustling. Harold hated the work, but I went gladly. I did it for my parents. I still recall my constant chant, invoked at the end of each evening when the customers returned for their coats: "Please don't forget the hatcheck boys, we only work on tips." It was humiliating, but even more so when my mother was forced to do the asking.

I was distressed for my parents. It was a terrible, unseemly way to make a living, to be dependent on the charity of other people. It was honorable work, but tiring, boring, and mindless—and it was demeaning to have to ask for tips. The humiliation of those nights has never left me, and I have never forgiven my uncle for the way he treated us, or for putting my parents in that situation, even though I am sure he saw things a little differently. From his perspective, it was likely just a matter of offering his sister's family an opportunity that he could have given to others, but I still resented him. We all did. Once, Uncle Louie threatened to give the concession to someone else. My brother got so mad at him one night, over an issue I no longer recall, that he actually threw a punch at him. That was a moment when we thought things were absolutely over. As distasteful as this arrangement was, it was the only steady job my father had, and it seemed Harold's anger would cost us the concession. The blowup occurred during the depths of the Depression, and we had no place else to go. I don't recall how long the fallout from this incident dragged on, but it was clearly a major crisis. Eventually, Harold was made to apologize, which made me dislike my uncle all the more.

The years checking coats at Kruger's left me with two indelible family portraits, and one lasting scar. The first picture has my sister, Pat, at its center. She was too young to help us with the concession, and she stayed home with a baby-sitter on the nights we all worked. Those nights, we would all return home at different times. I was the youngest, and I went home first. Often it would be as late as midnight, even during the week. Pat was a bed wetter, and our system was that whenever one of us came home, we woke her up and took her to the bathroom. So I would drag her out of bed and sit her on the toilet seat. Sometimes I ran the faucet to help her urinate. When she was finished, I put her back to bed. Harold would come home an hour or so later, and he would repeat the procedure. Then it was my mother's turn. We tortured that poor child. By the time my father came home she was crying to be let alone. "I don't have to go," she would say, but nobody believed her.

The other family scene took place on Sunday mornings. Saturdays were always the busiest nights at Kruger's, and Sundays would find us in our parents' bedroom, counting the take from the night before. We would sit on their bed and roll the dimes and quarters (mostly dimes) into bank papers. As awful as the night before may have been, there was something joyous, celebratory about those mornings. After a busy Saturday night we'd count out fifty dollars; on a typical day it would be about half that. Twenty or thirty dollars was a lot of money in those days, even for a night's work involving four of us. And there were many nights when the dance hall was dark and we earned nothing.

The lasting scar from that period has been my reluctance as a fund-raiser. I am plainly lousy at it. I hate asking for money, especially for my own political campaigns, and I am sure my distaste stems in some way from those long nights at Kruger's. When I ask for a contribution, I can still hear that plaintive cry: "Please don't forget the hatcheck boys, we only work on tips!"

Our second Newark apartment was at 61 Milford Avenue, in a lower-middle-class, Jewish neighborhood. The street was a mix of private houses and small apartment buildings; the apartment was several steps up from our place on Spruce Street. Quitman Street was the acknowledged dividing line between the black and Jewish communities, and our apartment house on Spruce Street had been only one block away. Milford Avenue was in a much more affluent neighborhood, relatively speaking. Of course, everybody liked to think of themselves as middle class in those days, as they do today. People haven't changed much. A Depression-era economist could accurately have described us as poor. Indeed, there were some days when my hardworking father had only five dollars in his pocket, and no savings.

Still, we thought of ourselves as middle class, and we saw the Milford Avenue apartment as the height of luxury. By our standards, it was. Harold and I no longer slept in the dining room, in a pull-out cot near the radio. We shared a bedroom with twin beds. Pat had the back bedroom.

We still didn't have a living room, but things were looking up. In fact, our financial picture looked so encouraging for a while that my mother eventually moved us into an even nicer apartment next door. We would have moved within our own building, but there is a superstition among Jews that you cannot move to a lower floor in the same building. You must always move up. I don't know where this superstition started. The symbolism is clear, but the logic is lost on me: it's okay to move to a lower floor, as long as you're going to another building. To my mother, though, the logic was sound. We moved next door, to a lower floor.

I went to South Side High. The school was about 25 percent black, and 75 percent Jewish. I always like to say I went to an integrated school before it was fashionable, and I think I had a pretty good education. I went to Monmouth Street Elementary School when we lived on Spruce Street, and to Miller Street Elementary School when we lived on Milford Avenue. Both schools were about 50 percent black and 50 percent white.

Newark was a relatively safe, peaceful city in the 1930s, but it was not without racial tensions. Even as late as 1941, when we moved from Newark, there was considerable prejudice against the city's black population. It's unbelievable to me now, but some Newark movie theaters restricted black patrons to balcony seats in those days; many landlords refused to rent to black tenants; blacks were treated horrendously in some restaurants. Disgraceful discriminations like these occurred in Newark just as they did in many parts of the country. Remember, even our armed forces were segregated until Harry Truman integrated them in 1948.

For the most part, though, relations between blacks and whites were harmonious. There was no violence that I can remember. I was friendly with some of the black kids in school. I shared a desk one year with a black student—we had double desks in those days—and the two of us were friends in school, but not out of school, which was more or less the order of the day.

I am no authority on adolescent friendships. I once remarked that I cannot recall a single close friend from my ten years in Newark, and while that is not entirely true it is close enough to the mark to cause me some regrets in the remembering. I did have two good friends then: Stanley Rocklin and Donald Fischer. We all saw a lot of each other. They were friendships born of proximity: Donald and Stanley both lived in our buildings at 61–71 Milford Avenue. We went to the movies together, to the Cameo Theater around the block from our building. It never mattered what was playing. We'd go anyway. There would always be a double feature and a chapter of a serial. A bargain.

I still remember the food in Donald's apartment. I would sometimes go on picnics with Donald and his family, and I envied him and the way he lived. They had a car. I thought they were extremely wealthy people. Donald's father was part-owner and manager of one of the most popular Newark restaurants, the Tavern, and I remember my delight in going to his apartment and eating wonderful things that we never had in our house. The restaurant was famous for its coconut custard pie, and even after fifty years, I still remember it as the best I have ever eaten.

The person I spent the most time with throughout my childhood was my brother. He was a dominant figure in my life. He was my protector against neighborhood bullies. (Once, when our drunken superintendent threatened to hit me, Harold intervened: "If you hit him," he challenged, "I'll knock you down." The super withdrew.) Still, despite Harold's supposed role and all the time we spent together, we were not close. We had no special feeling for each other. As adults, we are unalike in a number of ways, but we have found the basis for a close fraternal friendship. (Indeed, my brother, his second wife, Gail, and Gail's daughter by her previous marriage, Joey, have become very close to me over the last few years.)

Of course, then we were unalike, too, but we never thought finding a common ground was worth the effort. Harold thought I was a crybaby, and I was. Whenever my parents were out—often, during these hatchecking years —he would chase me around the dining room table and punch me when he caught me. It hurt. This was a game to him. To me it was pain. I survived by holding back my tears all the hours until my parents came home, then starting to bawl when their key turned in the lock. Of course, the next time my parents went out, Harold meted out his punishment for my previous squealing, and the cycle would start again.

The other way Harold would torment me was to play dead. We shared the same bed for many years, and on some mornings, or in the middle of some nights, he announced that he was dead and indeed appeared to be. I tried to shake him awake, and when simple nudges proved futile, I hit him. He withstood an enormous amount of pain, my brother. I pounded on him, and still he wouldn't flinch. Finally, when he had me convinced he was really dead, he opened his eyes and scared the hell out of me. He'd tease me for hours for having believed him, and remembering all those blows I'd rained on his body, he'd beat me up.

When Harold was in high school, we both found other diversions. As a teenager Harold wanted less and less to do with the family, and chose more and more to be by himself. Or with the baby-sitter. He used to fool around with all the baby-sitters Mama brought in to look after Pat. I never actually saw him with these girls, but he bragged about his exploits afterward. I knew his claims were true.

Slowly, Harold made a place for himself outside the family loop. When we went on marvelous family outings with my mother's sister, Alice, and her family, Harold always found an excuse not to go. Alice was married to Izzy Bodner, whom we all called Uncle Bodner, for some strange reason. (Even his wife called him Bodner.) We spent a lot of time with their family. They lived in a cramped apartment in West Orange, New Jersey, behind Uncle Bodner's tailor shop, and we visited with them almost every weekend. On Sundays we'd bundle into Uncle Bodner's car—my parents, Pat and I, Uncle Bodner, Aunt Alice, and their two children, Seymour and Pearl—and we'd go to a state park for a picnic. I don't know what Harold did with his days, but we spent most of ours driving and eating. Mama and Aunt Alice packed wonderful picnic lunches, and I could never understand why we had to drive to the park (or sometimes even to the Catskill Mountains) before we could eat. Fifteen minutes into the trip, we children would shout, "Let's eat!" The two mothers always brought extra sandwiches, anticipating the routine.

Uncle Bodner drove us to the few true family vacations we had in those days. (We didn't have a car, and were happy for the ride.) Harold rarely joined us. We shared a bungalow on Swan Lake in the Catskills with the Bodners. The bungalow was so small the two families had to eat in shifts; we put our name on our food in the icebox, and they labeled theirs. One summer, we were lucky enough to have our own house. On some vacations, as the Depression retreated, we even stayed in hotels. In those days, the five of us could have stayed at a nice hotel for less than seventy-five dollars per week, including three delicious meals a day.

On one of these vacations I managed to prevent a huge tragedy. It was at Kutsher's Country Club. I was thirteen years old. There was a platform out in the middle of the lake, a kind of float where people would gather to sun-bathe, or to practice their dives, or rest up before swim-ming back the few hundred feet to shore. Everybody, men and women, wore rubber caps to keep their hair dry in those days. I stood on the platform, looking out on the rubber-capped heads in the water. Suddenly, I spotted a familiar cap, bobbing up and down in the water. It was Pat, about six years old, struggling to make it to the plat-form. She was drowning. Swimming was one of the few sports I did well, but I didn't think about that at the time. I would have jumped in after my baby sister even if I couldn't swim at all.

I swam to her, and dragged her to shore. It was one of the most terrifying moments of my life. Pat had swallowed a great deal of water, some of which was spilling from her mouth. I don't remember if she was conscious or not, but I was absolutely petrified. My fear turned to delight mo-ments later, when Pat opened her eyes and started to cry. As I recall, Mama spanked her for going in over her head.

That same year marked another turning-point in my growing up. Donald Fischer and I were playing tag in our building. It was a Sunday. Donald ran down the steps to the front door, and I raced after him. When he reached the plate-glass door, it closed behind him. I was unable to stop and my left hand went through the glass, shattering the pane. There was blood everywhere. I don't remember feeling pain so much as horror at the sight of my hand. I didn't know it at the time, but I had sliced through every tendon in my left hand and wrist, except the thumb.

Luckily, I had the presence of mind to run to our family doctor, Dr. Lowenstein, the father of two boys I occasion-ally played with. I was in no real pain, but I was very afraid.The pain would come later. On a Sunday, there was no reason to expect that the doctor would be home, but God was with me.

I don't think Dr. Lowenstein was the greatest doctor in the world, but he was on that day. We arrived just as he was coming in from golf. (You have to understand, in those days Jews didn't play golf; Jews didn't even play tennis; clearly, the doctor was moving up in the world.) He took me into his office and made a quick examination, then made a decision that saved the use of my hand. Instead of simply closing up the wound, which some doctors would have done (and which happened to one of my cousins), he determined that the tendons were cut and drove me to Beth Israel Hospital in Newark. He had someone call my parents at Kruger's for permission to operate.

They were operating on me even before my mother and father got to the hospital. They put in 150 stitches. Almost a year of physical therapy brought my hand to where it currently is, about 80 percent of full strength. The handicap has not prevented me from doing anything I have ever wanted to do, but some tasks are difficult. I can no longer grip as tightly with my left hand as with my right, the left fingers being a little atrophied and about a half-inch shorter, but the hand is functional. Most people are unaware of it. Indeed, when I was drafted during World War II, the injury might have made me eligible for 4F status and deferment from the service, but I never mentioned it, and it was never noticed.

In high school, though, I was only too happy to use my injury as a crutch. I hated gym classes and avoided them "on account of my hand." Even outside of school, I shunned any kind of athletic activity. I had no interest in it, and after my accident, I had the perfect reason to avoid it. Because I was tall for my age, people assumed I was a good athlete. "You must be a great basketball player," they would say. Knowing I wasn't made me not want to play at all, so as not to disappoint them or be the subject of ridicule. I was never well-coordinated. And I had absolutely no interest in the professional sports that so occupied the attentions of my brother and the other neighborhood boys. If I couldn't do it well, I must have figured, I wouldn't do it at all. After my accident, if the other kids teased me about my disinterest or inability, I blamed my hand.

The injury also gave rise to one of my favorite (apocryphal) anecdotes, which I used in later years to explain why my brother was a jock and I was not. The scene, as I paint it, has my mother standing in the kitchen, looking at her two sons. She turns to my brother and says, "Harold, you go out and play baseball." Then she turns to me and says, "Ed, you sit in the corner and study to be mayor."

I settled quietly into this new role, and over time developed a routine with home, school, work, and family that would last me through high school. The few friends I had were enough. My weekends were busy with the hatcheck concession, or with family outings, or movies. I filled my school days with the requisite extracurricular activities. I was, for a time, the president of the debating society at South Side High School. I also had an interest in stamp-collecting and, later, in photography, and for a while spent a good deal of time in the school darkroom.

I was a fairly solid, unspectacular B student in high school. I never worked hard at getting good grades, although I would never claim that if I had I would have been an A student. I confess that I have never fully trusted anyone who graduated at the top of his class, or scored highest on tests. There was almost always something wrong with those people. I was quite happy to be in the academic middle, although in retrospect it seems I wasn't happy for long. I managed to skip two years of elementary school without too much effort—in those days students able to pass basic, grade-level tests were accelerated—and I graduated at sixteen years old.

I was eager to get on with the rest of my life after high school. And it started in Brooklyn.

2

Spartanburg, South Carolina

WE MOVED TO BROOKLYN IN 1941. Today I joke that we escaped from Newark, but in truth, when we left, Newark wasn't a bad place. The seeds of the 1968 riots had yet to be planted there.

My mother found us an apartment at 320 Ocean Parkway. Uncle Bernie and his family lived next door at number 330, and when Mama returned from one of her visits, she unilaterally decided we were moving. Ocean Parkway, in 1941, was a beautiful avenue. It has still retained a good deal of its sweep and grandeur, but back then it was something special. (I especially liked the fact that it led right into Coney Island and Nathan's hot dog stand.) The street is one of the city's historical treasures, designed by the architect Frederick Olmsted with a wonderfully wide sidewalk and a tree-lined path on one side, which was divided into pedestrian and bicycle paths. There were lovely park benches along the path, where neighbors spent warm summer evenings. Across the street was a bridle path, which I used on occasion; horses were available at stables near Prospect Park, about ten blocks away.

For this move, Mama gave us a complete make-over. She sold a great deal of our furniture, and one of the things she got rid of was our dining room set. She sold it for twenty dollars, including the chairs, and threw in her cut-glass bowls—ten of them—which had fallen into disfa-

vor. The Depression was just ending, with the approach of
World War II, and few people were interested in dining
room furniture at bargain prices. When people came to
look at our furniture, my sister complicated the problem
by pointing out all the little flaws, the cracks and loose
slats. Mama was apoplectic.

Our Ocean Parkway apartment had two bedrooms (and
one bathroom), but it might as well have been a palace.
There was a long hallway leading from the front door to
what was supposed to have been the dining room but
which Mama decided would be the den. These days, it
would be called a study or family room. It also doubled as
my bedroom, shared with Harold at first, before he moved
out on his own. I slept on one of the two couches. The
room was separated from my parents' bedroom by wide
French doors. There was another, smaller room in the
back of the apartment, which became my sister's bedroom, and a small kitchen, where we ate all our meals.

The absolute highlight of the apartment was our living
room, Mama's pride and joy. Of course, she used the
room, as nearly everyone did in those days—almost never.
She bought beautiful furniture, probably more expensive
than we could afford, and then kept the room off limits
unless we had important guests. The furniture was protected under old sheets, the way people do when they
close up their summer cottages for the winter. Who could
blame her? It would be a long time before she would be
able to replace the furniture. There was a stunning Queen
Anne chair, upholstered in a delicate cream and gold fab-
ric. And there was a blue mohair couch, which was absolutely gorgeous, and, according to Mama, particularly
perishable.

So we used the den. Seven days a week. The living room
was for special guests, or for Mama's mah-jongg friends.
Then she would put the bridge table in the living room. I
still have her bridge chairs, all six of them. I just had them
re-covered, about fifty years after they were first purchased, at a cost of one hundred dollars a chair; the entire

set cost my parents one hundred and twenty-five, including the table, which I no longer have.

Our rent was sixty-five dollars a month, which was a lot of money in those days (and twenty dollars more than we were paying in Newark), but Mama decided we could afford it. My father was back in the fur business in Manhattan by this time, and my parents were finally free from the hatcheck concession. For the first time since the Depression, my father's business prospects were good. At one point, things were going so well Papa tried to get Harold to become a furrier, but Harold was too smart to accept that honor. He helped out in Papa's fur loft when called on, but he never went willingly, and my father soon reached the inevitable conclusion that his plans for Harold were not going to work out.

No one ever thought of me as furrier material, which is just as well; even then, everyone knew I would become a lawyer. I never had a good grasp of the fur business, at least as it was explained to me by my father. Papa said he was losing money every year, although he was doing better financially. "Papa," I once asked him, "how can you lose money every year and still stay in business?"

"Sonny," he said, making what he thought was perfect sense, "we make it up in inventory."

I arrived in Brooklyn in circumstances that made it difficult to blend into my new neighborhood. I was sixteen years old, already out of high school, so chances of forming neighborhood friendships were few. I didn't mind. Of course, I quickly learned who everyone was on our block, and everyone soon knew me, but I didn't form any close attachments. Besides, I had college to keep me busy. I enrolled at City College of New York—CCNY—that fall; every day I took the subway to Harlem. Even then, this was chancy. The safest route was to go to 145th Street; this was not the most direct route, but it was the recommended one. Once in a while, when I was running late or feeling particularly daring, I'd get off at 135th Street and walk through St. Nicholas Park. The college warned students against this because of the frequent robberies and muggings, but I never had a problem.

The war put an abrupt end to my college career. I was drafted in March 1943. Though Mama insisted I seek a deferment because of my injured hand, I didn't reveal it to the draft doctors. I was not about to volunteer, but I certainly would serve when called. I was not then, as I am not now, of heroic quality. I hate the sight of blood, particularly my own. But, like most young men my age at that time, I was absolutely willing to fight for my country. And, like most young Jewish men from New York City (which translated into almost everyone I knew), I was eager to fight Adolf Hitler and his murderous anti-Semitism. At the time, we didn't know of the concentration camps or the extent of the German atrocities. We just knew Hitler was evil, and that he wanted to destroy the Jews. That he was actually doing so, on such a sweeping scale, we would not learn for some time.

I was assigned to seventeen weeks of basic training, at Camp Croft in Spartanburg, South Carolina. It was the most grueling, intense physical experience I have ever had. I think I went into the army at 185 pounds, and left Spartanburg at 160. Most of the weight was sweated off. South Carolina was so oppressively hot, it was like a constant sauna. But at only 160 pounds, I would literally get chilled if the temperature dropped from 120 degrees to 110. Still, I was in terrific shape, but much too thin. When I went in, I was out of shape—at first, I couldn't make it over the obstacle course, which wasn't unusual, as I would learn. I think our platoon was about 25 percent Jewish and all of us found it difficult to get over the obstacle course. The others would ridicule us, so I practiced at night in order to avoid their taunts. The toughest part of the course was scaling the sheer face of a wooden wall to reach the top. You had to master it. Ultimately, I did.

Basic training was a cultural revelation as well. The Jewish kids might not have shone on the obstacle course, or in other tests of physical strength or agility, but we dominated the two to three hours of seminars that were held each day. The classes always included a question-and-answer session and, generally, the ones with the questions and the answers were the Jews. We could be studying map reading, or world events, and every day it would be the same. One of the instructors would ask a question, and one of the non-Jews would mumble, sotto voce, "Which Yid is gonna raise his hand?" I resented it terribly but didn't know what to do about it. As basic training wore on, I burned with rage at this kind of treatment, but I knew I wasn't strong enough to battle back. I vowed to myself that I would become strong over the next several weeks, in order to stand up to our tormentors.

If memory serves, there were only two of us Jewish kids who were able to scale that wooden wall—myself, and a good friend of mine, Jacques Lennon, originally from Luxembourg. Over time, he and I were accepted by the others, for whatever reason; I think the assumption was that we weren't Jewish. The others apparently never thought their anti-Semitic comments referred to Jacques or me. I suffered them all silently, waiting for the right moment to take them on.

My time came soon enough. About fifteen weeks into basic training, I was tougher than I had ever been before, or have been since. I had no boxing skills, but I figured I could make a decent showing. Fate pitted me against the strongest guy in the outfit, who had actually been friendly toward me and Jacques. His name was La Rue, and he was a natural leader. I suppose he thought he was just kidding around. His disparaging comments were a big joke to him. He said something particularly hurtful about Jews one afternoon, out on the field—I no longer recall the remark—and I became enraged. I waited until the session was over, then I went to him. I must have looked crazed, but in truth I was scared out of my mind. I had never done anything like this before, but I was determined to stand up.

I grabbed him by his collar and said, "You and me are gonna have it out when we get back to the barracks."

La Rue was clearly heavier than I, and much stronger; he undoubtedly had experience as a street fighter. He was also the best athlete in the platoon. He had no idea what he had done to cause such fury in me. "What's wrong?" he said. "What are you talking about?"

I was too embarrassed to explain, so I shouted, "You know! You know!" At that point, he knew.

A crowd had gathered by the time we got back to the barracks. There must have been about a hundred guys in a big circle, waiting for me and La Rue to fight. People were running around and shouting, "They're gonna kill the Jews! Come and watch! They're gonna kill the Jews!" What that meant I am not sure, but I can still hear their cries. It was like a scene out of a bad movie.

As I was preparing to fight, one of the Jewish kids came to offer his help. This guy was fat, ugly, smart, and one of the main targets of the anti-Semitic insults. His name was Pearlstein. He was actually a nice, unassuming guy, but I was furious with him for putting me in this position, even though he had done nothing wrong.

"Get away from me!" I railed as he approached. "This is all your fault!"

Pearlstein was just trying to help, but I was so angry that I was going to be beaten up that I couldn't think straight. When I remember this incident from the perspective of fifty years, I am still ashamed at the way I treated poor Pearlstein. My own fears made me irrational. I was striking out at the wrong target.

The time came to fight. I was focused on my opponent. We donned gloves. I was no boxer, but I couldn't back down. I was entirely overmatched, and absolutely petrified. The crowd swelled in size. Everyone except the Jewish kids was rooting for my opponent and yelling for my blood. La Rue did not disappoint them. He knocked me down. Several times. I scrambled back up, parrying his jabs the best I could. After three rounds, someone stopped the fight. My nose was bloodied. I had landed a few good blows, but I had clearly been beaten.

I may have lost the fight, but I won the battle. In the two weeks remaining, I did not hear one anti-Semitic comment in that whole battalion. I feel very proud of that now, as I did then, and look back on this encounter as an important event in my life. I stood up for something I believed in, even when I knew I would lose. This was the kind of thing my brother would have done, and indeed often had. But Harold always won. It was new for me, though, and it felt exhilarating, liberating, even just trying and not winning.

I hadn't been exposed to the real world before the Army, and my time in Spartanburg was an education and an epiphany, both. As I said, the entire world seemed Jewish to me, growing up, but the Army quickly set me straight. Suddenly, being Jewish was not the norm. Anti-Semitism revealed itself directly to me for the first time, and I did not like what it looked like, or what it felt like: it wasn't only Hitler, it was here in America.

I matured in Spartanburg—physically, through the ordeal of basic training, and intellectually, through the unexpected exposure to a barracks-full of Southerners, Northerners, and the various ethnic populations that make up America. It took the Army to introduce me to this larger, broader world.

I kept a journal throughout my basic training. A lot of the other guys had a diary going. It was a way of unwinding, and putting things into perspective. I wrote mine in a brown leather number, about the size of a small paperback book, which was given to me by my mother before I left home. "God bless you, my son," she inscribed on the first page, to which my sister added, "Come back soon. Kill a few Japs for me." When I reread it I am transported back over the past fifty years.

That journal was my constant companion. Its sight and scent are as familiar to me as yesterday. Most of the entries are mundane, describing meals or regimens, or the difficulty we soldiers had in getting used to an open latrine, or to the 3.2 beer that was available there. Though most of it would bore anyone else, some entries are powerful and evocative: In one, I described a Southern soldier I had just met as "extremely likable and intelligent, except on the Negro question. He says as a matter of course that when he gets old enough he will join the Ku Klux Klan."

Other entries are still able to tug at my heart. "One of the boys was drowned in the lake," I wrote on October 23, 1943, after I had left Spartanburg for a six-week academic orientation tour at Rollins College in Orlando, Florida. "He wasn't in for bed check yesterday, nor reveille today. They found his body down near the pier. They put the flag at half-mast, and played taps. I hear taps every night, but it never sounded like this call. It just cut through everybody."

My parents came to visit me midway through basic training. I had never been away from home before, and I was eager to spend time with them. I was also looking forward to showing off my new physique. But we never knew when we would be pulled for KP. When our turn came, we draped a towel at the foot of the bed, and then someone else woke us up at four-thirty in the morning for duty. I didn't want to take the chance that I'd be chosen, although it was not my turn, because my parents would only be at the camp for a few days. Sometimes, if we weren't in bed at four-thirty, they'd simply pull the guy in the next cot. So I got up at four o'clock and left the barracks. I went to the guest house and sat on the porch in a rocker until I could wake my parents for breakfast.

The rest of those seventeen weeks are a blur. On weekends, unless the sergeant had revoked our passes in punishment, we went to town for steak dinners and speculated about where we would be sent after Spartanburg—to Europe, or to the Pacific. It was a tense, uncertain time.

I have a very vivid memory of a terrible accident at the end of our seventeen weeks. We all went through a ritual of burning whatever personal items we would be leaving behind. I don't know if this was a Spartanburg or an Army tradition, but we made fires in big oil barrels, into which we discarded our trash. It was all very festive. It was just a harmless, parting display, until someone stupidly threw a cartridge into the flames. A good friend was standing near the barrel and lost an eye as a result of the explosion. My friend was shipped home (I would never see him or hear of him again), and I wondered how many more of us would follow him, how the war would end for each of us. I thought I would die in battle.

One of the prize assignments after Spartanburg was a slot in the Army Specialized Training Program, or ASTP. The program was intended to train GIs as foreign language specialists, doctors, engineers, and other professionals for various special assignments. ASTP naturally favored the brighter kids: we had to take a test to be accepted; as I recall, it was a general intelligence test, not in any discipline. Once we were accepted, the Army assigned us to an American university for specialized training.

In retrospect, ASTP was not a fair or equitable program, and in fact it would be dismantled later that year for those very reasons. Nevertheless, I applied, took the test, and was accepted. I was sent first to Rollins College for a six-week orientation program. Rollins had a reputation for being a playboy school: golf and tennis took priority over classes. I applied for the foreign languages program to be a German language interpreter. I couldn't speak German well; I had had two years of high-school German and another two semesters at CCNY, but I couldn't really carry on a conversation; I certainly was unable to communicate in a substantive way with a German. Still, I thought it was worth a shot.

I was sent to be interviewed by the school's German-language professor. His name was Feuerstein. "Speak to me in German," the professor said, quite reasonably. "Anything at all."

The best I could do was recite a passage from William

Tell, which I thought I had committed to memory. As it turned out, I had not.

"You can't speak German," the professor announced, also quite reasonably, after the first or second stanza. "Not well enough for this program."

"Professor," I countered (in English), "you have an option. You can fail me. Or you can pass me. If you fail me, I leave tomorrow and return to the infantry. I really don't want to do that. I much prefer this program. If you pass me, you will see I am a quick learner. And I will learn. I will very quickly learn to speak German fluently."

The professor looked at me with a blank face. For a long time, he didn't say anything. But he passed me. God bless Professor Feuerstein, who is surely long dead by this time.

I was assigned to the German program at Fordham University in New York, on the Bronx campus. I could not have imagined a more convenient tour of duty. I would live at Fordham during the week, and go home to Brooklyn on weekends. My evenings, even during the week, would be entirely my own. It seemed too good to be true, which in fact it was: At Fordham, there were no Professor Feursteins to charm, or to reason with. The program there was administered by a priest who approached me with the same request: "Speak to me in German."

I tried my William Tell bit.

"You can't speak German," the priest observed.

"You're right," I allowed. "I cannot, but . . ."

"Soldier," he cut me off. "If you want to stay in this program, you'll have to become an engineer."

So I became an engineer. I did not like engineering, but it was better than being an infantryman. I was still assigned to the Fordham campus, still free to return home each weekend and to go out to the movies or to dinner at night.

Fortunately for the country, the ASTP program ended about a year later, after which I was sent to Camp Carson, in Colorado, for additional combat infantry training. A

group of us ASTP soldiers were assigned to fill the de-
pleted ranks of the 104th (Timberwolf) Infantry division,
which had been on maneuvers in the California desert for
many months. They had lost nearly half their personnel.
At Camp Carson, our ASTP group joined a division of
GIs from the Deep South. Our new cohorts were a bunch
of self-described redneck Southern hillbillies, and we
ASTP kids stood out like ninety-eight-pound weaklings in
a Charles Atlas ad. I don't use the terms "redneck" or
"hillbillies" pejoratively here. In fact, I came to like and
respect these guys a great deal. These terms, and "ridge
runners," which they particularly favored, were the way
they referred to themselves. Their brand of humor was to
tell stories about screwing chickens. It had never occurred
to me that this was something you could do with a
chicken, and I'm still not sure that they were joking. My
fellow soldiers made it sound like a common occurrence.
We ASTP kids didn't press them for details.

Initially, the contrast between us and the ridge runners
was frightening. We were students; they were soldiers. For
most of us, basic training was a year-old memory, while
these guys were just coming off maneuvers in the California desert. If we had been in good shape a year ago, we
weren't now. These hillbillies seemed like giants compared with us; they were extraordinary, athletic-looking
guys, their skin burned to leather by constant exposure to
the sun. I could not imagine a more disparate group, and
there was a good deal of tension between us at first.
Within a few weeks, though, we adjusted to each other. In
the end, the two groups became one.

By the time we were overseas, our rough spots had
evened out, but we learned to make use of our cultural
differences.

In Europe, my new friends and I were never satisfied
with the army C or K rations, and tried to supplement our
diet wherever possible. I quickly became the number one
food scrounger, with assists from everyone else; the ridge

runners had their own special talents in the food-gathering area.

There was one episode I will never forget. We found a pig on an abandoned farm, near the evacuated German town of Aachen. We all decided this pig would make a nice meal. The trouble was, first it had to be killed. I had never known anyone who had killed a pig or even knew how, but for the ridge runners, it was easy. One of them strolled casually to the pig, then shot it in the head with his rifle. Then he took out his knife and cut the pig's throat. To me, the scene was like some bizarre documentary; to the hillbillies, an ordinary event.

The big deal came moments later, as the poor pig began to shake itself blood-dry. It went into shock. When the animal shook, the blood flew in a swirling circle all around him. We were all very superstitious soldiers, and nobody wanted to be touched by the blood, figuring it would bring bad luck. So we ran to the side. The pig finally shook itself to death, but I will never forget the sight of the six or seven of us fleeing in every direction, trying to avoid the curse of its blood.

We all helped to butcher and skin the animal, under the tutelage of one of the ridge runners. We took it to a barn and hoisted it up by a rope tossed over a beam. It was a very professional, albeit makeshift, operation. When we were finally finished preparing the meat, one of the ridge runners cautioned that we should wait twenty-four hours before eating it. He said we had to let the life force leave the animal. It seemed to us practical (and hungry) New Yorkers that the animal's life force was long gone, and we proceeded with the meal. The pig got its revenge later that evening.

We should have listened to the country boy. All of us were up half the night, sick as dogs. None of us was seriously ill; most of us just had diarrhea.

For the most part, our meals were far less eventful, but many were equally memorable. I was forever being sent to the countryside or the nearest town, to make friends with the locals and get us invited to a nearby farmhouse for a meal, or to forage for chicken and Calvados that we could consume in our foxholes. I was a good talker and better with languages than the others, so I became the designated scrounger. I did this with considerable success in France, Belgium, Holland, and Germany. In Normandy, for example, I got a group of us invited to a French farmhouse for a delightful evening. Our hosts were not farmers but a well-to-do refugee family from Paris. There was a piano in the farmhouse, and one of the members of our squad was a marvelous jazz pianist. I cannot remember any of the details from that night, but it was congenial, with food and wine and song.

In Holland, I knocked on a farmhouse door and went into my standard spiel in halting German. The Dutch woman who answered was quite frightened at first, but when she realized I was an American soldier she laughed at my poor German. She became friendly as soon as I was able to make myself understood. We agreed on a price for a roasted chicken, and she told me to come back for it in two hours. I returned to my foxhole, and at the agreed-upon time I went back. But in the meantime, the house had been occupied by our company lieutenant, for his command post. I didn't know this when I knocked on the door.

"Come in," an American voice barked from the other side. The lieutenant was very nice about it. Though he could have kept the bird himself, he simply said, "Koch, your chicken is on the stove." He even smiled. I retreated back to my foxhole with our roast, where it provided a good meal, and a good laugh.

There is a great deal of ugliness underneath these happy memories. Our division was often in grave danger. We Timberwolves were part of the combat infantry and Ninth Army; we fired at Germans, and they fired back. Some of us never made it home. I am still haunted by four incidents among many unpleasant memories.

The first, once again, centers on food. (I have long wondered why so many of my wartime recollections are food-related.) We were in Breda, Holland. There was fighting around the city, and we were dug in on a dike. In the dikes, we were able to make good foxholes; when we dug into the fields, we were two feet down in the water. As I remember our position, there was a farmhouse behind us, in the middle of a big, open field. Across the field in front of us, on the next dike, were the German foxholes.

Someone in the squad had ventured into the farmhouse during the day and discovered it was abandoned, but well stocked with food. We decided to go back for the food that night. We were in a precarious position, but we were also hungry. One soldier was opposed to our plan, a Polish guy named Bolechoski. He was a religious Catholic with thick glasses. We got along well enough. He was pretty much a loner, but on this night he made a point of talking to all of us about the sinfulness of taking food, that it would be stealing from the absent Dutch family.

We tried to reason with him. This is war, we said, as we started to cross the field. Don't be foolish. These people have left their home. It is not stealing. We are soldiers. We're expected to eat their food.

Bolechoski was unwilling to join the feast, which consisted mostly of pickled green beans. He tagged along, though, urging us not to take the food. We argued with him and eventually prevailed on him to eat. He did so reluctantly. As soon as he finished, he lamented his decision. "I shouldn't have done it," I heard him say. "It's not right." It weighed heavily on his heart.

Later that night, back in our foxholes, a mortar scored a direct hit on Bolechoski's foxhole, and he was killed instantly. The rest of us were lucky. We could hear the mortars exploding, and I later imagined our religious friend, hunkered down against the attack, chastened by his deeds of the night and thinking, This is God's punishment. We all felt responsible for his death.

The second story has nothing at all to do with food. It concerns a shoe mine and a good friend named Mike Berrigan. A shoe mine was a three-pronged mine which protruded slightly out of the earth. It was designed to maim, not to kill. It detonated when it was stepped on, destroying the victim's leg and groin. We saw it at the time as one of the cruelest weapons of warfare; when deployed effectively, it left the victim in tremendous, agonizing pain, critically but not fatally injured. If the medics reached the victim quickly, he would live, but the wounded leg most likely would have to be amputated; if they did not reach him, the victim probably would bleed to death.

Our squad was crossing a field when Mike Berrigan stepped on one of these mines. He cried out in pain, then called for help. I was standing about twenty feet away, with another soldier; we were the only ones near enough to hear him, and we started our own cries of "Medic!" as we headed toward Mike.

I was pretty much scared to death, not just for Mike but for myself. If there was one mine, there would be others. I approached him with extreme caution, on hands and knees, probing the ground ahead of me with my bayonet. The other soldier did the same. We both proceeded as quickly as safety allowed.

Mike was moaning all the time. He was crying when we finally reached him. He thought he was dying. For all I knew then, he might have been. "My foot," he said to me. "My foot. It's gone."

He was right. It was. I wasn't going to tell him this, so I lied. "You're gonna be alright, Mike," I said. "Help is coming."

"How bad is it?" he wanted to know.

I looked at his leg again. There was no question he had lost his foot. It was still in his boot. It might have been hanging on by a tendon, but it was clear he would never have the use of it again. "Mike," I said, "you're a lucky guy. You're okay. You're gonna go home. The war's over for you. And it's really not bad. You're foot's okay. They'll fix it."

I have no idea whether or not Mike believed me. Probably not. I simply could not bring myself to tell him the truth. I kept wishing that the medics would hurry up—to administer to Mike, of course, but also to allow me to get back to the company, now almost across the field. The medics came soon enough. They were by far the bravest people in the entire war. These guys didn't use their bayonets when they crossed that mine field to Mike, as I had. They knew they were in mortal danger, but they were so focused on saving that soldier and so fearless that, most likely, they didn't think about it. They just did what they had to do. Two of them arrived, placed Mike on a stretcher, and took him away.

I never saw Mike Berrigan again, although we did correspond for a short time after the war. He did lose his foot but was fitted with a prosthetic device, and he was able to live a full, productive life. He married, and had children. He was a wonderful friend. We lost touch with each other, eventually, although years later, when I was mayor, Mike's son came to see me at City Hall while he was in New York for a visit. Regrettably, I was not in, but he left his name at the gate and told the guard he wanted to see me because I had saved his father's life. Now, I did not save Mike's life. I want to make that very clear. The medics did. I didn't even administer first aid before the medics arrived. All I did was try to comfort him. But in Mike's head and heart, I had something to do with his rescue from that mine field, enough so that he passed the story of my involvement on to his son.

The third incident has survived in memory as more of an image than a story. I didn't know the person involved— and so it resonates in a different way than the others. Still, it is perhaps the most grisly image I took home with me from overseas. The scene also took place in Holland, on the same day as Mike's accident. Our squad was attempting to cross a field when we were fired on by German 88s. The 88s were the most feared and most famous artillery in use at that time. They were extremely accurate, and only the Germans had them. They were designed to destroy tanks, although the Germans often used them directly at the troops. During this fire, we all broke into a dead run for cover. As I ran, I was looking forward, just as the soldier in front of me suffered a direct hit. His head was actually severed from the rest of his body. It is hard for me to imagine now how that happened—perhaps a fragment from the cannon shell hit him in the neck—but this man's head was literally hurled up into the air. His body simply crumpled to the earth.

It was a ghastly sight, and I will never forget the horror of it and the terror, but at the time I just kept running. I had to get across that field, or I too would die.

The last incident that I recall took place in Germany. I do not remember what German division we were chasing, but we were bogged down with several other squads, returning heavy fire. At one point, we retreated into a farmhouse. There were a couple of squads, each with twelve men, so there was a lot of activity in this fairly small space. It was night, and we took turns on sentry duty. After a while, we all woke at the sound of a shot. It was the guy on watch. He had heard some activity outside and fired into the night. The shot was followed by a cry for help, in English, from the field on the other side of the farmhouse door.

All of us realized what had happened in the same instant: the sentry had shot one of our own men! I went outside with two or three other soldiers to help drag him in. It was one of the country boys. He was a big, sweet man. He used to carry the "portable" radio on his back (in those days, the portable radios weighed about fifty pounds). We struggled to bring him inside. He was still conscious when we carried him through the farmhouse door, but he died quickly thereafter. There was nothing any of us could do for him, and no place to go for help.

In the morning, I checked his body. Rigor mortis had set in, and he was stiff as a board. I remember feeling an intense sorrow at the cruel accident, the unnecessary loss of such a good man. For me, this was perhaps the saddest personal moment of the entire war.

My frontline duty was curtailed after about three months by another accident, this one decidedly less serious. We were in the German Rhineland, in the city of Aachen, the site of our pig roast. We had taken the city after it was evacuated. I was searching an abandoned building at night with a few other soldiers when I tripped and fell down the cellar stairs. I didn't break any bones, but I did injure my knee and sprain my foot pretty badly; the knee later became infected. I wasn't in any great pain, but it hurt a good deal, and I had trouble walking.

I was hospitalized the next day and never saw combat duty again. It was November 1944. I was later reassigned to the Army's European Civilian Affairs Division, or ECAD. At the time, they were looking for people who could speak German, so I volunteered for the job. Of course, I knew about as much German as I did when they wouldn't let me into the ASTP German program, but there was no one at ECAD to make me struggle through my William Tell recitation. They took me at my word.

I was sent to Bavaria, where I remained for the balance of the war. No one in the detachment of ten spoke any German, and I was assigned to be the interpreter. So I had to learn. I did this by practicing with the German help working in the house. As I had vowed to do a year earlier in the ASTP program, I learned the language fairly quickly. Before long, I could speak it quite well. I was given a job broadly described as denazification, removing German public officials from their jobs and finding others to take their places.

Denazification basically meant whatever the Army wanted it to mean. The ECAD's denazification units assigned to the small towns around Bavaria consisted mainly of ten or so soldiers. One of the jobs in our unit was to seize property when we needed it. We never seized it simply to remove it from one group of bad Germans and give it to a group of good Germans. We would seek out the locals who had been enemies of the Nazis. We weren't always right, but that was the way it was done. In my whole time in Bavaria, I never met anyone who admitted to being a Nazi. Many told me about their Jewish grandmothers. How could they be Nazis? they argued. And then, when the evidence against them was clear, they claimed they were in the Nazi Party because it was forced upon them.

I was honorably discharged from the United States Army as a sergeant with a combat infantry badge, and two battle stars buck, in April of 1946. A new life was to begin for me, and I was to have company.

I bought a beautiful boxer puppy while I was in Bavaria, and she became my constant companion. I got her when she was about nine months old. Showing great imagination, I called her Boxer. It was a stupid name for such a splendid dog. She became a kind of trophy to me, a legacy from the war. I couldn't bear to leave her behind so she came home with me. Actually, I sent her on ahead. It was uncertain whether I would be able to ship the dog overseas, but for eighty dollars the Army provided a box and sent her as freight. So Boxer arrived in Brooklyn a few days before I did.

Boxer and I moved into my parents' apartment on Ocean Parkway. In later years, as a politician, I would often be asked to explain why I lived for so long with my parents, but it never even occurred to me to live anyplace else. This was home. And, after the war, I had no place else to go. I was now twenty-two years old. I didn't have a job. I had only two years of college. I had no idea what my next move would be.

So Boxer and I moved into the den. My mother was happy to have me home safe, but she wasn't too keen on the dog. Mama was smart enough to know that she'd wind up taking care of her. At first she even refused to let Boxer stay for more than a few days, but I pleaded with her to give the dog a chance. My sister Pat instantly fell in love with the dog, and she joined the campaign to let her remain. As I recall, we won a stay on her case one day at a time.

Boxer didn't exactly help her own cause, at the beginning. When we left her alone in the apartment, she destroyed the furniture. She tore up the carpet. She peed on my mother's bed. The dog was angry at being alone in the house. When Mama was home she chased after the dog, trying to discipline her, and as Boxer continued in this way, Mama's resolve to get rid of her deepened. Every day, we'd come home and hear what new havoc Boxer had wreaked, and Pat and I would cajole Mama into giving the dog one more chance.

Over time, Boxer wore Mama down. The dog drew out my mother's affection and within a few months she was doting on this animal as if she were hers, not mine. Boxer had two litters of puppies while she lived with us, and Mama doted on those animals as well. I think Mama grew to love Boxer more than we did. (Mama was right; she did wind up taking care of that dog.) Boxer stayed with us for nearly ten years, before she died of cancer. She first developed symptoms when she was nine. I took her to the veterinarian, who recommended that we put her to death. I couldn't do that, so I took her to another vet. His opinion was that they might be able to operate to remove the cancer, but it would cost one hundred and fifty dollars. People thought I was crazy to spend that kind of money on a dog; these days, of course, it is commonplace to spend much more.

Boxer lived for another year after her operation, and then the symptoms returned. I brought her back to the second veterinarian, who recommended immediate additional surgery. I consented, without a second thought. Two hours later, the doctor came out and told me he had put her to sleep. The cancer had metastasized and was too extensive, he said. He couldn't save her. The vet asked if I wanted to bury Boxer privately. I said no, but I did want to see the body. I wanted to make sure she was dead. I loved that dog, and I couldn't stand the thought that they might be doing experiments on her.

My adjustment to civilian life after the war was fairly smooth. I was only overseas for about twenty months, which does not seem enough time for any kind of culture shock to set in. What surprised me most upon my return was the singing commercials that seemed to proliferate on the radio. I didn't remember jingles from before the war, and now they were everywhere: "Pepsi Cola hits the spot. . . ."

Apart from the jingles, everything else seemed the same. I even remember thinking how strange it was that I had seen so much—indeed, we had fought a monumental war to free the world from Hitler's grip—and yet I returned home to find things pretty much as I had left them. My plans for the future were still up in the air. I had my two years at CCNY on which to build, but returning to my undergraduate studies seemed a waste, a step backward. After all, I had lost nearly three years of my life, and I needed to catch up.

For a long time, I had wanted to be a lawyer, so I applied to New York University Law School. In 1946, it was not unusual for someone to enter a law school without having a bachelor's degree, but it certainly wasn't the order of the day. Today, a college degree is required to gain admission, but back then, occasionally it was waived. In fact, in earlier days, even law school wasn't always necessary; you could become a lawyer by clerking for another lawyer and then passing the bar exam.

One of the attractive features of NYU Law School in those days was an accelerated course of study. They offered three semesters in one year, with no summer vacation, allowing students to graduate in two years instead of three. I applied for admission to this accelerated program. I had it all figured out. I would finish law school in two years, at the age of twenty-four (remember, I had graduated from high school at sixteen).

For a while it looked as though things wouldn't quite

work out this way. At NYU, I was interviewed by a professor who was not entirely convinced that my unfinished undergraduate education at CCNY was enough of a foundation on which to build a legal career.

"Mr. Koch," he said, after hearing me plead my case, "I am going to recommend that you go back and finish college. Come and see us again in two years."

I was terribly disappointed, but only for a moment. As I stood to leave the professor's office, crushed, I had a wonderful stroke of luck. Another professor walked by to exchange pleasantries with his colleague.

"I have a young man here who was a student at your alma mater," my interviewer said, by way of introduction.

"Ah," said the second professor, Paul Kaufman, extending his hand to me. "Will you be joining us next year?"

"I'm afraid not," my interviewer said, before I could answer. "Mr. Koch only finished two years at CCNY before he was drafted and sent overseas. I told him he should consider going back to college and then visit us again."

"What kind of grades does he have?" Kaufman asked, looking at me.

My interviewer informed him I had a B average at CCNY.

"A B average at CCNY is like an A anyplace else," my surprise benefactor said to his colleague. "I think we should take him."

And, with that, they took me. The chance encounter was one of the most important events of my career. If Paul Kaufman had not come by at that exact moment, I might never have gone to law school at all. Who knows what I might have done with my life? This moment was the first time I benefited from an old boys' network. (There would be a second and final time, two years later, when I was looking for a job.) I never owned a school tie in the usual sense. I should point out that there was some truth in Kaufman's evaluation of my CCNY grades. In those days,

CCNY was a tough school, and a B might well have been the equivalent of an A elsewhere. The school was known as the poor boy's Harvard. Nowadays, regrettably, a CCNY diploma will open no doors, and many old-time CCNY alumni are ashamed at the way the student body, the school newspaper, and a racist professor named Leonard Jeffries have made Jews feel unwelcome there with anti-Semitic claptrap.

I never did go back to CCNY to complete my bachelor's degree, because I never had to, although ultimately I did receive a degree from the school. After I became mayor, university officials invited me to their commencement ceremonies to give me an honorary bachelor's degree. I thought the invitation ironic, because I knew there were several on the CCNY board who did not like me. I wasn't radical enough in my politics for them. I knew this decision could not have been unanimous. I joked that it was probably decided by a six-to-five vote. They said they would credit me for my years of service in the Army and to the city. They also said it was to be a full-fledged, legitimate degree, but I never considered it so. I appeared at the commencement ceremony and accepted the degree with appreciation, but I have never cited it on my curriculum vitae. As far as I'm concerned, I still don't have an undergraduate degree.

And so, without the benefit of a degree but with the full force of an old school tie, I was accepted to law school. Unfortunately, even Paul Kaufman's nod of approval was not enough to get me into the accelerated class beginning that summer, because it was already full. I was admitted for the fall, and I decided to fill the summer ahead with a job in the mountains. I needed the money and the vacation. I thought a job as a busboy at one of the Catskill mountain resort hotels would fill the bill. Unfortunately, I was turned down by several employment agencies because I had no experience. So I had to lie. I told the man who hired me I'd been a busboy for many years, although I had never carried a tray that did not have my own food on it. I was so convincing they offered me the job of busboy captain at the Adler Hotel in Sharon Springs, New York. There were to be only two other busboys on the staff, but I was captain, even though I couldn't carry a tray with one hand.

I never anguished about misrepresenting myself to the Adler Hotel, because the job and the hotel did not exactly come through as advertised. I had imagined my summer this way: a little waiting on tables, a little tennis, a little waiting on tables, a little swimming. The Adler Hotel had imagined my summer this way: a little waiting on tables, a little painting, a little waiting on tables, a little light repair work. They actually brought us up there two weeks before the season to paint the place. What an operation! I was so miserable. There was no tennis or swimming. Worse, the food was terrible, and what there was of it was pretty spare. It was as though they took one meal, breakfast, divided it into three parts, and served it over the course of the entire day.

I was rescued from this miserable summer by a phone call from home. The NYU admissions office had called to inform me that a space had opened up in the accelerated summer program. Someone had dropped out, and they were offering the slot to me. I immediately gave notice to the Adler Hotel, put down my paintbrush, and went home.

3

Brooklyn

I PASSED THE BAR EXAM ON my second try, in the spring of 1949. I was troubled, but not overwhelmed, by my initial failure. I could have done without the additional anxiety, but as I said, I have never been first in anything, and it seemed the law would be no exception. (I graduated in the middle of my class at NYU Law.)

Actually, that I failed the bar the first time out is not entirely accurate. I passed one half of the test and failed the other, so I only had to take the second half over. Nowadays, you must retake the entire exam, no matter what. The exam was only the first of my worries. I also had to be recommended to the New York Bar Association's character committee, which struck me then, and does still, as an intimidating procedure. I didn't know anyone who knew members of that committee, so I had to scramble. With some effort, I collected the recommendations I needed, but it was a distressing ordeal, as I imagine it is today.

Finding a job was even more distressing. I didn't have any connections. There were no lawyers in my family. Many of my law school friends had at least one family acquaintance on whom they could call for help. I had no one. Others also had far better grades than I did. And I had not yet passed the bar. I got to the point where I knocked on doors cold, walking the pavement for what seemed like weeks, until I finally found myself sitting across the desk from a benevolent CCNY graduate. He didn't have a job to offer me, but he did send me to see a friend of his named Joe Finkelstein, who he thought might have a position available.

Mr. Finkelstein had a small Manhattan practice, in a small and very Spartan office at 38 Park Row, across the street from City Hall. He hired me on the spot. I started out at fifteen dollars a week, with the understanding that I would be raised to twenty-five dollars a week once I passed the bar. The money barely paid for lunches and carfare. But I did not resent Joe Finkelstein, who was a very nice man, for paying me so little. He was doing me a favor. He didn't need me. I couldn't find a job anywhere else, and he knew it. He took me in as a great kindness. And I was happy for the chance.

Of course, I wasn't happy for long. Even at twenty-five dollars a week, and even living at home with my parents, I wasn't making enough to get by. If I wanted to go out with friends for a first-class lunch, it cost about seven dollars. My classmates and I stayed in touch by lunching once a week, a practice I could hardly afford on my salary. And I wasn't particularly enjoying the work Joe was assigning— mostly research, which is the lot of almost every first-year associate. I was not brilliant at research. I wanted to try cases.

After a few months, I got a job at Regosin & Edwards, a small corporate law firm at 70 Pine Street, at sixty dollars a week. Now I could afford those seven-dollar lunches, although I was still waiting for my chance to try cases. I did research there, too, and answered calendar calls in court. I even wrote some briefs, but those were never my specialty.

After two years at Regosin & Edwards, I decided that the only way to do what I wanted was to practice on my own. You have to understand, I wasn't risking all that much with this decision. I had no family to support. My living expenses were minimal. I was young enough to find

another job if things didn't work out. More important, a
GI program at the time helped veterans to start their own
businesses, with a stipend of one hundred dollars per
month for one year, above expenses. I no longer remember exactly how the program worked, but I figured I would
wind up with twenty dollars each week. That was about
what I had been making at my first job. It was a tremendous incentive.

Joe Finkelstein, my first boss, did me another kindness
to get me started: he gave me a room free of charge at 38
Park Row. It was an old, third-rate building, but the rent
was clearly affordable. I moved to a nicer office, at 52 Wall
Street, as soon as I could afford to pay rent.

My first case as a trial lawyer was special. It actually
dated back to Milford Avenue in Newark, and my brother,
Harold. Harold was not the world's best student. He was
difficult, unruly, constantly in trouble at school. He gave
his teachers a very hard time. He sold school rings without
having the school concession. He was found in a burlesque
house when it was raided by truant officers. Mama spent a
lot of time at the principal's office. School and Harold
simply did not get along, and he had no interest in going
on to college. After graduation, he needed a job, but they
were scarce during the Depression, particularly jobs with
good career prospects attached to them.

Enter Milton Wiener. Wiener, we would later learn, was
a crook. He conned a lot of people, including my father,
into believing he could obtain a Teamsters union card for
them or their adult children. The Teamsters, in Newark,
was a closed union, and for five hundred dollars (a lot of
money in those days) Milton Wiener promised a lifetime
job and a union card. He told my father he could get
Harold a job delivering newspapers, at a good salary
(forty-five dollars a week, as I recall), and with excellent
benefits. So my father paid the five hundred dollars.
Milton Wiener earned Papa's trust by taking Harold out
on the trucks as an apprentice for many months, while he
taught my brother the business. The business consisted of

Harold's binding the papers into bundles and delivering them to the truck, all the while waiting for his union card.

The card never came. Wiener disappeared. He abandoned his wife and children. He left Newark, we later learned, with about ten thousand dollars, filched from trusting people like my father in similar scams. There was a big scandal, and an investigation, but no arrests were made. My father never heard from Milton Wiener again. Harold never got his union card (instead, he married his first wife, Frances Schottenfeld, who owned a carpet business with her brothers, but that's another story), and my father did not get his money back.

Ten years later, the scene of this since-forgotten crime shifted to New York. I had just left Regosin & Edwards. By sheer coincidence, Harold spotted Milton Wiener on a Manhattan street and convinced a policeman to detain him. There were several outstanding warrants for Wiener's arrest. The resulting police report revealed his address, which turned out to be a sleazy midtown hotel. I decided to pursue Milton Wiener in a civil case. I had nothing else to do, and the years had not diminished my distaste for this man who had cheated my father out of his hard-earned money. Acting as my father's attorney, I sued him in municipal court for the five hundred dollars, plus interest. And I won. I had to attach his salary in order to collect, but he paid ten dollars a week for well over a year, until his debt, including lots of interest, was paid.

What satisfaction! It wasn't the money that made this victory sweet. It was the justice: I had sued Milton Wiener and made him accountable for his actions. It was a special triumph, underlined by the fact that this was my first real trial. I believe I was a good trial lawyer, but not a great one. I had good instincts as a cross-examiner, since I was always able to think pretty quickly on my feet. What I was never very good at, and indeed pursued with great difficulty, was soliciting business. I recognized this gradually but soon enough. I was not particularly aggressive in hustling up work, but my overhead was low and my needs modest, so I managed.

One of the ways lawyers traditionally add to their store of clients is to become active in local groups. In my case, though, the impulses for these outside activities were more social than professional. For example, I had been active at our synagogue since 1946, when I returned from overseas. The Flatbush Jewish Center was a conservative synagogue at the corner of Church Avenue and Ocean Parkway, about two blocks from our apartment. (It is still there, incidentally.) Indeed, my interests in the center were more social than religious. The temple sponsored a Young People's League, which I quickly joined and in which I soon took a leadership position. We went on retreats and held dances, and staged theatrical productions. Eventually, I became president of the league, or YPL, as it was known.

Even then, I was a good administrator. I increased membership to record numbers and raised a good deal of money by sponsoring Saturday night dances and a regular lecture series. The YPL was part of a national organization of young adults affiliated with the conservative movement of the Jewish religion. There were about five or six of us at the core of the Flatbush group, and we spent almost all of our free time together. I have not seen any of them for many years, and only a few of their names still come easily to mind—Irv Sultan, Harold Kalb, Mike Rosenfeld—but I recall the period with great fondness. While it may have been a frustrating time for me professionally, it was a happy period socially, one that enhanced my feelings for the history and traditions of my religion and the Jewish nation.

I don't recall that I generated a great amount of legal business as a direct result of my YPL presidency. My emerging political involvement had a more direct impact on my career, although this too began as more of a social outlet than anything else. I wanted to meet people, and exchanging ideas and lobbying for a common cause seemed to me a good way to do this. My active role in politics began in 1952, when I campaigned on street corners for Adlai Stevenson's presidential bid. I was even more active in his 1956 campaign. Street speaking was an effective tool both times; there is considerably less of it today, in the age of television and radio sound bites, paid and unpaid, and that is too bad.

In 1952, the New York State Democratic Committee provided its speakers with an American flag of specific dimensions, then required to be displayed by law. We generally used a chair, or a plastic carton, to elevate ourselves over the crowds. I would spend most of my lunch hours lauding Stevenson's candidacy. My office was then at 52 Wall Street, and I used to go down at noon to the corner where Broad, Nassau, and Wall Streets come together and place my chair on the steps of the Federal Hall National Memorial, the historic site of George Washington's inauguration as the first President of this country. It seemed a fitting spot for my efforts. Moreover, it was probably the busiest place in downtown Manhattan during lunchtime.

I enjoyed these speeches a great deal; they were almost always successful. On most days, a handful of people would gather, then grow to a crowd of two to three hundred. I wasn't using an amplifier of any kind (that required a five-dollar police permit), so it was sometimes an effort to make myself heard, but I managed. I was always a good street speaker, and I like to think these big crowds were a reflection of my abilities, but I also realize there wasn't much to do during the lunch hour but sit outside with a sandwich and listen to me, or one of the Holy Roller street evangelists across the way.

What thrilled me most about Adlai Stevenson was his speeches. He was a solid candidate and had my full support. In retrospect, I don't think he would have made as good a President as Eisenhower; he was such a remote personality that he never could have galvanized the nation the way Eisenhower ultimately was able to do. Stevenson's major attraction for me was his opposition to the development and use of the hydrogen bomb. Beyond that, he was not of heroic dimensions.

I have never had a hero—everyone has clay feet—but, for me, Harry Truman probably came closest to filling the role. He was the only President in my lifetime that I consider extraordinary. What I loved and admired about Truman, and I suspect what the country loved and admired, was that he was an ordinary man who rose to the occasion. He was one of us. He had common sense, and he never lost it in thought or action. Of course, he also had clay feet. He was anti-Semitic and anti-black at one time in his life, but I believe he overcame those prejudices and became a fairer and more effective leader.

My admiration for Adlai Stevenson was much less, but he was clearly my candidate of choice. Stevenson's great legacy was that he was a magnificent writer, and a truly wonderful speaker. I can read his speeches and actually be moved by them. They were quite extraordinary. My speeches on his behalf were not quite on the same level, but they got the point across. I used to orate about the hydrogen bomb, stating that Stevenson would stop it and Eisenhower would use it. That was the campaign.

There is a story that emerged from the street campaign that I have retold many times over the years. It is one of my favorites. I had the crowd worked up to a pretty good lather one afternoon, when I was suddenly approached by a burly Irish cop. He interrupted my speech and asked to see my permit. I reminded him, politely, that I was displaying the American flag, that I was not using a loudspeaking device and was therefore not required to have a permit. Despite my explanation, the cop threatened me with a ticket if I did not stop.

"Officer," I tried again. "I am an attorney. My office is just a few blocks from here. I am protected by the Constitution. I am allowed to speak. Trust me on this."

"Listen, Bud," the cop said. "This is the last time I'm tellin' ya. You've got no permit. Stop, or I'm gonna take you in."

Now, I knew this police officer was just trying to do his job, but what bothered me was that he wasn't doing it well. He was a beat cop assigned to patrol a busy downtown business district. Surely, he should have known the laws regulating public speaking. I was totally frustrated by the interruption and the hassle, especially because I had a good crowd and a nice momentum going before this cop came along. I also knew that I would lose them if I allowed this exchange to become heated in any way, so I tried to reason with this unreasonable man.

"Officer, look," I said, indicating one of the evangelists across the street. "That guy is there every single day, preaching about the coming of the Messiah. He's got a crowd the same size as mine. You never ask him for a permit."

"He's different," the cop said, with total sincerity. "He's a fanatic."

On a personal level, a few significant things changed for me before I campaigned for Stevenson again four years later. The first was that I rented a house one summer, on Fire Island, with four or five other guys. We were in a community called Fair Harbor. I didn't know any of those people before the summer began. My sister introduced me to one of them; Pat worked with him at the Theological Seminary of America, and she knew he was looking for another summer shareholder to help defray the group's expenses. I thought the change in routine would do me good. It did. I enjoyed that summer enormously, and it led me directly to the next big development: I decided the time had come for me to move out of my parents' apartment and get a place of my own. My father didn't take the news too well. He thought that I should not move out until my sister was married later that year. It didn't make any sense, his thinking, but he was absolutely firm. He was beside himself at my decision. Remember, I was thirty-two years old at the time, and Pat must have been about twenty-four. Pat didn't care one way or the other. Still, Papa was irrational, to the point where he tried to forbid me to move out until Pat married. He also threatened he would never talk to me again. Jewish grudges are funny.

I moved anyway. My father continued to talk to me. Pat was already engaged, by this time, and the summer's taste of living on my own had whetted my appetite for more. I wound up taking a place at 81 Bedford Street, in Greenwich Village, with one of my Fair Harbor housemates, Bill Sommer. The rent, which we shared, was $145 a month, which was a lot of money in those days, although reasonably cheap for the Village. After a while, Bill married and moved out, and I was on my own. What I remember best, and most fondly, about the neighborhood was a bar called Louie's, at Seventh Avenue and Fourth Street, in Sheridan Square. It was a cellar bar, with a restaurant. It's no longer there, but at the time Louie's served the best (and biggest) plate of veal parmigiana in the city. The meal cost a dollar seventy-five, and beer was ten cents a glass. With Louie's so close and so cheap, eating out was the thing to do.

Almost immediately, I sought out the group of Village Democrats that was supporting Stevenson—Citizens for Stevenson was the alternative to the organization of the local Democratic county leader, Carmine De Sapio, who had refused to endorse Stevenson's candidacy. The group later became known as the Village Independent Democrats and played a pivotal role in my rising political career, but I'll get to that. During the 1956 campaign, I became the group's major street speaker, reprising my role from 1952. Of course, the venue was changed this time around, and I moved my soapbox from Wall Street to Sheridan Square, or sometimes to the corner of Eighth Street and Sixth Avenue, where I gathered even bigger crowds than I had downtown.

I simply loved talking to these neighborhood crowds. And I had a flair for it. Even then, my remarks were always extemporaneous. I was particularly effective in responding to questions. I especially loved disarming the hecklers, who would regularly turn out to hear me speak.

Hecklers are a regular component of street speaking. As long as they are not drunk or violent, they are an asset. They actually keep the crowd listening to the speaker.

The Citizens for Stevenson group was run by a young man named Dick Kuh, who was an assistant district attorney under Frank Hogan. (He was later appointed district attorney, but when he ran for a full term, he was defeated by Robert Morgenthau.) I was the group's most enthusiastic speaker, maybe its best and certainly its busiest, but for some reason I never quite fit in. I left the group shortly after the election, deciding it was too cliquey and that I would never be happy there. I didn't do anything politically for the next several months. It may have been even a year.

I never lost my distaste for club politics, although I did eventually return to it. Carmine De Sapio sent two of his young supporters to ask me to join his Tamawa Club, the Democratic club that essentially controlled Greenwich Village politics from its loft offices at 88 Seventh Avenue South. The club was about to be reformed, they said; the old guard would soon give way to some of the younger members; they were looking for new blood. I figured I'd give the Tamawa Club a shot, so I signed on. I needed an outlet for my energies. I had come very quickly to enjoy Village politics, the exchange of ideas with neighbors deeply involved in the community, the ability (or at least the perceived ability) to make some impact on my corner of the world.

Of course, all the talk about club reforms turned out to be just talk. De Sapio was the traditional kind of political leader—a deal maker, dispenser of favors, and collector of IOUs—and he was not about to relinquish control of anything. Still, I stayed on at the Tamawa Club for a number of months. It was run like an Orthodox synagogue: women sat on one side of the room, and men sat on the other. Women did not pay dues and were accorded only honorary-member status, and I remember being particularly appalled at their exclusion since, under the party rules,

Carmine shared his position as Village district leader with a woman coleader named Elsie Gleason Mattura.

I came to see the Tamawa Club as ridiculous. It represented everything that was wrong with city politics, so I left. Politically, I was once again adrift, and I remained unaffiliated for the next year or so. Professionally, my practice was beginning to prosper. I was surviving. Maybe my short-lived career in politics had some carryover benefit to my law practice. Personally, this tentative period was marked by the most wrenching and painful tragedy of my adult life: the death of my mother, from cancer.

It was not at all sudden. It might have been easier on all of us, Mama included, if it had been. She had been under treatment for a gallbladder condition for five years. At first, she didn't tell any of us she was sick. Of course, she didn't know she had cancer at the time, but she was in a great deal of pain. One Sunday, by chance, I stopped at my parents' apartment the evening before my mother was to check into the hospital for surgery, something she had not told us about. It was August 1960. I had rented a cabana/locker at Lido Beach for the summer, and I often stopped off in Brooklyn on my way back to the Village.

"Oh, Ed," Mama said as I came through the door. "I'm so happy you're here." She hugged me.

Now, Mama was always glad to see me, but she seemed more pleased than usual by this visit. She seemed agitated, on edge. I suspected something. "What's wrong, Mama?" I asked.

"I'm going into the hospital tomorrow," she announced, as if it was nothing at all.

"What's wrong?"

"Nothing," she assured me. "Just a little heartburn, gallbladder trouble. It's nothing serious."

But it was serious. After five years, Mama's incompetent doctor advised her to have her gallbladder removed and had a surgeon check her into a small, undistinguished private hospital on Kings Highway in Brooklyn. When I spoke to the surgeon, he assured me the procedure was a simple matter and told me not to worry.

Thank God I didn't listen to him. Of course I worried. How could I not? I had never heard of this surgeon, or this hospital. And Mama's doctor did not impress me as a man who knew exactly what he was doing. It took some effort, but I finally convinced my mother to let me bring in a well-known surgeon, and to move her to a first-class hospital. Several days later she checked into Brooklyn Jewish Hospital. Her surgery was rescheduled for the following day. My father and I waited downstairs during the operation. After about two hours, the doctor came down to the waiting room and approached my father. The doctor's face looked completely blank. "Mr. Koch," he said. "There is no way to tell you this except straight from the shoulder. Your wife has cancer. It's inoperable. She's going to die. I'm terribly sorry."

"When?" Papa said.

"My guess is three months."

Papa and I began to cry. Through our sobs we heard the doctor explain that Mama's cancer, which she probably had had for the past five years, had spread throughout her stomach and abdomen. "There is nothing you can do to save her," the doctor said. "Please believe me. Don't take her from place to place. You will only torture her. There is nothing anyone can do. Let her die in peace."

We didn't know what to do. It all seemed too much to us. But someone had to tell Harold and Pat, someone had to make arrangements for Mama's care, and that someone was me. First, though, Papa and I pulled ourselves together and went to Mama's room. We sat by her side, waiting for the anesthetic to wear off. When she woke up, she looked at me and asked how the operation had gone.

"Mama, you're fine," I lied. "It was just gallstones." We never told my mother what was wrong with her. In those days, people were not told that they had cancer. The news was considered too crushing. For our family, it was a bad decision. It meant that none of our conversations from

that day on were honest. People do things differently today, and with good reason.

We took Mama home a few days later. For the next
several weeks, we took turns taking care of her. I com-
muted between my parents' apartment and mine. I took a
lot of time away from my law practice to help out at home.
I was on my own, and I had more time to spare than Pat
or Harold, so I was with my parents at some point every
day. Harold lived in New Jersey, and Pat had just had a
premature baby and was recuperating at home in River-
dale. I stayed at my parents' apartment some nights, although mostly I went home. The time alone in my car,
driving back and forth, was awful. When I was with my
parents, or with Harold and Pat, I was usually okay, but
driving home late at night, I would break into sobs. How
could this be happening to such a strong, wonderful
woman? I wondered in my private moments. Why, God?

The logistics of arranging for Mama's care were simpler
than the caretaking itself. She was in great pain. Some
days were better than others, but most were worse. Her
colon was blocked, and she couldn't move her bowels. She
became jaundiced. We called in a local doctor to help, but
there was nothing he could do. We never called the original doctor, the one who diagnosed her condition as gallstones. If I had seen that man again, I would have killed
him. He had misdiagnosed my mother for five years. I
don't know that those five years of non-treatment caused
her death, but I certainly thought so then and still do.

My poor, dear mother was in agony. She knew there
was something wrong beyond what we were telling her,
but we still kept the news from her. It seemed like the
compassionate thing to do. When she asked about her
jaundice, which was caused by her cancerous liver, we told
her it came from adhesions. We told her they were block-
ing her colon, that they would go away, and she would be
fine. We were as consoling as we knew how to be, lying
every day. I don't think Mama believed us, but after a
while she stopped asking what was wrong with her.

In a few weeks, she became too much for us to handle. The doctor was coming to the apartment twice a day to administer pain medication. My father and I tried to resume work. My brother and sister had their own families and schedules to juggle. The housekeeper we employed during the day was unable to provide adequate care; it was too much for her, and not enough for my mother.

Finally, we all agreed that Mama could not go on like this. It was too painful for her. It was too painful for us. We were still not prepared to tell her the truth about her cancer, but we were determined to do something for her. I went back to the surgeon at Brooklyn Jewish and sought his help in obtaining treatment.

"Mr. Koch," he insisted, "there is really nothing we can do for her."

"What about X-ray treatments?" I asked.

"In your mother's case, I wouldn't recommend them," he said. "The cancer has spread too far."

"Will they hurt her?"

"No," he said, "but they won't help her and I wouldn't recommend them."

I knew the doctor was right, that pursuing this type of treatment would probably be a waste of time, but I could not let someone I loved, my own mother, die before my eyes without doing something. She was in such pain. So, more for us than for her, we decided to subject her to X rays. I set up an appointment at a clinic. I went with Mama on her initial visit. I walked in ahead of her and told the doctor that my mother didn't know she had cancer. I asked him please to tell her she was being treated for adhesions. He said he would. Then I went back to the waiting room to try to keep my mother from talking to any of the other patients. Everyone there had cancer.

I should have known Mama better. We all should have. She was a brave, smart woman. She knew what was going on. If she didn't know before that trip to the X-ray lab, she did the moment the doctor opened his mouth. "Mrs.

Koch," he said, after looking at her chart, "I am prescribing twenty X-ray treatments."

In that precise moment, Mama knew. I feel sure of this. She put her hand on mine, and for a long while she said nothing. Finally, she said, "I didn't know I was that sick." Now she knew.

Even so, we never talked about it again. We never talked about her cancer, or about her dying, or about how much we all meant to each other. It was a tragic mistake. We all knew the truth, and we could have been a great comfort to each other.

Predictably, the X-ray treatments did not help. The only thing they did do was confirm to all our well-meaning cousins and aunts and friends and neighbors that Mama had cancer. Our phone started ringing off the hook. Everyone knew a doctor who had a cure for cancer, and everyone expected us to give their doctor a try. We didn't know what to do. We wanted to listen, and to give each suggestion our serious consideration, but we didn't want to drag Mama to every quack in New York City, searching for a cure the surgeon told us did not exist. We had already been to many well-known doctors seeking second opinions, and all had said there was no hope.

I drove Mama to all of these appointments, sometimes too fast. On one trip, as we were heading up the East River Drive to Mount Sinai Hospital, I was pulled over by a cop. We were late for our appointment, and I was going ten miles over the speed limit.

"Officer," I said as I got out of the car, out of Mama's earshot. "Whatever you're going to do, please do it quickly. My mother has cancer. I'm taking her to the hospital. We're already late for her appointment." It must have been obvious to this man from my bearing and demeanor how distressed I was, and I thought surely he would send us on our way with a warning and his good wishes. Instead he made us wait while he wrote out a speeding ticket. It struck me then, as it does now, as a perverse act of inhumanity. I have never forgotten it.

Finally, my cousin Sylvia Seasonwein called with the name of a doctor who had, she said, cured several cancer patients. Sylvia actually knew some of these patients. Dr. Revicci was affiliated with a hospital called Trafalgar, on Manhattan's Upper East Side, which later became an abortion center but back then was an accredited Blue Cross hospital. What could be bad? Blue Cross and Blue Shield wouldn't allow a quack in their hospital, I thought. So I made an appointment.

Dr. Revicci examined my mother and said, "I can cure her." Just like that.

We all wanted to believe him. I thought, Maybe he can, maybe he can't, and I was grateful that he was willing to take her on as a patient and admit her to the hospital. No other hospital would take a terminally ill patient; in those days, they were expected to die at home. For this alone, I could have kissed Dr. Revicci's hands.

His method of treatment involved an elixir he had developed—a serum taken, as I recall, from horses—which was administered to my mother once a day, in a tiny paper cup. Mama drank it down without complaint until the day she died. Dr. Revicci charged twenty-five dollars a day for this medication, which reinforced my first impression that he was not a quack: a quack would charge much more than twenty-five dollars a day.

This treatment went on for a period of weeks. Dr. Revicci kept telling us my mother was getting better, but she continued in terrible pain. She seemed to be getting progressively worse. One afternoon, I arrived at the hospital and found her screaming in pain. I had never heard my mother cry out like this. It was agonizing to hear.

"Eddie!" she cried, as I came into her room to comfort her. "Why don't you let me die? I can't take the pain. I want to die."

I took her hand. "Mama," I said, in my most reassuring voice, stifling my need to cry, "would we be keeping you alive, and watching you suffer in this way, if we didn't know you're getting better?" It shames me now to admit it, but even her violent suffering was not enough to shake me from my white lies. I knew that she knew that she had cancer, and that she was dying, but I wanted to believe she was getting well. I wanted her to believe it.

When my mother was calm and the pain had passed, I sought out Dr. Revicci. "How can you do this to my mother?" I yelled at him, when I found him downstairs. "She is in agony! You're not curing her! She's dying. Why don't you stop prolonging the pain and let her die, as she wants to?"

"She is getting well," he insisted. "I am going to cure her. Would I allow her to suffer this way if I didn't think I could cure her?"

What could I say? He was the doctor. I wanted to believe him.

Mama lived a few days longer. The pain came and went. We all took turns at her side. One of us was with her around the clock. Finally, on her last day, three months almost to the day after her surgery, she went into convulsions. She shook and shivered; she seemed to be freezing. My father and I looked on, unable to help her. We held her hand, stroked her hair, kissed her hands, but we couldn't help her. It was clear to us that she was collapsing. The doctors scrambled to perform a procedure called a cutdown. That was the term; I'll never forget it. They did that cutdown on her foot, looking for a vein to get an IV started, her other veins having collapsed. Mama died as we stood at her bedside. Even after thirty years, I weep at the memory. I was overwhelmed with grief—in his own way, Papa was, too.

Much later, the end to my parents' long years of fighting with each other reminded me of an old joke: An elderly man is standing at the grave of his wife, crying hard, bitter tears. His son approaches the man and says, "Papa, why are you crying so? You know you didn't love her. I can't believe you're crying now that she's dead." And the father says, "Why did she take so long?"

I believe my father's tears were real. He and Mama had

considerable differences over the years; they drove each other crazy; they didn't belong together. But they were together; they had built a life, and a home, and a family. And now my father was alone.

I made the funeral arrangements. Though we were not Orthodox, we decided on an Orthodox funeral. I took my father to the Riverside Funeral Chapel, at the head of Ocean Parkway near Prospect Park. We needed to pick out a casket. We told the director we were looking for something in the Orthodox tradition, and he ushered us into a room with a twenty-five-hundred-dollar casket. Undertakers were famous for doing this, and I suspect they still are. What a despicable racket! He knew that we were looking for something simple, but he figured he'd work his hard sell on us just the same.

He took us into several rooms, and in each room the caskets cost less. He didn't skip a room. Probably he thought our resolve would weaken and we would be shamed into buying an expensive one. Finally, he took us into the basement, where he showed us two pine boxes, which is what we had told him we wanted in the first place. My mother would not have appreciated an expensive casket; she would have thought it a tremendous waste of money. And besides, an Orthodox funeral requires a simple wooden casket without nails or ornament. The idea is that the body should go "from dust to dust" as quickly as possible.

The funeral-home director knew this, and yet he persisted in his pitch. Even here in the basement, he wanted to sell us the more expensive of the two pine caskets. One of them had a Star of David on the top, and it cost fifty dollars more than the plain model. We were so humiliated by the ordeal that we said yes to the Star of David. We could resist no further. I've never forgotten that. That man made us feel cheap, and we succumbed.

A bizarre story surfaced during this time. I didn't recognize it as bizarre until years later. I didn't even recognize it as a story. I'll explain. When it came time to collect my mother's belongings from the hospital, I discovered that her diamond engagement ring was missing. I was certain she was wearing it when we brought her there; indeed, I have a picture in my mind of my holding her hand, her fingers clasped around mine, and she is wearing the ring. I can still see it. It was just a simple diamond ring, but it was of tremendous sentimental value, particularly at the time. I was incensed that it had disappeared. I was convinced one of the hospital orderlies had taken the ring from my mother's finger after she passed away, and I was enraged at the thought: what ghouls!

My anger never subsided. There was nothing I could do about it, but it continued to bother me, even after many years. I felt better when I talked about it, so I told the story often. I wrote about it. It worked its way into several of my public statements as Congressman and mayor, before my sister finally heard it and set me straight.

"That ring wasn't stolen," Pat said. "I've had it all these years." Now, at least, we have one thing we can laugh about when we think of that time.

I am now five years older than Mama was when she died, but even now, I can recall her agony and feel her pain. She was such a tough, smart, and resourceful woman. Her death also left me with a great many regrets. At the core of most of them was the deception we all engaged in to try and keep the fact of Mama's cancer from her. I often wish I could undo those lies. I wish we could have told Mama the truth, that we were there to help make her remaining days as full and comfortable as possible. I wish I had had an honest conversation with her about what was happening. As I said, we underestimated her. She could have handled it. In fact, she did. She undoubtedly knew, at least on some level, but we all chose to go through it silently. She should have been given the opportunity to decide on her treatment. Maybe she didn't want to be schlepped all over town from one doctor to another. If she knew what was really happening to her, she would have been able to make her own, informed decisions. Maybe she wanted to die at home, in peace.

Most of all, we all wish we had had the chance to say an honest good-bye, to tell Mama how much she had meant to us.

4

Greenwich Village

LIFE WENT ON AFTER MY mother died, as I knew it always does. My father adjusted to his new role of widower better than the rest of us did to life without Mama. I think he actually became a better, nicer person after my mother's death. He felt freer, happier. He was never very happy in his marriage. He and Mama were never a good fit. Mama was smarter than he, he was nicer than she, and more caring to others. Papa quickly decided he did not want to live alone. Luckily, he found someone else right away. His friends introduced him to a widow named Rose Klein, who was also hoping to marry. Like my father, Rose was the antithesis of sophistication; she had ordinary intelligence and very little schooling. They liked the same things. They were a good match, and they married about a year later. Rose was a good, kind woman, and we children were delighted that Papa had found someone to take care of him, to love him and keep him company. Besides, we all knew, if he didn't remarry, ultimately one of us would have had to take him in.

But I'm getting ahead of myself. Let me get back to 1960. I returned my full energies to my growing law practice and started looking for a partner. And I stepped up my involvement in Village politics. By this time I had rejoined the Village Independent Democrats. I had worried that I would not be welcomed back, since my break with the club a few years earlier had been somewhat acrimonious, but they were glad to have me. They were looking for new people, particularly those who were willing to give a good deal of their time and take on leadership positions. I became chairman of the speakers' committee and played a major role in the group's unsuccessful district leadership campaign in 1959.

After my mother's death, I was even more active in the club, becoming its law chairman, which essentially meant that I was responsible for the preparation of all of our election-designating petitions and other highly technical matters involved in getting on the ballot. In 1960, we ran two candidates for state committee. As with the district leader position, the state law called for a male and a female candidate to be jointly elected. Our candidates were Jim Lanigan and Sarah Schoenkopf. Carmine De Sapio, a very smart politician, decided not to run his usual party hacks, as we at the VID referred to the Tamawa candidates; instead, fearing public support for our reform platform, he recruited two reformers of his own, Charlie Kinsolving and Eleanor Clark French. It was a shrewd move. His candidates had impeccable credentials; our candidates' were good, but not as good. As ever, the Tamawa Club would be tough to beat.

Of course, we were really running against De Sapio, although his name was not on the ballot. That was clear to everyone. To the VID, the state committee seats represented a significant first step toward gaining full control of party politics in the Village; to De Sapio, the seats promised at least the status quo, allowing him to maintain his strong political base and clout, for himself and his club. I spent most of that campaign on a soapbox, often on the corner of Eighth Street and MacDougal, attacking De Sapio and extolling our own candidates. I always made it a point to praise the records of service of De Sapio's candidates, who were not members of his club and were themselves leaders in the reform movement, while attacking De Sapio as district leader. It seemed to me that it would be unfair to attack Kinsolving and French, with their better credentials, simply because they were being used by a boss. In truth, I wasn't particularly fond of one of our own candidates, Lanigan. I thought he was weak and somewhat foolish. I wasn't about to undermine his candidacy in any way, but I tried to be honest in my soapbox oratory and let the people know that the real issue was whether we were going to let De Sapio continue to control Village party politics, or send a message by defeating his dupes, as good and decent as the two of them were.

My candor stunned a lot of people in my own club, but it won us a lot of support as well. Many politicians would not have done what I did, but my approach has always been to be straightforward and intellectually honest. Say exactly what you think and what you know to be true, and people will generally believe you. If it makes sense, people will understand it, even if it ruffles some feathers. Luckily, in this election, my message came through. (If it hadn't, the VID might have found someone else to put on its soapbox.) We trounced De Sapio's candidates. I honestly thought we would win, but not by such a wide margin. De Sapio's tight grip on Village politics was loosening. It was our first victory, and it gained us a firm footing in the district.

The district had three official clubs: the Tamawa Club, the Murray Hill Club, and the Tilden Club. The Murray Hill and Tilden groups had already defeated the old-line clubs in their neighborhoods and were recognized as official. The VID was seeking to do the same in the Village by defeating the Tamawa Club for the district leadership. We had unsuccessfully opposed De Sapio's club in 1957 and 1959. But even our dramatic victory in the 1960 state committee election was not enough to gain us official club status; that would have to come in the next district leadership election, in 1961.

Suddenly, we were well positioned to unseat the Tamawa Club, and in the 1961 district leader race we ran Jim Lanigan and Carol Greitzer against Carmine De

Sapio and Diana Halle. Our campaign received an unexpected assist from Mayor Robert F. Wagner, who ran for reelection that year and came out strongly against De Sapio's county leaders. The mayoral campaign clearly destroyed De Sapio, and helped the reform clubs throughout the city. Lanigan and Greitzer won the race, making the Village Independent Democrats the official Democratic club for Greenwich Village.

Unfortunately, the thrill of this victory was short-lived. Less than two weeks after the election, Lanigan appeared on television and announced his intention to run for county leader in Manhattan. We were all stunned. Now, whether or not this was something he intended to do, he should never have announced it so soon after his election. It wasn't even two weeks! He made us and himself look foolish.

One of the big issues of the 1961 campaign was the changing face of Washington Square Park, and it led in a roundabout way to a story that would stretch out over twenty years. I'll explain. The Italian community in the south Village was up in arms back then because the park had become a hangout not only for the beatnik set but for what seemed to be every disaffected young person in New York City. The older Italians didn't care for the crowds, or the noise, or the filth. Their quiet enjoyment of the park had been stripped from them, they maintained. Specifically, they protested the fact that folksingers were allowed to sing in the park on Sunday afternoons, often surrounded by large crowds. It was a sham issue, but that was where they directed their efforts. After all, singing in the park was nothing new; it was an old tradition. Community leaders approached Mayor Wagner and demanded that he eliminate singing entirely from Washington Square Park. The mayor, seeking reelection, was obviously looking for issues that he could seize and make his own. Foolishly, he seized on this one, and he directed the parks commissioner to issue a regulation banning all singing in Washington Square Park.

What an outrage! Let us forget, for the moment, the First Amendment rights violated by such a regulation. The mayor had missed the point entirely. The folksingers, for the most part, were students. Certainly, the majority of them did not behave in any objectionable way. There were indeed problems throughout the Village, but it was those student folksingers who became the focus of the anger of the Italian community.

When the singers were banned and the regulation enforced by the police, a number of us decided to do something about it. We formed what we called the Right to Sing Committee. I was the committee's lawyer, and we set to work to protest the ban. A group of about twenty singers gathered on the first Sunday after the ban to test the enforcement of this new regulation, and they were all arrested. Even some of the listeners were arrested.

I was not skilled in criminal law, so we asked the *Village Voice*, the alternative weekly newspaper, to run a box on its front page, soliciting volunteer lawyers to defend the students and others who had been arrested. We had a tremendous response, and it fell to me to interview the volunteers. One of them was a young man named Sandy Katz. He said he was a specialist in criminal law, and I was delighted that he had come forward to help. Wonderful, I thought. This man is the answer to our problems.

Katz then very decently warned me of a potential problem. He told me that his major client was the Communist Party. I thought, Oh, great, what do we need this for? I knew our group would be attacked as a bunch of disreputable left-wing radicals if our principal trial lawyer's major client was the Communist Party.

So I said to him, "Sandy, listen. You're a nice guy, and obviously a good lawyer, and I want you to understand it means nothing to me that you're representing the Communist Party, and they're your major client. Absolutely nothing. But I do want you to know, I don't think we can afford that additional problem right now." I went on to say that if I couldn't find anyone else, I would be back to him. He took it very well, and displayed no rancor. As it turned out, other criminal law attorneys volunteered, and the problems Katz might have brought with him were avoided.

That was the last I saw of Sandy Katz until we were brought together some twenty years later, in an adversarial way. The incident that connected us was, for me, pretty frightening. As mayor, I was invited to address a group of several thousand medical professionals at the New York Hilton Hotel. The group consisted of doctors and paraprofessionals from all over the country, and I was asked to welcome them and introduce Patricia Harris, who headed the Department of Health, Education and Welfare under President Jimmy Carter. The conference was held shortly after the Shah of Iran was overthrown by the Ayatollah Khomeini. International tensions were high, and a mob in Tehran had taken over the American embassy. For some reason, the Ayatollah's supporters determined that this conference would be a good forum for their positions.

The episode was given a good deal of coverage in the press, and I have written about it on several occasions, so I will give a shorthand version of what happened: As I stood up to welcome the crowd, I felt a hand around my throat, a fist in my eye, and something wet oozing down my cheek. I thought I was being assassinated, or someone had thrown acid in my face. For a moment, I had no idea what was happening. I reacted on impulse, grabbing my assailant's right hand from around my throat, and forcing him to the ground. Then I sat on him. All of this happened in the space of a few seconds, in front of several thousand people.

I had only one security guard with me at the time. His name was Ron Simoncini. He could not come to my aid right away because he was busy chasing down and handcuffing two others who were throwing eggs at me. (The wet stuff I had felt dripping down my face turned out to be a raw egg, and shell, which my attacker was rubbing into my eye.) Finally, Simoncini came over to me and said, "Get up, Mayor. I'll take care of him." Then he cuffed the guy.

I stood and looked down at my attacker lying on the floor. I was furious. My life and dignity had been threatened. I was so angry at this guy that all I wanted to do was hurt him. I wondered, Will it cause greater pain if I kick him in the balls or the head?

Simoncini looked into my eyes, guessed exactly what I was thinking, and said, "Mayor, please don't kick him."

He was right, I knew. If I kicked this terrorist he'd claim mayoral brutality, and I'd wind up as the defendant. So I held back. Instead, I returned to the podium and said to the assailant's supporters (who were by now displaying anti-American banners throughout the auditorium), "This is not Iran, and as soon as I welcome everybody I'm taking this guy to jail."

And that's just what I did. I escorted my attacker (who turned out to be a doctor from San Diego, originally from New York City) to the police precinct, where he was booked. Later District Attorney Robert Morgenthau kindly offered to send his people to my office to take my complaint, but I insisted that the case be handled in the ordinary way; I went down to his office and completed the paperwork.

The case came to trial about a year later. That's how slow the criminal justice system is in New York City. Enter, again, Sandy Katz, who now appeared as the defendant's counsel. He was a little heavier than at our first meeting, but it was clearly the same man. When I was called to give my testimony, he approached to cross-examine me. "Mayor," he said, "you did not see your attacker at the time you were attacked, is that correct?"

"Yes, that's true, counselor," I replied.

"Then you really don't know who attacked you," he went on, "isn't that true?"

"No, counselor," I said. "I know who attacked me, and I will tell you how I know." Then I turned to my left to talk directly to the jury, forgetting all about Sandy Katz and the judge. I explained to them that I was standing on the stage, that I felt a hand around my throat, and another hand grinding something into my eye. I demonstrated how I grabbed the guy's hand from my throat and wrestled him to the ground. No, I did not see him when he approached me from behind, I allowed, but we were face to face when I got him down onto the floor. I acted out the whole scene, as it had happened. And then I turned and pointed to the defendant, who was sitting at a nearby table, and said, "And that's him!" It was very effective.

My attacker was found guilty, and given a thirty-day sentence and a thousand-dollar fine. (That's the heavy punishment in New York City for assaulting the mayor.) Nothing passed between Sandy Katz and myself before, during, or after the trial, other than the business at hand. Neither of us mentioned our years-ago encounter. I mention it here to reinforce my belief that it's a small world, and New York is a small city.

Our efforts with the Right to Sing Committee ended on a far more pleasant note. We threatened Mayor Wagner that we would not support him for reelection until he called a meeting at Gracie Mansion to reverse himself and allow the folksingers back in the park. He did. It was a huge victory, and it ultimately won our group a lot of support among young Village voters.

I sought the state assembly nomination the following year, 1962. To be accurate, it sought me. De Sapio's candidate was the incumbent, William Passannante, who held the Sixty-third District seat. Nobody in our club wanted to run against him, and understandably so. Passannante, in 1962, was considered to be a bridge between the old-liners and the reformers. He was regarded as unbeatable because he had De Sapio's support, but he also had a reputation as a liberal, progressive legislator. It was hard to find someone to oppose him. After all, nobody wants to run in an election they know they are going to lose.

I had been elected president of the VID, and I thought

it was extremely important that we put forward a candidate in this election; without a candidate, I feared the club would not advance politically. By default, that candidate was me. I couldn't find anyone else to take the job. It was my first try for elected office, and it was a difficult race. I had a tough time soliciting support; in fact, the single major endorsement I received was from Eleanor Roosevelt; everyone else lined up behind Passannante. Senator Herbert Lehman actually sent out a letter to every registered Democrat in the district, in which he urged voters to oppose my candidacy. Mayor Wagner endorsed Passannante.

In the rare, quiet moments of the campaign, I wondered what in the world I had gotten myself into and why. I never questioned myself for long, though. I was proud of the issues I was raising in my campaign. I vowed to seek the repeal of the sodomy laws and to allow divorce on grounds other than just adultery. I also sought to make abortions legal, without restrictions. These were daring and controversial positions to take in 1962—my big-three issues were nicknamed "the SAD committee," for sodomy, abortion, and divorce—but I was firm in my beliefs, even if they might have been unpopular. It is easy to be firm in your beliefs when you know you're right. Indeed, with the passage of time, all three goals were achieved, as a result of the efforts of others.

The campaign set the scene for yet another cherished story. To be accurate, the story took place before the campaign even began, as I was petitioning voters in the district to ensure I had enough signatures even to get on the ballot. I was schlepping from apartment to apartment, knocking on the doors of registered Democrats. Remember, this was new to me. I had petitioned before, on behalf of other candidates, but never for myself. It was not as bad as asking for campaign contributions, which everyone I know finds distasteful, but it was nevertheless difficult to sell myself at every door. All candidates, of course, are required to go through these same motions, and after a while it becomes second nature, but it is not easy at first.

The key, I learned with practice, is never to sound blasé or to appear to be doing it by rote.

At one point, still uncomfortable with the routine, I found myself knocking on the door of a brownstone that belonged to Mel Brooks, the comedian, and Anne Bancroft, the actress. Even then, they were well known. Bancroft answered the door.

"I'm Ed Koch," I said, "and I'm running for the assembly against William Passannante."

"I'm sorry," she cut me off curtly, "but I don't sign petitions."

She was nice enough about it, but she was also firm. I thought I would at least try to tell her about myself and I started to, but her dog changed my plans. I don't remember the breed of the dog, but he was big and very excited. The dog burst out the door and ran down the street. Mel Brooks came bounding out after him. I ran to the street to see if I could help.

So there I was, with Mel Brooks, chasing his dog down a Greenwich Village street. After a few moments, I managed to grab the dog by his collar and walk him over to Brooks, who was very grateful. "Mr. Brooks," I said, jumping on this opportunity to go into my pitch. "I'm Ed Koch. I'm running for assembly in your district. Would you sign my petition so I can get on the ballot?"

"Sure," he said, and he signed, happy to return a favor to the man who had just collared his dog.

Anne Bancroft still refused to sign, even after I walked back to the apartment with Brooks and their dog. A part of me wondered what I would have to do to get her support.

And that was the end of the story, at least for many years. It now has a great kicker, which came nearly twenty years later after I had been elected mayor. I was in Paris in 1979, dining at Maxim's as a guest of Mayor Jacques Chirac's deputy, who had been assigned to entertain us, when I noticed Brooks and Bancroft across the room. I walked to their table to say hello, as a fellow New Yorker abroad. They could not have been nicer. They were even very flattering, Anne Bancroft in particular. She went on and on about how delighted she was that I was mayor. She even remembered being one of the first in the neighborhood to sign my petition for the assembly, back in 1962. I did not correct her. My thinking at the time was, if that's the way she remembers it, so be it; she supports me now, as I hope she will in the future, so why embarrass her with the truth?

I collected enough signatures to get my name on the ballot, but that was the last victory of my first (and most difficult) campaign. I lost the primary, but the real trauma was how badly I was beaten. I was devastated, and disheartened. I was also humiliated. A part of me wondered why I had ever put myself through it in the first place. On the night of the primary, I conceded the election with these words: "Politics is a dirty business. I will never run again. I'm through with the whole thing."

I now realize I was lucky to have lost. I have since told people that losing that primary was the best thing that ever happened to me. I sincerely believe that if I had won and then triumphed in the general election, I would probably still be an assemblyman. Passannante remained in the assembly for the balance of his political life, never rising higher than deputy speaker, of which there are several. I don't mean to disparage Passannante or any of the good people who have served so long and with such dedication, but for me it would have been a wasted life, a boring life.

I recovered from the loss soon enough, and set about repairing the divisions within the VID. I also set about expanding my law practice. I had been working on my own as a lawyer for eight or nine years and was becoming increasingly frustrated with the demands that are made on a solo practitioner. I couldn't be in two places at one time. I hadn't had a vacation in longer than I could remember. My political involvement was taking up more and more of my time, and I had been thinking about finding a partner for some time. Indeed, I had initiated conversations with any number of potential associates, but I had yet to come across a likely candidate. I wanted to find someone who would work as hard as I did.

My next political campaign, for district leader in 1963, provided my introduction to the man who would become my first law partner. It also gave me my first election night victory. Once again, I did not want to run but felt I had to. The VID had repudiated Jim Lanigan, who had deserted us in the 1962 assembly campaign and refused to place himself at odds with Mayor Wagner and Senator Lehman, who were supporting Passannante. We launched a frenetic search for a new male candidate to run against Carmine De Sapio, who was seeking to win his district leader seats back after the upset victory of Jim Lanigan and Carol Greitzer two years earlier. The VID first approached Theodore Bikel, the actor and folksinger, who lived in the Village and was active in club politics. He declined. We then approached James Baldwin, the writer, but he too declined. Five other people turned us down. Why? De Sapio and his machine were too formidable and threatening, and the uphill campaigning must have appeared too daunting.

I think another reason we had such trouble finding a candidate was fear. Not just fear of losing the election, but fear of violence. De Sapio may never have threatened anyone in his life (at least I'm not aware of any threats), but he had a reputation that suggested otherwise; he even looked intimidating, with the dark glasses he wore as a result of an eye ailment. He was also the victim of ethnic identification; fair or not, there were many who thought of mobsters when they thought of him.

Eventually, and again reluctantly, I stepped forward. As in the year before, I did not want to run, but even more, I did not want De Sapio to run unopposed. Tellingly, there were some in the group who objected to my reluctant candidacy, and I told them I objected to it too. There was always a lot of internal backstabbing within the VID. Some among our ranks did not think too highly of me or my bid for the district leadership. I challenged these opponents to run in my place, but no one did.

I became a candidate out of sense of obligation, not one of mission or purpose. Much has been written about me over the years, about how I had cleverly laid the groundwork for a political career, quietly building my power base, but that simply wasn't the case. I never wanted to be a candidate in those early years, at least not until my try for the city council some years later. In 1962 and 1963, I would have much preferred to continue working for the candidacy of others, and for the VID. But I was president of the club, and there was no question that we needed to field a candidate. I felt I had no choice.

I teamed with Carol Greitzer, who was the incumbent female district leader, to oppose De Sapio and his replacement running mate, Diana Halle. It was a heated and exciting campaign. There were no incidents of violence directed at Greitzer or myself, save for one; it may or may not have been accidental, although I was inclined then, as I am now, to believe it was intentional. I was living at the time at 72 Barrow Street, in the West Village, in the same building as many of De Sapio's friends and relatives; my apartment was next door to George Tombini, De Sapio's uncle. They all knew who I was, and I knew who they were. One night, at about two-thirty in the morning, after a club meeting, I stopped in front of my building to talk to the VID campaigner who had walked me home. This was an early form of security for the candidate. We talked for a few minutes. The street was well lit. It was a quiet night, and our voices, I am sure, carried to the open apartment windows above the street. I stepped away from the building just as our conversation ended, and as I did, I was startled by the crash of a heavy clay flowerpot, exploding on the pavement. It landed right where I had been standing. If I hadn't stepped away when I did, it would have hit me; if it hit me on the skull, I would have been killed. It might have been an accident, but I'm not sure.

This time out, I had the unexpected support of many

who had previously opposed the VID reformers. The most influential of these was Edward Costikyan, the Manhattan county leader who had opposed me in the assembly race against Passannante. His turnabout was really quite remarkable. Costikyan's personal interests got in the way of his politics, and I suppose I should have not been surprised that he chose to help me; he stood to lose the county leader seat if De Sapio regained his district leadership, so he endorsed our reform ticket. We accepted his support even though he had done us great harm in the past. To refuse it would have been foolish.

One of my biggest supporters, though, was my proud father. I don't believe Papa cared about politics one way or the other until I became politically active. Even then, his concerns did not reach too far beyond how the various issues affected me. I don't think he ever really understood what the district leadership position was all about, or why the VID was important to me, but he was enthusiastic just the same; if it was something I wanted, then he wanted it for me. The personal highlight of the campaign was when Papa draped a homemade banner from his eleventh-floor factory window at 208 West Thirtieth Street. The banner stretched from the eleventh floor to the third floor, and said, "Vote for my son Ed Koch, the district leader. [Signed,] Lou Koch." It got a lot of media attention, and I remember how proud I was of Papa and flattered at his gesture.

It turned out we needed all the support we could get, even of the homemade variety. We won the election by a margin of forty-one votes, out of about nine thousand cast. It was the closest election I have ever been involved in, and the battle did not end on election night. In fact, that was when it kicked into high gear. That night, all of the precincts but one had reported; the race was extremely close, and the last precinct was a high-rise apartment house on East Tenth Street that was so big it was a stand-alone precinct. The building, Stewart House, happened also to be the home of De Sapio's running mate,

Diana Halle. Knowing this, I was ready to concede the election, because tradition and logic held that most candidates carry their own buildings, just as I had carried 72 Barrow Street, even though it was filled with old-line residents.

But then the final returns came in, with Carol and myself on top, and everything turned to chaos. I stood up at campaign headquarters and ordered our people to guard the voting booths and ballot boxes. With a margin of only forty-one votes, I knew De Sapio would challenge the election and demand a recount. He did that and more. He took us to court. He claimed that we stole the election from him! I could not believe it. How could the VID reformers steal an election from Carmine De Sapio, the man whose machine ran on the fuel of political corruption? The charge was patently ridiculous, but De Sapio implied that we had opened the graves to stuff the ballot box.

At the ensuing trial, the court ordered a second election to be held the following year. The judge was honest; it had been close, and the decision could have gone either way. I can laugh about the aftermath of this election now, from the perspective of thirty years, but at the time I was absolutely enraged that our victory had been stolen from us and our ethics unfairly challenged.

And so, a special midterm election was held the following year. This time around, we won by a more comfortable 164 votes. This surely enraged De Sapio, and he fought back again; he aggressively (and successfully) sought redistricting, to include a larger section of Little Italy, thinking such a move would help to shore up his eroding neighborhood support in time for the next election. It was a shrewd, calculating move—after all, he assumed the additional twenty-five hundred (mostly) Italian voters would (mostly) support him—but it didn't work. In the regular 1965 district leadership election, we won by more than five hundred votes out of eleven thousand cast. De Sapio's career was over. The days of old-line boss politics in Greenwich Village were finally at an end.

Actually, it would take a jail sentence to remove De Sapio from Village politics once and for all. He was later convicted of extorting twenty-five thousand dollars from Con Edison. It was a tremendous scandal. After he was found guilty, a reporter asked me what I thought of the verdict and the man. Even then, De Sapio's influence colored my remarks. "He is a crook," I said, "but I like him."

Most politicians still like De Sapio. He always gets the most applause when he is introduced at Democratic dinners.

The district leadership was not a paid position, but it was very time-consuming. I still had to earn a living and keep my law practice going. The need to find a partner was increasingly apparent. Suddenly, I did not have to look too far. One of the major forces in our 1963 district leader campaign was a young lawyer named Lester Evens. He struck me right off as a tireless and dedicated worker, and a very nice man. He also seemed to be a good lawyer. We became fast friends over the course of the campaign, and as soon as it seemed appropriate I introduced the idea of our going into business together. Lester was already in partnership with two other attorneys at that time, but he had begun to voice his unhappiness with the arrangement. He was more than open to the possibility.

We talked it over for a few weeks, before finally agreeing to team up. At the time, my practice was more substantial than his. My income was about twenty thousand dollars a year in 1963, which was not a grand amount, but it was comfortable; his practice earned him considerably less. Still, I offered a fifty-fifty split, and Lester naturally agreed. That has always been my philosophy in establishing a working partnership: share equally, whether or not the contributions to the enterprise are also equal.

We had our problems almost immediately. Lester's tirelessness turned out to apply overwhelmingly to politics and to the various *pro bono* causes that sparked his interest, while I was out there trying to make a living for the two of us. Now, you can be involved in causes, as I was, but you have to try to carry your weight. He did not, and I wanted to dissolve our partnership almost as soon as it began.

It was not easy to do this. Lester had just left his partners to join up with me. It would not have been fair for me to simply terminate our agreement on thirty days' notice, so I gave it a year to work itself out. Sadly, but probably also predictably, it never did. I suffered every single day, asking myself, Why am I putting up with this? I finally told Lester it wasn't working out. If I didn't tell him I knew I would get ulcers.

Still, our unhappy association did not sour me on working with a partner. Actually, the opposite was the case. Working with Lester Evens (who went on to become a civil court judge, elected as the VID candidate) confirmed for me how desperately I needed a partner, particularly as my duties at the VID and as district leader increased. I pursued another partner aggressively after Lester and I parted, and this pursuit led me to perhaps the closest, most enduring association of my professional life. I was having dinner one night with a friend, Leonard Sandler, who went on to become an appellate judge (and who died of a heart attack at sixty-two), and a friend of his, Allen Schwartz, who was then an assistant district attorney under Frank Hogan. I did not know Allen. We went to dinner at a restaurant called the Ninth Circle, which was a wonderful steak house before it became a gay bar. The steaks were excellent and cost only five dollars. The meal was memorable, though, for my introduction to Allen. I was very impressed with him, and after the dinner I asked Leonard if he thought Allen would consider going into private practice in a partnership with me.

At first, Allen didn't even want to talk about it. He passed the message on through Leonard that he was flattered at my interest, but he was comfortable in his present job. I was disappointed and began looking elsewhere. Nine months later, almost to the day, Allen called Leonard to see if I still wanted a partner. It was as though the idea needed time to gestate. Allen and I met to iron out the details. We went into business on a handshake. Once again, I offered a fifty-fifty split, even though my income exceeded his. He moved into my one-room office at 52 Wall Street, where we became Koch & Schwartz. We even shared the same desk for a while, and it was over this single desk, I am told, that I first voiced my intention to someday seek the mayoralty of New York City. I do not remember this particular moment but Allen does, and he has a superb memory. As Allen recalls it, I turned to him one day, shortly after the birth of his first child, David, and said, "Allen, when I become mayor, your son can be bar-mitzvahed at Gracie Mansion."

Allen reminded me of this conversation shortly after I was elected mayor and he had begun serving as my corporation counsel. "Now, Ed," Allen said, gingerly, "you're not bound, and you might not even remember, but if you were serious, I would like that for David."

"Of course I remember, Allen," I said. "And of course we can have the bar mitzvah at the mansion."

And so, as far as I know, David Schwartz, the son of one of the best corporation counsels the city has ever seen, was the first and only boy to be bar-mitzvahed in Gracie Mansion—a little footnote for Jewish history buffs. (Similarly, Harold's stepdaughter, Joey, was bas-mitzvahed in the mansion's Susan E. Wagner Wing.)

Allen and I enjoyed a great and fulfilling partnership. We took on every client we could find, in all aspects of the law. Allen was and is an exceptional litigator and an astute businessman. Years later, when I won the mayoralty, Allen was my first and only choice to serve as corporation counsel. Happily, he accepted (after thinking it over for a day or two), and he really turned things around. The office had fallen into sad disrepair under Abe Beame's corporation counsel, Bernard Richland. There were thousands of legal files piled on the floor. The place was a disaster. There were five thousand default judgments against the city, because we didn't have enough lawyers to answer the cases. The lawyers we did have didn't even have their own phones; there was about one telephone for every three lawyers, an untenable situation.

Beame was not a lawyer, and when he was required to trim his budget he failed to realize the importance of the corporation counsel's office. It was one of the agencies hardest hit by his cuts. I had a lot of damage to undo. I determined that, more than anything else, the city's fiscal salvation rested with the performance of two agencies: the corporation counsel's office, to defend us from predators bent on ripping off the city; and the Office of Management and Budget, to provide the financial blueprint to pull us through our short- and long-term financial crises. As a result, I always gave these two offices preferred treatment at budget time, and I am convinced my judgment was right.

Allen did a stellar job of cleaning up the office's operations, helping to set the city on a sure course, and he remains one of my closest, most supportive friends. Every doctor has a doctor, and every lawyer has a lawyer. He is my lawyer.

Our partnership was such an immediate success that our thoughts turned to expansion. We invited an old friend of mine, John Lankenau, whom I had known since my Fair Harbor days, to join our small firm. He accepted and moved in with us at 52 Wall Street. Eventually, we took over more space in the same suite there, and to help fill it we took on another partner, Victor Kovner, who had organized the New York delegation for Martin Luther King's march on Washington the previous year. I had known Victor for a number of years. I knew his wife, Sarah, even longer. She had been my campaign manager in the 1962 assembly race. Victor and I first met during his tenure as executive assistant to Senator Lehman. I liked him and admired his work and convictions.

Koch, Schwartz, Lankenau & Kovner enjoyed a few strong years together. We shared everything equally. Regrettably, my friendships with Victor Kovner and John Lankenau have not survived the years. The fallings-out, in each case, took the same form: betrayal, as I saw it. As mayor, I appointed John to serve as chairman of my Cultural Commission, because I knew he was interested in classical and medieval music. I also asked him to serve on the board of the Jacob Javits Convention Center. He was delighted to accept both positions. I remained close with John and his wife, Allison, until 1989. When I was seeking my fourth term as mayor and trying to overcome the problems of a corruption scandal that I will discuss later on in these pages, he decided not to support me. I lost a lot of support by 1989, but John's defection was among the most hurtful. He knew I was an honest man, yet in my moment of need, he withdrew. For that, I will never forgive him.

I will never forgive Victor Kovner either, for much the same reason. He withdrew his support in 1981. I had named him to my committee for the selection of criminal and family court judges, a position he had asked for and admirably filled. Nevertheless, he decided the city had had enough of me after one term, that I wasn't progressive enough for his tastes. He actually went out and formed a search committee to find a candidate to run against me, as he did again in 1985 and 1989. I removed him from the selection committee after our first break.

Early on, though, we had a nice partnership going. We handled a wide assortment of cases, and represented a disparate group of clients. We did a good deal of *pro bono* work, but we also wanted to make a decent living as lawyers. One of my highest-profile clients was the *Village Voice*. We were on a six-hundred-dollar-a-year retainer for that newspaper, which even in 1965 was a ridiculously low fee. We took them on for prestige. Victor Kovner eventually became the major libel lawyer for the *Voice*, after I was elected to Congress and dissolved the practice, and he undoubtedly billed the paper many thousands more than under our original agreement.

My first involvement with the paper was not propitious. It came in a case stemming from a landlord-tenant dispute in an old-law tenement at 40 MacDougal Street. The dispute led to a lifelong friendship with the *Voice*'s editor, Dan Wolf. I'll explain. At the time, I was representing the tenants in the building against the landlord, who was seeking to substantially rehabilitate the property, thereby freeing the building from rent-control restrictions. He was working within the existing laws, and his hope was to upgrade the apartments in his building so he could collect market rents for them. I believe he was getting forty or fifty dollars a month for apartments that, if renovated, could fetch as much as $350, based on the established rents in neighboring buildings. All of this was subject to the landlord's getting a permit for substantial demolition.

The *Voice* ran an item denouncing me for being prolandlord, after a lawyer representing a different group of tenants against the same landlord said that I had refused to provide an affidavit alleging the landlord was violating his agreements with my clients. In fact, he was not. Further complicating the issue was the fact that I provided the landlord's attorney with a letter attesting that he had carried out his agreements with my clients. I thought the *Voice* attack against me was unfair, and I went to see Dan Wolf, seeking a retraction.

Our first meeting did not augur well for our friendship. Dan did not care whether the landlord had carried out his agreement. He could not look past the fact that I was helping him. I argued that there were good landlords and bad ones, just as there were good tenants and bad. He countered that even if this particular landlord was honest in this particular case, it did not warrant my helping him by providing the letter. I defended myself, as I would today, by arguing that I had an obligation to stand up for what is right and speak out against what is wrong. I am a compulsive truth-teller, even when it is not in my best interests.

Dan would not retract the *Voice*'s condemnation and refused to accept my defense, but we moved on from that shaky beginning to become good friends. He even hired me as the paper's attorney. Dan used to have regular Friday afternoon get-togethers in his office at four o'clock, and pretty soon I became part of the crowd. The cast changed from week to week, but I was always there. We talked about everything from Village politics to national issues. Sometimes we'd stay long into the evening. Dan impressed me then as one of the smartest people I had ever met, and we remain close friends to this day. I still have the same opinion of him. When he retired from the paper, he came with me to City Hall, where he served as an adviser; when I left office, he returned with me to the private sector and now edits my various newspaper columns and speeches.

One of the more notable legal judgments I won for Dan was in a slander suit. Dan and I, independently, heard a radio commentator make the claim that the editor of the *Village Voice* used marijuana. This was untrue. In 1965, it was also a crime.

"I think you have a case," I told Dan, when I saw him later that day.

"Yeah," he agreed, "but who's gonna believe that the editor of the *Village Voice* doesn't smoke marijuana?"

We both laughed. Dan had a point, but the fact was that he did not use drugs. So we sued. We settled the case for seven thousand dollars, of which I collected one-third for my firm. It turned out the radio commentator had confused the *Village Voice* with another underground paper. He simply made a mistake, but it cost him.

The practice thrived. The four partners complemented each other nicely. We also got along, which is a rare thing in a law firm. We were all active in various outside activities, so no one minded too much when the district leadership and my campaigning pulled me away from the office.

Besides, there was always the unspoken belief that my political involvement would be of long-term benefit to the firm, mitigating any short-term drop-off caused by my occasional absences.

By 1966, things were working out so well among the four partners that I thought the firm was well positioned to absorb another of my short leaves for an all-out campaign. I wanted to run for city council, because I thought I could win and because I thought I could make a difference. Unlike my previous tries for elected office, the impulses for this move were entirely my own. It was something I wanted to do; it wasn't something I felt I had an obligation to others to do.

My decision was set in motion by a political game of musical chairs. Specifically, I sought the seat in the Second Councilmanic District vacated by the Republican, Theodore Kupferman, who resigned his position to seek the Congressional seat left vacant by the city's new mayor, John Lindsay. In many ways, though my decision to run for city council was based on an earlier decision, one that was perhaps the most difficult and also the most influential of my early political career.

5

Washington, D.C.

THE 1965 MAYORAL ELECTION TURNED New York City politics upside down and inside out. It also changed the direction of my own political career. Traditionally, the city is a Democratic town. It has been axiomatic: the Democratic candidate for mayor will wind up in City Hall. That is, it was axiomatic until John Lindsay came along. Lindsay, the charismatic United States Congressman from New York's posh Upper East Side (the so-called Silk-Stocking District), was the Republican Party candidate. He also had the backing of the Liberal Party. He was opposed in the general election by Abe Beame, the city comptroller who had won the Democratic nomination.

Despite party loyalties, I simply could not bring myself to endorse Beame. There were a lot of people, in government and elsewhere, who shared my distaste for his old-style clubhouse politics. I didn't like what he stood for, and I didn't think he could lead the city effectively. Indeed, most of my Greenwich Village constituents enthusiastically supported Lindsay, who as a Congressman was seen as an independent and liberal voice, with cachet because he was a Republican. Like many liberal Democrats, I was in a difficult position. I could not bring myself to campaign for Beame, but at the same time, as Democratic district leader for Greenwich Village, it would have been heresy to support Lindsay. For a long time, I did not know what to do.

I remained neutral for as long as I could, until I finally decided to trust my instincts. Whatever successes I had enjoyed until then in the political arena, I had come by them honestly. Whatever successes I hoped to enjoy in the future would have to come on the same terms. The people knew that I spoke my mind, sometimes uninhibitedly, and I realized I would have to do so now. Life is too short to compromise on those things that are really important. To me, choosing a mayor is important.

And so, two days before the election, I committed political heresy and came out in support of Lindsay. To say that this was not an easy decision is to underestimate the power of the regulars in the Democratic Party. I honestly thought that this would be the end of my political career, but I was determined to vote my conscience and didn't have any other options.

I reached this decision with the help of my friend Henry Stern, a Liberal Party district leader. He was a power in the Liberal Party and a political pro. I met with Stern in my apartment at 14 Washington Place on the Sunday before the Tuesday election, and we made hasty plans for a press conference the next morning, to be held in my law office at 52 Wall Street. The polls were extremely close at this late date: the *Daily News* was predicting a victory for Beame; the *Herald Tribune* showed a slight lead for Lindsay; the other papers said it was too close to call. We knew my announcement would generate a lot of attention, and possibly even help to decide the race. We sent out the customary telegrams, informing the press that I had an important announcement to make regarding the mayoral election. We were not explicit in telegraphing the next day's bombshell—a Democratic district leader, breaking ranks to endorse the Republican!—but reporters were able to read between the lines and sensed what was coming.

I didn't sleep at all that Sunday night. I was racked, and

wrecked, by indecision and fearful of the consequences of my choice. Don't misunderstand me: I was firm in my support of Lindsay, but I was uncertain and tentative about opposing Beame and breaking with the party in such a public way. Perhaps, I second-guessed, I should simply stay quiet, and vote for Lindsay in silence. It was a very tough call, but the telegrams had gone out, and there was nothing I could do but go forward with my decision.

At six o'clock in the morning, still unable to sleep, I got dressed and went outside for a walk. I thought the fresh morning air would clear my thinking, but more than that I was out to get the advice of my friend Dan Wolf, whom I had already come to regard as a very wise man. I expected Dan to be at his office at the *Village Voice,* but because it was so early no one would be there to answer the telephone or to let me in at the front door. This was a problem. As I walked, I lost all track of time, but I finally found myself standing in front of the newspaper offices at the corner of Christopher Street and Seventh Avenue South. I looked up at his second-floor window. Dan was a confirmed early riser and often arrived at work before the sun. Sure enough, he was there. Thank God, I thought. A sounding board. Maybe Dan would talk me out of my decision. Or maybe he would support me in it. Either way, I knew I had to talk to him. I threw some stones at his window to get his attention, and he came downstairs to let me in.

Dan was surprised to see me at this early hour and asked if there was anything wrong. I told him I had decided to come out for Lindsay and had called a press conference for ten o'clock that morning. It was clear to Dan that I was quite distraught. "I'm going to be destroyed," I said. "It's the end of my political career."

"I don't think so," Dan said, concerned for my dilemma but also intrigued at my news. He reminded me that I had already annoyed a great many in the Democratic Party by opposing and defeating Carmine De Sapio; there was nothing I could do that would be worse.

"But this is different," I suggested. "This is completely different."

"It is," Dan agreed, "but I don't think it will matter as much. There's a lot of support for Lindsay out there. You're not alone."

Dan's instincts were almost always on target, and I desperately wanted to believe him. "I hope you're right," I said. Underneath, I was not so sure.

"Have you told Carol?" he asked, meaning Carol Greitzer, my district coleader.

"No," I said. "It didn't even occur to me. I haven't really told anyone."

"Call her," he advised. "It's a big mistake not to."

Dan was right about this, as he was about most things. He reminded me that as soon as I made my announcement the press would be all over Carol Greitzer for a comment. If she was not alerted to my plans, then she might be made to look foolish and out of the loop. Caught unaware, she might feel compelled to denounce me; alerted, she might be kinder in her comments. I liked Carol a great deal, socially and politically, and I did not want her to look or feel bad. Most of all, though, I did not want to have her lash out at me, for making a key decision without consulting her.

So I went to my office at 52 Wall Street and called Carol. She had an inconvenient habit of leaving her phone off the hook at night. She usually put it back at about ten in the morning; with God's providence, her phone would be working early. I reached her at about nine o'clock. "Carol," I said, "I have something to tell you. I'm coming out for Lindsay this morning, and there is nothing you can do to stop me. I just wanted you to know before I tell the reporters at the press conference."

I was completely surprised by her response. "I wish you had told me sooner," she said, almost conspiratorially. "I might have come out with you."

She was as astonished at my willingness to endorse Lindsay as I was at hers. I was not as alone as I had feared. Great. Maybe this wouldn't be my political down-fall. "It's not too late," I replied. "The press conference is not for another hour."

"I still have to shower," she said. "I can't get there in time."

"I'll put it off until eleven."

"Can you do that?"

"Sure," I said. "The reporters will wait. They sense what's coming."

"I'll be there."

I was delighted at Carol's position, and at her support of mine. I then called Marty Berger, a lawyer who succeeded me as president of the VID after I was elected as district leader; he also wanted to come out for Lindsay, and the three of us planned to present a united front. At eleven o'clock, we stood in my too-small (for press conferences, anyway) office, made our prepared statements, and fielded questions from the incredulous pack of reporters. We all handled ourselves pretty well, considering, but I was still anxious over my decision. A part of me was certain that this would be my last great political act.

Election Day dawned with the following front-page headline in the *Daily News:* LBJ AND HUMPHREY PUSH BEAME; REFORM DEM KOCH BACKS LINDSAY. The words, in a type size that should be reserved for the outbreak of war, were presented in a banner headline. It was the biggest splash I had ever made. I was not at all prepared for this. In the eyes of the paper's headline writers, at least, my endorsement carried almost as much weight as the White House endorsement of Beame. Of course, I realized that the heavy play had more to do with my crossing party lines than it did with any clout I might have otherwise wielded, but I was floored by the attention just the same. And that was just the morning. Later that day, I was asked to join Lindsay at Republican headquarters, and to make a statement on his behalf on live television. I had no idea my endorsement for mayor would be seen as such a big deal. It was a big deal to me, of course, and I knew it would not go unnoticed in political circles, but Lindsay's campaign people were telling me it was all the voters on the street could talk about. This I did not expect. Lindsay called me later in the afternoon from a campaign stop in Coney Island, to tell me personally how important the announcement was and to thank me for it.

To tell the truth, I relished all the attention, at least for the moment. I had had about enough by that evening, though. Bob Price, one of Lindsay's top aides, asked me to appear on a television program with Carol Greitzer and Marty Berger, to expand on our endorsement. When I arrived at the appointed time, I looked around the room at all of the Republican faces and reminded myself why I was a Democrat. These are not my kind of people, I was thinking. These are richies. I don't like them politically or socially. They don't like me or what I represent. We have nothing in common. What the hell am I doing here?

I told Bob Price that I felt like a monkey on a string, and preferred not to go through with the planned television appearance. He understood, and I left. Price and I went on to become very good friends and remain so to this day. Of course, my relationship with John Lindsay turned out somewhat differently, but I'll get to that.

There are some who say my last-minute endorsement pushed Lindsay over the top. I do not believe that, even though he only beat Beame by about one hundred thousand votes. I'm flattered that some people think I helped decide that race, but I am also smart enough to know that my support was a reflection of the mood of liberal Democrats throughout the city, just as it was a reflection of my own. It is true, though, that my endorsement gave some Democrats the explanation they needed to realize their hands wouldn't fall off if they pulled the lever for a Republican, even if it was on the Liberal Party line.

I was made to pay for my independence. As I expected, the Democratic regulars arranged to exact their revenge. They did this through a rather silly kangaroo-court proceeding at the Commodore Hotel, where they put Carol and myself on trial on charges of party disloyalty, and then sought our resignation from the district leadership. We refused to step down. The regulars, realizing that if they deposed us we would likely win overwhelmingly in any new election, then sought a simple apology. We refused even that. The County Democratic Executive Committee, also known as Tammany Hall, ultimately passed a new rule for district leaders crossing party lines to endorse a candidate. It was called "the Koch-Greitzer rule"—how's that for an honor?—and it provided for what was tantamount to automatic expulsion from the district leadership.

I suppose the old line Democrats came away from these proceedings thinking I had been censured in some way, that I had been made to atone for the transgression of endorsing the Republican mayoral candidate. I saw things a little differently. To me, their action did not even amount to a slap on the wrist. It was nothing. Tammany Hall couldn't touch me. I had spoken my mind—honestly, brazenly, and with conviction—and the people in my district turned out to be tremendously supportive of my position and my candor.

Lindsay vacated his Congressional seat in January 1966, when he was sworn in as mayor, setting in motion the curious game of musical chairs I referred to earlier. Theodore Kupferman, the Republican-Liberal, resigned his Second Councilmanic District seat to run for Lindsay's Congressional slot. The city council appointed Woodward Kingman, also a Republican, to take Kupferman's seat on an interim basis, and called for a special election in November 1966 to formally fill the vacancy.

The district covered most of Greenwich Village; Chelsea, just north of the Village; and wide swatches of the Upper East Side. At the time, it was one of the few Republican seats in the city. As I recall, it had been held by a Republican for the past thirty-eight years. I was out to change that. I had by this time developed an exceptionally strong voter base in the Village. As a result of my very public support of Lindsay, I was enjoying a popularity unlike any I had experienced in my short time in politics. People stopped me on the street to thank me for what I had done or to engage me in discussions of what I might do in the future. For the first time, I began to think that I might indeed have a political future. To liberal Democrats, and now to some Republicans, I began to be seen as a kind of maverick, a straight shooter who was not afraid to challenge the political system, or to confront the various problems facing the city without regard to party lines.

I liked this new high profile, and I wanted to use it to advantage—mine and the public's, which I saw as basically the same. I never looked to politics and government for what they could give to me; rather, I looked for what I could bring to them. I had no private or hidden agenda, as many of my critics have suggested over the years. I was not out for personal gain or advantage. For me, government was a kind of call to duty, to which I responded.

After Lindsay, I started to see myself in a unique position to do some good, to change the system that had dominated the city and harmed it. The council seat promised a challenging first step, an opportunity. Realize, I had never held elected public office. I had been defeated in my one race, for the assembly—the district leadership, to which I had been elected in three consecutive years, was only a party position. I was eager for the chance to see how government worked, from the inside.

So I ran. At the time, the city council position paid twenty thousand dollars a year, but the job requirements were only part time. Nowadays, council members earn more than twice that amount, and many devote their full schedules to the position. Back then, though, the city council met formally only once each week, and there were very few committee meetings. Essentially, the job was as easy or time-consuming as the councilman wanted it to be. Constituent service was optional. I decided that, if elected, I would continue with my legal practice and put in an additional forty hours a week as councilman. Remember, in my case, I got up at five-thirty each morning, and I went to sleep at around midnight, so I had a lot of available hours in the day.

I did take a leave from my law practice in order to campaign full time. After all, it would not have done me much good to be out on the streets greeting voters only at the crack of dawn. My partners understood my decision and indeed were quite supportive. I'm sure they thought my election to the city council and my resulting high visibility would yield some positive benefits to our small firm. Perhaps it did, although I don't think so. Everyone knew me well enough to know I would never use my public office to help a friend or client.

But first I had to get elected. It was a difficult, even ugly, campaign. My opponent in the general election, Woodward Kingman, started with strength: as the quasi-incumbent, he was holding the position I was seeking; as a Republican, he had the advantage in the Second Councilmanic District. I had hoped to receive Lindsay's endorsement as a kind of payback for my endorsement of him; at the very least, I expected Lindsay to remain neutral, which the voters would see as unspoken support. That's the way things worked in politics, and even though I didn't always play by the rules, I assumed everyone else did. I assumed wrong. Lindsay's assurance that he would never forget what I had done for him turned out to be nearly worthless, but he did allow his parks commissioner, Tom Hoving, to endorse me.

The Kingman camp played the usual dirty tricks. His campaign people tore down my posters the night before the election. I know this because my own supporters saw them do it. Well after midnight, my workers putting up posters were being shadowed by a car with its lights off. At nearly every corner, someone would get out of the mysterious car and tear them down. Finally, the Koch car doubled back to catch this guy in the act. My workers discovered it was Kingman's assistant campaign manager. It was contemptible.

One of my supporters, Mary Piazza, became a lifelong

friend that night for what happened next. Mary asked Kingman's volunteer, quite reasonably, to stop what he was doing. He was free, she said, to put up Kingman's posters next to ours, but it was despicable to tear our posters down and stuff them in the trash. It simply wasn't good form, and they cost us fifty cents apiece, to boot. The Kingman assistant, apparently unable to muster a verbal response, began to push Mary.

Mary's husband, Tony (another lifelong friend), rushed to his wife's defense, but she called him off. "Don't touch him," she told her husband, "he's mine." Then she slugged him. God bless her.

The *Village Voice* made the difference on election morning. The paper had been extremely supportive throughout the campaign, but it was nothing compared to the page-one editorial written by my good friend Dan Wolf. It was the most glorious endorsement I have ever received. "Koch is something else," he wrote. "He has had more effect on the government of this city while out of office than most men have had while in office."

I recall that editorial endorsement as the most satisfying of my political career. It also gave me a variant on a trite line which I will repeat here. On election night, after the polls had closed and Kingman had conceded, I joked, "I got my job through the *Village Voice.*" Indeed, I had. My support throughout the Village and Chelsea, where the *Voice* readership was greatest, was enough to overcome Kingman's strong base on the Upper East Side.

Whatever got me there, I was overjoyed. And I was determined to do great things for the city. As a councilman, I vowed, I would be beholden to no one. The old-line Democrats had sought to run me out of town just one year earlier; I owed nothing to either party, and everything to the voters in my district. The only way to legislate, I determined, was as an independent, with the hope of swaying Democratic party officials to my point of view.

That was not always as easy as I thought it would be. Or, perhaps, I did not make things as easy for myself as I could have. There were times, I'll admit, where it might have been prudent to simply vote my conscience and keep my mouth shut. I just wasn't built that way. People came to know that about me over time, but this was their first taste of me as a public official. I voted my conscience, to be sure, but I wanted the people of the city to know why I voted the way I did; I wanted them to know what I knew. If something needed to be said, I spoke up. Loudly. And often. If something smelled, I denounced it.

One of my frequent targets, in those days, was Lindsay's budget; I was openly critical of the way he was managing city funds. About a year into my term I was even confronted on my outspokenness by Hoving, the parks commissioner, who was the son of Tiffany president Walter Hoving. The younger Hoving had supported me in my campaign for city council (on January 1, 1967, the day of my installation, he called me a "rebel with reason," and proclaimed me his favorite councilman), and I suppose the Lindsay forces dispatched him to talk to me because they thought I might be better called to task by a friend than a foe.

"Ed," Hoving said, on the telephone, "the mayor is very upset that you're sniping at him and attacking him."

"What does he want me to do about it?" I wondered. I knew what was coming, but I wanted to make Hoving say it.

"He wants you to stop it," he said.

I was incensed. How dare the mayor seek to silence me. He was giving the city away to the labor unions and creating special-interest programs intended to buy supporters. I was not about to keep quiet.

"Listen, Tom," I said. "I am not the mayor's man on the city council. I am not your man. I am my own man on this council, and I will vote the way I want to vote." My message was clear: there was no one in New York City who could intimidate me or tell me how to vote, not even Mayor John Lindsay.

After this conversation with Hoving, I made it a special

point to attack the Lindsay administration whenever the opportunity arose. As it happened, that was more often than not. I was always careful to attack the mayor only with cause and not out of spite, but I imagine there were times when I enjoyed it more than was seemly. Certainly, I never gave him the benefit of the doubt; if I did, I didn't mean to.

The next big erosion in my relationship with Lindsay came the following year, 1968, when I decided to seek his old seat in the city's Seventeenth Congressional District, being vacated by Theodore Kupferman whose former Second Councilmanic District seat I was occupying. It was as though we took turns keeping the seats warm for each other. As in the 1966 city council race, I foolishly hoped Lindsay would either endorse me or remain neutral. He did neither. But what really soured me on Lindsay was the way he botched the entire matter on a personal level. He wouldn't even see me to explain his decision, at least not at first. To me, it was an insult.

Let me backtrack a little. The Seventeenth Congressional District was a disparate collection of neighborhoods with a variety of divergent interests. It included the lower-income immigrant neighborhoods of the northern end of the Lower East Side, Italian and largely eclectic communities in Greenwich Village, the upper-middle-class enclave of Murray Hill, the internationally flavored Turtle Bay, and the higher-income communities of Yorkville and the Upper East Side. The district ran the length of the East Side, from Houston Street to Ninety-sixth Street, including small sections of the Village west of Fifth Avenue. It covered the city's richest neighborhoods and some of its poorest. Quite a mix.

I was opposed in the general election by Whitney North Seymour, Jr., the Republican state senator for the Upper East Side. Seymour, a Wall Street WASP, was known as a progressive state senator. By contrast, I was seen by some as a Greenwich Village flake. I saw myself as a liberal with sanity, a phrase I first used publicly in 1971. If I had thought of it in 1968, I would have used it then. Others, of course, regarded me somewhat differently. At the start of my Congressional campaign, my influence had only recently begun to reach outside my Village base. My reputation, if I had one at all, was based on my place of residence. I've never been a radical or a flake, but I was dogged by those labels for a number of years simply because I lived in the Village, where the radicals and flakes were supposed to reside.

During a radio debate with Seymour, I learned that my opponent was about to receive Lindsay's endorsement. I should have expected this, but I was furious nevertheless. I called Bob Sweet, Lindsay's deputy mayor, requesting an appointment. (Sweet is now a very able Federal District Court judge.)

"What do you want to see the mayor about?" Sweet asked. I'm sure he knew.

"That will be between me and the mayor," I said.

"I'm afraid that's not good enough," he said. "I have to know in advance what it is you want to discuss with him."

I couldn't believe it. Since when did the mayor make himself unavailable to a city councilman without an approved agenda? It was an outrage, and I not-so-subtly suggested to Sweet that the mayor might want to rethink his position before I called a press conference.

I was given an appointment immediately. Sort of. The appointment was scheduled for the next week. As it turned out, I had to wait over a month to see him, because a teachers' strike was consuming much of the mayor's attention. I was raging, still, but I figured I'd keep quiet about it until we had our meeting. Then I'd see what happened.

I arrived at City Hall at the appointed time, and Lindsay kept me waiting for over an hour. By this time I was fit to be tied. Then, when the mayor tried to filibuster our meeting with innocuous small talk, I stopped him and said, "Mr. Mayor, we have about twenty minutes and shortly your secretary will come in and end the meeting and we won't have gotten to the reason for my coming here." Then I cut right to it: "Seymour says you're endorsing him. Is that true?"

"Yes," Lindsay said, "it is."

I was prepared for this response. I took out a copy of the banner *Daily News* headline from the 1965 mayoral election, the one trumpeting my support of Lindsay's candidacy, weighed against President Johnson's endorsement of Abe Beame. "Maybe you don't remember this," I said, placing the headline on the table, "but a lot of people do." I played it up as a dramatic moment, vowing that I would win the election even without his endorsement. Then I walked out of his office, and that was the end of any civility between me and John Lindsay. Years later, after I became mayor, I tortured him at every opportunity. He deserved it.

I campaigned the pants off of poor Whitney North Seymour, Jr. He had no idea what hit him. He assumed the election would be a cakewalk for him, as it had been for Republicans in the past, and as the political oddsmakers had predicted it would be again. But I campaigned tirelessly. And I won the endorsement of the Liberal Party, which proved to be the key to the whole election; with my Village support pitted against Seymour's Upper East Side backing, the Liberal endorsement became even more important.

My law partners good-naturedly forbade me to practice law during this time, again thinking my election would bring some benefit by association to the firm. They wanted me out there twenty-four hours a day, making sure the people knew my name and my face, and what I stood for. I was glad my partners felt this way, because this was exactly what I had in mind. I may not have been out campaigning twenty-four hours a day every day, but it was pretty damn close. I'd say sixteen to eighteen hours a day was about average.

I was all over the place during the campaign. I personally gave out over a million pieces of campaign literature, by count. My favorite places to meet potential supporters were the bus and subway stops throughout the district. I was there to greet the first commuters at seven o'clock in the morning, and again on their way home between five and seven o'clock that night. Over time, I was seeing the same people again and again, and they came to know me. I even bumped into my opponent once, as he drove by the bus stop at Fourteenth Street and First Avenue in his campaign station wagon about eight-thirty one morning. The scene was typical of our opposing strategies and appeals: Seymour, warm and cozy in his car, somewhat above the fray; and me, down there on the street, talking and shaking hands. I was the candidate of the people, he was the candidate of the rich elite, or so I felt.

Seymour stopped his car to offer me a ride uptown, and to ask me how things were going. He probably wished right away that he hadn't. "Ed," he said, "what time did you get here this morning?"

"Seven o'clock," I said.

"And how long have you been doing this?" he wanted to know.

"For about a year."

I saw an ashen look overtake my opponent. I can't be sure, but I think this was the first time he realized what he was up against, and it was followed by a second, more alarming realization that the first one had come too late.

Whitney North Seymour, Jr., was actually magnanimous in defeat. I won by about twenty-five hundred votes, which was a respectable but not overwhelming margin, and Seymour came over to my campaign headquarters after the polls closed to concede. I thought it was brave and gracious of him to do so, and I never forgot the gesture. Twenty-one years later, I offered to do the same thing for David Dinkins when I lost the Democratic primary in my bid for a fourth term as mayor. I was following Seymour's lead, because I thought it was the classy thing to do. I never made it to Dinkins headquarters, however: the new nominee told me my appearance there wasn't necessary.

At the time, I felt relieved but glad I had offered. I would have been booed by his crowd, much of it on the radical left. They hated me, and it had been a nasty campaign. I was suffering enough that night, without opening myself up for more abuse. My supporters, though, back in 1968, did not boo Whitney North Seymour, Jr., when he came to concede. They cheered him, and he was at his best. There is something to be said for a WASP upbringing.

John Lindsay was far less gracious in defeat than his candidate. "Koch's win is a catastrophe for the city," he said in a radio interview, after the results were in. What a stupid thing to say. I couldn't believe it. It was bad enough he had supported Seymour, but now on top of that he denounced my election. What he should have said was that Koch's win is a catastrophe for John Lindsay, because after his remark I stepped up my efforts to make his life miserable. Some time later, when he ran for President, a reporter asked me why a man who was by then revered almost everywhere in the country was not loved in the city of New York. "Well," I said, "to know him is not to love him."

Despite Lindsay's vicious comment, my election to Congress marked the beginning of an exciting time. Washington was not at all what I expected, although to be honest, I didn't know what to expect. I was like Jimmy Stewart in *Mr. Smith Goes to Washington*—I really saw myself that way. I was young, full of ideas, and determined to vote my conscience on all issues. I wanted to make a difference, to have an impact. I gave up my law practice, as I had pledged to do during the campaign. I knew some Senators and Congressmen had continued their practices, but that left them exposed to conflict-of-interest charges.

I was a little bit lost in Washington at first, but only for about a day. I worried how I would ever get around. My father came down for my swearing-in ceremony, along with my sister Pat and my brother Harold; I was more tourist than host. I didn't know where anything was. I actually had to consult a guidebook to figure out where I was supposed to be and how to get there. I remember being at lunch with my family in one of the restaurants on the Hill when I heard the bells ring. It was the first day of the session, and I didn't know about the bells. They signaled that there was going to be a vote, and were installed in every office and corridor on the Hill, even in restaurants on the Hill that were frequented by members.

I didn't want to miss my first vote. I didn't want to miss any vote. This first vote was important to me as a symbol, obviously, but also because of what was at issue: the seating of Adam Clayton Powell, the black Congressman from Harlem who had been held in contempt of Congress for, among other things, slandering a woman in his district. I planned to vote to seat him, but now, with the bells ringing, I thought I wouldn't get my chance. I was thinking to myself, God, how am I going to get back to the floor in time? There were all those tunnels to worry about. I should have used a strand of wool to help me retrace my steps. Of course, in the end, I simply followed the crowd and made it back in plenty of time. Powell lost the vote, but I was there and voted for him. I was part of the process. I had a voice in our national affairs. It was thrilling.

I adjusted to the rest of my new routine on the Hill soon enough. At first, I rented a furnished apartment requiring a car to bring me to my office. That was no good, so I took a furnished apartment in the southwest part of town, about five blocks from my office. It was a so-called English basement apartment. An English basement, for those who don't know about them, as I didn't, is one of those apartments below the ground floor, the kind with the very small windows, very high up on the walls. Generally, these windows look out on gardens, which you can't see from the inside because the windows are too high. The apartment was so damp my shoes actually turned white overnight. That's an English basement. For my first few years in Washington, it was home.

Home was also the Longworth Office Building, which was (and still is) the best and most beautiful of the three

House office buildings on Capitol Hill. The newest is the Rayburn Office Building, a huge, marble structure that reminded me of the Pentagon. It had no character, but it had a lot of room. Then there was the Cannon Building, which was the oldest structure. It had a lot of character, but not a lot of room. The Longworth was situated between the other two. To my mind it was the most desirable building, although I never seemed to have as much space as I needed.

My most pressing order of business was assembling a staff. First, I appointed an old friend, David Brown, as my chief of staff. Actually, he didn't want that title, even though he happily accepted the job. He wanted to be called "chief counsel." He thought it sounded more important. What the hell did I care? He was a lawyer, and if he wanted the title of counsel, he could have it.

I first met David Brown when I was a city councilman. He did some consulting work for me as part of a special task force I had set up to investigate certain problems within my district. I had taken a five-thousand-dollar stipend, which councilmen typically (and legally) pocketed for themselves, and used it to hire ten experts in various fields, each for a five-hundred-dollar honorarium. David was one of my experts. I was greatly impressed by him. He was smart, but very laid back. We hit it off right away. David, it seemed to me, was the consummate WASP—preppy and handsome, with a lovely wife and, ultimately, two beautiful children. He could and did wear frayed shirt collars with aplomb, and I'm still practicing. He played an instrumental role in my Congressional campaign. I was delighted that he accepted my offer.

After the election, and before the Ninety-first Congress convened in January 1969, David went down to Washington to fill our staff positions there. We decided we would have five staffers in my Washington office, and another five in New York. I planned to be a constituent-minded Congressman, and I thought this mix would help me to accomplish that. My strategy was to commute home on weekends. I would spend Monday nights through Thursday in Washington (in those days, Congress did not meet on Fridays, with rare exceptions), and weekends in New York. The two cities were close enough to make it an easy commute. I kept my Greenwich Village apartment on Washington Place, where I could live comfortably, after spending my midweeks in that damp English basement. I had virtually no social life in Washington beyond dining out with other Congressmen at the end of the day. I did not have any desire to go to Washington parties, after sampling a few and finding them very boring. I only stayed in Washington over two weekends during my entire nine years there.

So David Brown and I had about ten staff slots to fill. Unfortunately, we didn't have a lot of money to pay in salaries, and this almost cost me one of the best workers on the Hill: Ronay Arlt, a startlingly beautiful woman with an extraordinary mind. She had worked for Connecticut Congressman Don Irwin, who had supported the Vietnam War and had been defeated in the 1968 election. I was very taken with Ronay in our interview, and I decided to offer her a job. I asked her how much money she wanted in salary.

"Fourteen thousand dollars," she said, quite reasonably, particularly because I was considering her to run my Washington office.

Reasonable or not, it was more money than we wanted to pay. I offered her ten thousand dollars a year. When I think of that figure now, I cringe. Obviously, it represented more real money in 1969 than it does today, but even so it was ridiculous. "I'm sorry," I said, and I really was because I thought I would lose her over this, "but we are only paying ten thousand dollars."

"Listen," she said. "I'll come to work for you for ten, but in seven weeks you'll be paying me the fourteen."

So we had a deal, and I had someone to run my Washington office. Ronay was wrong about the seven weeks, though. She was making fourteen thousand after less than a month. She was so good, and so bright, and so thorough, that I couldn't afford to lose her. Everything she did was brilliant. She was, like me, a workaholic. A lot of people use that word pejoratively, but I don't. She loved her job. She loved public service. We became good friends, and she stayed with me into my third mayoral administration —at the end in a less involved way, giving up all of her posts except as my representative to the Metropolitan Transit Authority.

In Washington, Ronay and I would go out to dinner quite often; I was always looking for someone to have dinner with. I was lonely. My friends and my family were in New York. Most of the other Congressmen had their families living with them in one of the Washington suburbs. Indeed, the first friendships I developed there were with the other bachelor Congressmen, or communting Congressmen whose wives and families had not moved with them to Washington. We all had our evenings free, and were eager for company. A group of us even shared a house for a while, after I abandoned my basement digs.

The other important hire I made, very early on, was Diane Coffey, who would stay with me from 1971 until 1989, when I ended my career in public office. She became chief of staff beginning with my first mayoral administration. Together, Diane and Ronay kept my Congressional offices running smoothly and efficiently. They were, and remain, two of the most remarkable professionals I have ever met.

I was totally dependent on my staff during my first term in Congress. Ronay had a good deal of experience on the Hill, and when Diane later came aboard, I benefited from her expertise and intelligence as well. One of the ways I learned to make a quick impression among my new colleagues was to use the *Congressional Record* to advantage. I used to write three or four statements a day on subjects that I was interested in, and enter them into the record. Other staff members, including David Brown and some of the interns, wrote statements for me, as did Ronay and

Diane, but I wrote most of them myself, and edited all the others. I think I placed more statements in the *Congressional Record* than any other Congressman, and I'm quite proud of them. They're still there, and I think they've held up quite well with the passage of time. (There, for example, you'll find that I, along with others, proposed that double-hulled oil tankers be mandated, about ten years before the Exxon Valdez accident in Alaska; regrettably, the Congress didn't adopt the idea.)

The benefit of all this writing, as I anticipated, was that my name began to be associated with certain issues. I came to be perceived (by some, anyway) as an expert on child care, mass transit, Israel, the Vietnam War, and a host of other issues, simply because I had so much to say about each of them. It got to the point where some of the other representatives would wonder, Well, what does Koch think about this? I was able to get some of them to join me on the letters or resolutions that I was churning out, primarily for public discussion. But I was far too junior to get anything passed.

My influence on the Hill also benefited from something called the one-minute hour. The one-minute hour was the portion of the day given over to any subject of any Congressman's choice. It took place at noon, when Congress opened each day. The stipulation was that each Congressman could speak on any matter for one minute, until everyone who wanted the chance had been heard. During the rest of the day, debate was confined to whatever subject was on the floor, but the one-minute hour was open to any subject. We rarely needed the full hour; there were only a handful of members who saw it, as I did, as a great opportunity to be heard.

And so at noon, each day, I stood in the well of the House, asking for recognition from the speaker. The trick was to keep your commentary to two hundred words or less. If you did, it would appear in the front of the *Congressional Record*, where more Congressmen would read it. If you went on, or revised your comments later, or added to them, the statement would be consigned to the back of the *Congressional Record*. Only staffers read that far, so I tried to keep my statements short and up front. The habit served me well for the rest of my time in public office. I learned to speak in one-minute sound bites, rattling off coherent, even articulate, statements that would make their way onto the evening news. Most people can't express a full, clear thought in such a short space of time. Without the skills sharpened over nine years' worth of one-minute hours, I couldn't have done it either.

My years as a Congressman put me on a playing field with a number of powerful national figures. Chief among these, at the time, was President Richard Nixon. Like most liberal Democrats, I did not like him. Our first face-to-face meeting took place on the House floor, just a few days before his inauguration on January 20, 1969. As a former member of the House, he had the special privilege of appearing there. On that day, the rules of the House were suspended for the President-elect. Everyone got into line to shake his hand.

As I said, I didn't think much of Nixon in those days. I have a much higher opinion of him today, but back then I thought, I'm not going to shake his hand, why should I? It was foolish on my part; I had been a Congressman for less than three weeks, and I was already prepared to snub the next President of the United States. But then I thought, Well, he does live in my district. His residence then was on Fifth Avenue. So for that reason, since I made it a practice to shake hands with my constituents whenever possible, I got into line with everybody else.

Fishbait Miller, the doorkeeper, introduced each member of Congress to the President-elect. When my turn came, Fishbait said, "Mr. President, this is one of our boys"—meaning a Democrat—"who took one of your seats away. This is Ed Koch from the Seventeenth District in Manhattan."

I shook Nixon's hand, and the President-elect said, "Lotta money in that district."

I thought, What a tacky thing to say, particularly to a new Congressman.

Years later, after Watergate, my distaste for the man had not abated. I was so anti-Nixon that after he resigned from office in disgrace, I actually tried to cut off his pension in an amendment I offered to some legislation. That was how passionate I was. I could get only seventeen other Congressmen to stand up with me, so I was unable to get a recorded vote, which requires a show of twenty hands. Who knows if the amendment would have carried if it had been recorded. Thank God, it never got the chance. Despite his fall from grace, Nixon deserved his pension.

Time has left me with a different impression of Nixon's Presidency than I had as a Congressman. He was corrupt and made a huge mistake, but he has paid the price. And he has been rehabilitated with time. I have come to realize that Nixon was brilliant on many issues. He opened diplomatic relations and trade with China. He saved Israel in 1973 by resupplying it with desperately needed armaments, and for that alone he deserves a place in heaven in my book. He was, and probably still is, anti-Semitic, based on some of the comments he made in those Watergate recordings, but he recognized that the United States needed Israel as a democratic ally and bastion against the client states of the Soviet Union.

I have actually come to like Richard Nixon, so I was distressed when it appeared our new relationship—the mayor and the former President—might be upset by an unfortunate photograph. We were at St. Patrick's Cathedral, attending a eulogy for Italian Prime Minister Aldo Moro, who had been murdered by terrorists. I was still the mayor. As I was going into the church, I was stopped by a reporter. I always stop to talk to reporters when they ask. They have a job to do. The reporter was holding a paper cup of coffee. It was a fairly crowded spot, and the reporter, jostled, accidentally spilled his coffee on me. It was hot. Next, two things happened at the same time. Nixon walked by me into the cathedral, and a photographer decided to take a picture. The result appeared in the papers the next day: a shot of me, grimacing in pain from the hot coffee, with the former President passing by. The caption suggested that I was expressing my distaste for Nixon, which was absolutely not the case. I was mortified, so I wrote the President a note explaining that there was absolutely no offense intended by my expression and that the reporter had just spilled some hot coffee on me. It was an innocent thing, but a telling reminder of how the constant glare of the public eye can affect even the most benign personal exchanges.

These days, I find myself sitting next to Richard Nixon at funerals. We sat next to each other at Malcolm Forbes's funeral in March 1990. He was flanked on the other side by Elizabeth Taylor. Flanked is probably a good choice of words here, because Liz looked like a huge horse at the time. She wore a sable coat to conceal her girth, but it didn't do the trick. It actually made her look bigger. Anyway, Nixon and I sat there, as we had come to do on a number of these sad occasions, and talked collegially. He said he read and liked my columns in the *New York Post*, which was very nice of him, and I told him I enjoyed his most recent book. It was all very civil, and a long way from my parvenu attempt to have his pension terminated.

George Bush, of course, went on to become the most notable of my Congressional colleagues. Our service in Congress overlapped for one term. We had a collegial but distant relationship then. We never went out to dinner together or pursued a social friendship, but we were always cordial to one another. My favorite Bush story took place a few years later, after he was named director of the Central Intelligence Agency. I was by this time serving on the foreign operations subcommittee of the Appropriations Committee. I had been seeking to cut off aid to Uruguay, which I had come to see as a kind of charnel house of Latin America. Out of a population of 1.3 million, some five thousand were jailed as political prisoners. I was successful in eliminating the $3 million in annual

United States military aid to Uruguay. "This year, Uruguay," I said on the floor of the House. "Next year, on to Nicaragua."

One afternoon, shortly afterward, I was in my New York office at 26 Federal Plaza, when I got a phone call from Bush in his capacity as director of the Central Intelligence Agency. "Listen, Ed," he said, "my agents have gotten news that there's a contract out on your life. The Uruguayan Secret Service wants to kill you."

I was really taken aback. "George," I said, "you will provide protection, won't you?"

"No," he said. "The CIA does not provide personal protection."

I couldn't believe it, so I argued the point. After all, there was a contract on my life because of something I did as a representative of the United States government. I went into a desperate and passionate plea on why I deserved CIA protection.

"I'm sorry, Ed," Bush said, when I was through. "There's nothing I can do about it."

"But George," I persisted, "what am I supposed to do?"

"Be-e-e-e-e-e careful," he said.

Another Bush story, of more recent vintage, took place shortly after he was elected President, when I was asked by the United States Conference of Mayors to try to seek a meeting with him in the transition before his inauguration. I called on a Thursday to ask for an appointment for the following morning, when I would be in Washington for a television appearance. The only prominent Democrats the President-elect had seen during this early period were Michael Dukakis and Jesse Jackson, but he graciously made time for me, even on such short notice. I felt quite complimented; I had not expected it.

I met the President-elect on Friday morning in the executive wing of the White House. Jim Baker, John Sununu, and Brent Scowcroft were in the room. "How are you, Ed?" Bush said, putting his arm around me. He could not have been warmer. I knew we would only have a half-hour or so, and it seemed all the President-elect wanted to talk about were the good old days back in Congress, and his recent election. That was fine with me, at least at the out-set, but then I realized that when all this cheerful remi-niscing was over, I would not have gotten to my agenda.

"Mr. President," I said, interrupting our small talk at the first opportunity. "I have an agenda of eleven items. When I leave here the press will ask me if we discussed them. Please let me tell you what they are, so that I can go out and say we did."

"Of course," he said.

So I went through my agenda. I don't even remember what all the issues were, but I read through them like a laundry list. (One, as I recall, was a request to help the Armenians who had just suffered an earthquake; I also sought support for a South African boycott until apartheid was ended.) With each mention, Bush nodded or prom-ised to look into the matter, and then I moved on down the list.

I wanted to be able to say truthfully that I'd raised these issues with Mr. Bush, and that's exactly what I did. Sununu sent someone out with me to make sure I did not overstate the President-elect's position, but he needn't have worried.

But let me get back to those days about which George Bush was so nostalgic. Over time, I became a respected member of Congress. I hope that doesn't sound immod-est. I think if you asked any of my colleagues from that period they would tell you the same thing. I was well liked, which made me more effective as a legislator. I went out of my way to be nice. As mayor, I didn't think I could spare the time to be as nice as I really am. It was a mistake on my part. But I was a nice Congressman. I thought I had to be. One reason I thought so was that Congress was an institution dominated by Southerners. This is not so much the case anymore, but in the early 1970s it certainly still was. It was very gentlemanly, and courtesy was extremely important. It may have been a false courtesy; in many cases I suspect it was. Some colleagues may have disliked one another, but courtesy was always required. It was very genteel.

What all this courtesy meant, in Congress anyway, was that it took a long time to get anything done. As mayor, I would always get right to the point, and I expected everyone else to do the same. As a Congressman, though, I had a different role. After all, when in Rome . . . That's the difference between being an executive and being a legislator. Most of a legislator's job is to educate colleagues and the public. An executive must act, implement, change, get things done.

Emanuel Celler, the Brooklyn Congressman, was the chairman of the New York delegation when I joined the Congress. Manny and I became good friends. He recognized that I had administrative talents and made me secretary of the delegation, which effectively meant that I had some ability to maneuver the delegation in support of or opposition to any number of things. The way to do that was to get the delegation to meet. That wasn't always so easy. They didn't meet on any regular basis before I arrived. Manny told me there was no way to get everybody together, or even to get a good turnout. But I came up with the solution: food.

The way to get near-full attendance at delegation meetings was to give the members a great lunch. Not just a good lunch, mind you, but a great lunch. And to top it off, for dessert, there was a make-your-own-sundae spread, with vanilla and chocolate ice cream, chopped walnuts, and thick chocolate syrup. This is what I did, and with a lure like that, they came. I think most of the New York delegation met every two weeks after that, which taught me that good government is sometimes fueled by good food.

My first committee assignment was Science and Astronautics. The space program was not a major interest of mine, but I immersed myself in it. I was determined to learn all that I could, in order to intelligently judge the complicated issues facing the committee. I came to the conclusion that we should be spending less money on manned space exploration and more on nonmanned exploration, which cost about one-fifth what the manned efforts did. Most people did not share my opinion, and were not inclined to hear my reasoning. In 1970, one of the most heated debates on the floor was over a $3.4 billion bill to establish a permanent space station and space shuttle project, and to continue NASA's program for manned space flight after the scheduled completion of the Apollo series in 1974. I thought the amount was excessive, particularly considering our mounting needs in areas such as education, housing, mass transit, pollution abatement, and crime control. Our priorities were all out of whack, and I recommended that the NASA budget be reduced rather than increased.

I knew I was fighting a losing battle, so in desperation (and frustration) I entered the following comment into the record: "I cannot justify approving monies to find out whether or not there is some microbe on Mars, when in fact I know there are rats in Harlem apartments."

Now, that's a sound bite.

For my constituents on the East Side of Manhattan, perhaps my most important fight was against the war in Vietnam. I put together one of the first joint resolutions endorsed both by representatives who supported and who opposed the war, calling for peace. A number of Congressmen simply could not abandon their initial support for our military involvement, even if they had since shifted their positions; they found it hard to publicly admit error. It was a dilemma for them. The resolution succeeded in creating a climate in which some members who realized they had erred could change their position with dignity, now that the war appeared unwinnable.

My first run-in over the war was with Congressman Wayne Hays, a really mean-spirited bully from Ohio. He was very smart, and one of the great House debaters. At the time, he was the powerful chairman of the House Administration Committee. During the week of North Vietnamese leader Ho Chi Minh's death, I went to the floor and said that, to the Vietnamese, he was like George Washington is to us, the father of his country, and I suggested we use the occasion of his death to extend the hand of friendship. Wayne Hays, in response on the House floor, referred to me as "an emissary from Hanoi."

I did not appreciate the charge, so I took Hays's comments from the *Congressional Record*, placed them alongside my own, and sent them out in a newsletter to my constituents. "Who do you agree with?" I wrote. "Please write to Wayne Hays and tell him what you think."

A week or so later, Hays approached me on the floor. "What the hell is goin' on?" he said. "I'm gettin' all these damn letters denouncing me. Stop it!" And then he laughed. I don't think he really cared that he was being deluged with letters from a bunch of liberal New Yorkers. He was amused by the whole thing. I took the exchange with Hays as a kind of signal that I was finally accepted, even by those who thought I was a liberal flake from New York City.

With time, my opposition to the war grew to where I introduced legislation to give amnesty to the thousands of draft dodgers and deserters in exile in Canada. People really thought I was nuts, including some of my liberal Congressional friends who opposed the war. I knew there was no hope of its passing, not at that time, but I wanted to start the discussion. (As it turned out, I wasn't nuts at all, just ahead of the times; amnesty was finally granted under President Jimmy Carter.)

I remember walking down Eighth Street one Friday morning, and being stopped by one of my constituents, an elderly lady who approached me, wanting to talk.

"How'm I doing?" I said, in what was becoming the signature greeting of my political career.

"Congressman," she said, "you're doing terrible. You're doing just terrible. How could you support those yellow-bellies? My grandson is in Vietnam, and here you are supporting those yellow-bellies in Canada."

"Ma'am," I said, as gently as I could manage. "I don't want to try and persuade you, but let me tell you my position. I think the war is wrong. I think that ultimately we have to bring our boys home. We've ruined too many lives, the draft dodgers' and the deserters' among them. It is time to heal. Now, I understand you see things differently, and I hope your grandson is okay, but this is my position. I hope you'll ultimately agree with me, but it's not necessary that you do. We will never agree on everything." Then I added, "But other than that, how else am I doing?"

"Other than that, you're doing wonderful," she said, and we both laughed.

Incidentally, my "How'm I doing?" phrase grew out of my first term as a Congressman. I used to come home to New York every Friday when Congress was not in session, and hand out literature at the twenty-five major subway and bus stops in my district. Every Friday morning, I'd be at one of them. I wanted to stay in touch with my constituents and give them the opportunity to talk to me, so I did not miss a week. Typically, I would hand out a reprint of some statement I had made in Congress that week and include a little box telling people where to write to express their opinion and help me to implement my suggestions. I asked them to send me copies of their letters, and that's how I communicated with them. Hundreds of my statements were copied in letters in the course of a week, as a direct result of my bus and subway stops; the originals were sent to the President, or his Cabinet members, among others.

Of course, my constituents were not always happy to see me, particularly at seven o'clock in the morning when they were running to catch the subway. They had other things on their minds than communicating with their Congressman. Most of them were in such a hurry that they probably saw me as an impediment. Perhaps they thought I was crazy; after all, it wasn't an election year—what the hell did I think I was doing?

I was trying to get attention, but it wasn't easy. When I first started, I would say, "Good morning, good morning, good morning," and people would rush by me, into the subway. A few would say "Good morning," but that was about it. I don't think they were being rude, just indifferent, distracted. Then one morning, just to vary the routine a little, I said, "I'm Ed Koch, your Congressman. How'm I doing?" And people responded. They actually stopped. Sometimes they told me I was doing lousy, but they always stopped. And they talked to me, and I listened.

Right away, I knew I was onto something, so I kept at it. I started to use the phrase in my newsletters and press releases. When I campaigned for reelection, I used it in my speeches, and everywhere else it seemed appropriate. "How'm I doing?" became associated with me, as it still is to this day. Years later, after I became mayor, the writer Ken Auletta, among others, condemned me for my slogan. There were a lot of people who used to criticize me for using it as often as I did, but for some reason Auletta's derision has stayed with me. He wrote that instead of saying, "How am *I* doing?" I should be saying, "How are *we* doing?"

I thought to myself, You dope. Do you think anyone could stand at a subway stop at seven in the morning saying, "How are *we* doing?" and expect any kind of response. That's the way a teacher talks to her children: "How are *we* doing today?" It's patronizing. Worse, it sounds foolish. Corporations pay millions of dollars for slogans and logos, and most times people don't remember them. I stumbled on a great one, and people remembered it. And it didn't cost a nickel. I wasn't about to give up a good thing.

By the end of my first term, my reelection seemed assured. Again, I don't mean to sound immodest, but my popularity was high. After all, my style in office was much the same as it was when I was running for office. In many ways, with my regular Friday subway stops, my campaigning never stopped, and now that I had the high profile of an incumbent (and the continued backing of the Liberal Party), I knew I would be tough to beat. A two-year term goes by quickly. If you're smart, you think about reelection the day after you're elected. Practically speaking, you must gear up about fourteen months before the next election. In my case, I never geared down.

I received 62 percent of the vote when I ran for my second term in 1970, outpolling my Republican opponent, a businessman named Peter Sprague, by nearly a two-to-one margin. It was an overwhelming victory, and it signaled a long future on the Hill. After my second term, I was elected to three more, with as much as 78 percent of the vote. Eventually the Republicans seemed to give up, losing any hope of beating me. They couldn't find anybody who wanted to spend money on a losing candidacy, or to subject themselves to such humiliation. Still, I campaigned vigorously each time out, no matter how slim my opponents' chances.

The most notable issue of my second term was not a Congressional matter at all, but it did more to distinguish me among New Yorkers than anything I ever did on the House floor. In the early 1970s, the Lindsay administration was pushing what the mayor called scatter-site housing. The idea was to put small, low-income housing projects in middle-class areas. It was not a good idea, but I didn't say anything publicly when I first heard about it in 1971. The targeted scatter sites were not in my district, although I was by now on the Banking and Currency Committee, which had jurisdiction over housing matters.

The Lindsay plan was controversial from the start. Many tenants of low-income projects, because of the various eligibility requirements, were on welfare, as they still are today; most were black or Hispanic, as they still are. And there is no question that incidents of violent crime were common in those projects, and in their surrounding neighborhoods. That's just a fact, and it still is today. But if you come out against such projects being put in your neighborhood, you will be called racist. I don't accept that now, and I didn't then. Certainly, there is racism in New York City, although I think to a far lesser degree than in most cities. New York is integrated. You can live wherever you can afford to live. In Chicago, for example, you can't live wherever you can afford to live. You can live in a black area, or you can live in a white area. There is little housing integration there, and that's true of many cities— not by law, but by custom, sometimes enforced by racial violence. That's not true in New York City, at least not to any great degree.

When Lindsay tried to place his scatter-site housing projects in a middle-class Italian neighborhood in Queens, there was such resistance he knew it would never be done. The Italians don't flee their communities or sit by while the government tries to destroy them. I give them credit for their sense of community. They helped save the city in a lot of ways. The Lubavitcher Jews did the same, when they refused to leave the Crown Heights section of Brooklyn, after it became overwhelmingly black. All of these people should get credit for having stayed put.

So, having been rejected by the Italians, Lindsay decided to put the low-income project in Forest Hills, a predominantly middle-class Jewish community in Queens, because the Jews, he believed, would not resist. He knew that all he had to do to make the Jews cave in was to call them racist if they opposed his plan, and they would fall to their knees and say, "Please don't call us racist. We'll do whatever you want." I don't think I'm exaggerating.

But the people of Forest Hills surprised Lindsay and everyone else. They fought back. It was almost too late (ground had already been broken on three twenty-four-story high-rises, for some four thousand low-income residents), but City Hall was suddenly up against mounting resistance. The fight was led by a rabbi whose synagogue stood across the street from the scatter site. The rabbi roused his community. This neighborhood will die, he said. Property values will fall, the Jews will leave, there will be more crime. The city responded by maintaining that there was less crime in public housing than elsewhere. That was pure baloney, but Lindsay and his commissioner, Simeon Golar, would have said anything to keep his plan moving forward.

I continued to be silent on the issue, although I did tell my colleague, Ben Rosenthal, who was the Congressman in the district, that I would join him in any action he chose to mount against the plan. But Ben was not eager to publicly oppose Lindsay's project, so I held my tongue (and my nose) some more. Finally, on a Sunday in 1971, a friend of mine suggested we drive out to Forest Hills to see firsthand what all the fuss was about. We arrived to find a huge picket line (which I did not expect) in front of the building site on 108th Street, hard by the Long Island Expressway.

I was reasonably well-known as the second-term Congressman from the city's silk-stocking district. One of the protest leaders asked me to speak against the projects before about two thousand demonstrators. I took the mike and said, "Keep up the fight. You can beat City Hall. They can't impose this on you. It's wrong."

It was wrong, and I regretted having kept silent until that moment on the issue. Of course, I had no real authority over the matter, but I did have a platform, and I was suddenly determined to use it. People might not like what I had to say, but they would listen to it. I firmly believed that we should not destroy our middle-class communities, black or white, for any reason. They were all precious. You would find the same resistance on this issue in a black middle-class area as you would in a white middle-class area. People work all their lives to get out of poverty and the problems that go with it. I didn't think there was anything wrong, or contradictory, about my position. It was common sense, but it really pissed off the reformers and liberals who had been my political base until that moment.

My remarks were broadcast by many radio stations, and I was deluged with phone calls denouncing me.

One of my favorite stories grew out of the resulting hue and cry against me. Stanley Geller, a past president of the VID and one of the most active reform leaders, challenged me on the issue. "I don't care if the Jews move out," he said to me. "The Jews have to pay their dues."

"Stanley," I said to him, "that's easy for you to say. You have this wonderful brownstone on Twelfth Street in the Village. I wish I owned one like that. You have this marvelous home in the Hamptons, with an Olympic-size swimming pool, and you have invited me there. I wish I owned one like that. On the day your kids were born you registered them in private schools. And you're telling me that the Jews have to pay their dues? I'm telling you, they're willing to pay their dues, they just don't want to pay yours."

I told that story all over town because I was fed up. Stanley Geller and I have moved past our differences on this issue, and we remain good friends, but he has disputed the facts of this exchange. He claimed the story was false in at least one respect: he did not register his children for private school on the day they were born. It was some time later. Fair enough.

I had my first encounter with Mario Cuomo over the Forest Hills housing issue. Cuomo, a Queens lawyer, was appointed by Mayor Lindsay in May 1972 as an independent fact-finder charged with investigating every aspect of the Forest Hills situation. Over the next two months, Cuomo conducted exhaustive interviews with those involved in the dispute—community leaders, engineers, urban planners—to try to determine the most appropriate course for the city to take. I was very impressed with Cuomo in our meeting. He was bright, articulate, and thorough.

"What do you recommend?" he asked me, as he was asking everyone else.

"Reduce it by half," I said. I knew the city couldn't

abandon the project entirely at this point. Ground had already been broken, contracts awarded, and construction begun. It would have been too costly to cancel. But if the project was scaled down, I argued, and the buildings built to twelve stories instead of twenty-four, housing far fewer than the scheduled four thousand, the impact on the surrounding community would be much less traumatic. Others made similar recommendations, and this is essentially what Cuomo advised Lindsay in his report, laying the groundwork for the course Lindsay ultimately took.

Cuomo was lionized for his handling of the matter by the reform leaders, while I was nearly drawn and quartered. I was berated by the VID, whose members denounced me as racist and reactionary for opposing any low-income project, no matter what the size. I did not retreat. I do not think it is liberal to destroy the middle class.

The reformers really beat me up over this. At one point, Cuomo was asked to speak at the VID and said, to his credit, "You are praising me and attacking Koch when we both concluded the same thing. I don't understand it."

I lost a lot of support after Forest Hills, but I also won new support. Early on, though, I thought the political fallout hurt me. I was censured by the Lexington Democratic Club, a powerful East Side reform club that was as old as the reform movement. I responded to them by saying, "The East Side reformers are for low-income housing projects, just so long as they're built in Forest Hills."

In the end, the issue was important for me both personally and politically. It was my baptism under political fire. It strengthened my resolve to say and do what I thought was right, even if my position was politically incorrect or unpopular. After Forest Hills, I no longer felt comfortable in the reform movement. I had been one of only three prominent reform leaders to support Bobby Kennedy for United States Senator in 1964 (along with Stanley Geller and Bob Clampitt) when the rest of the reformers were supporting Sam Stratton. Bobby Kennedy ultimately became a hero to the reform movement, but not when he ran in 1964. They hated him then and supported Congressman Stratton.

In many ways, Forest Hills was my Rubicon. It set me on my own independent path. It allowed me to persuade people that I was not some crazy reformer from Greenwich Village. But it did more than just change the way people thought of me; it changed the way I thought of the reform movement, which I had been a part of for so long. The reformers were dominated by young Jewish idealists —led at various times by Eleanor Roosevelt, Senator Herbert Lehman, Mayor Robert Wagner, and others who had an intense but pragmatic desire to change the world—but the troops on occasion were out of touch with reality. Some of their goals, if achieved, would have inflicted a great deal of pain on many people, but they didn't care. After Forest Hills, I came to see the reformers more as ideologues than mainstream Democrats. It was at this time that I coined the phrase I have used to describe myself ever since: a liberal with sanity.

But, again, I'm getting ahead of myself. Let me get back to Washington. Over time, I made a place for myself there. Or, I should say, I made a place for myself in Congress. I was never crazy about Washington, but I liked being a Congressman, and I was extremely dedicated to my work and to my constituents. I liked the prestige of the office, and having the power to change things and to educate people on the need for change. I liked the fact that I was able to get things done that directly benefited the voters in my district, and the city at large. I could have been a Congressman for the rest of my life (96 percent are returned to office in every election, and I did not then aspire to any higher office), except that it became increasingly difficult for me to continue to live in Washington. I was miserable there. I hated being away from New York, away from my family and friends. I was lonely.

I wanted to come home.

But I was torn. I was having an impact as a Congressman, and I did not want to give that up. Yes, I wanted to change my day-to-day life-style, but I did not want to give up my office. I didn't want to go back to the practice of law. The more I thought about it (and I began to think about it a lot), the more I realized there was only one position challenging enough to lure me away from Capitol Hill and home to New York City.

6

City Hall

I FIRST SOUGHT THE MAYORALTY OF New York City in 1973, but I didn't get very far.

I ran for a number of reasons. The main personal reason was that I wanted to get out of Washington. It doesn't sound like much, but I think that was my dominant impulse. I was suffocating there and longing to return to New York. I don't know that I realized that then, but it seems clear now. I felt I belonged in New York, where I thrived. I have always said that when I go north of the Bronx I get the bends, or that when I leave Queens I get nosebleeds. The lines are not original and I never passed them off as mine, but I do wish I had thought of them. I saw everything outside New York City as a kind of wasteland, and in some ways I still do. I love the pulse of the city, its energy, its tumult. Everything is in constant turmoil. On occasion, you worry that you may have to run for your life in the subway, or be prepared to do battle just to hail a cab, that's how exciting the city is. Every day has something new in it, and to top it off we have the best restaurants, the best theater, and the best museums in the entire world. In 1973, no other city could match what New York had to offer, and Washington didn't even come close. Besides, I was lonely there, and the weekend commute to New York was not sufficient to renew my spirits. One year I flew to New York more than a hundred times.

Politically, I ran to rescue the city from itself. I know that makes me sound a little naive and probably more than a little full of myself, but that's honestly the way I saw things. I was one of the first among the New York Congressional delegation to pay specific attention to the city's increasing problems, and I began to think I was almost uniquely positioned to help address those problems. Even though I was a third-term Congressman, I was still independent of the city's political system, and I thought a fresh perspective was one of the things the city needed. I also knew Abe Beame would make an inadequate mayor, and it was becoming increasingly apparent to me, and to other Democratic Party leaders, that he would land the nomination. I didn't want that to happen.

My campaign lasted for just forty-five days before we ran out of money. We had raised one hundred thousand dollars, which sounds like a lot of money but really was not. When you pay salaries to a campaign staff (I think I had six people on the payroll), pay for rent, and pay to print and circulate campaign literature, one hundred thousand dollars disappears quickly. Most of our money, as I recall, came from hundred-dollar contributions, when it came in at all. I'm surprised we made it through forty-five days. David Brown was my campaign manager, and he believed that the way to get credibility was to hire well-credentialed, buttoned-down-collar campaign people, rather than to seek out the eager and talented young men and women who would have been only too happy to volunteer their time to a candidate they believed in. The only problem with David's strategy was it didn't leave us with money for anything else. Commercial time, on television or radio, was out of the question.

Most of our campaign efforts were, out of necessity, conducted on street level. The highlights, I like to think, were my speeches. My major issue in the race was the frightening rise in the city's crime rate, and for those forty-five days I talked more about crime than anything else. The full-blown fiscal crisis that would nearly destroy the city under Abe Beame was still several years away. It was brewing, of course, and the city's profligacy was talked about in government circles, but it was not a front-burner public issue.

Violent crime was the number one concern to city residents and business owners. These days, we all take for granted that New York is not the safest place in the world and we make the necessary adjustments to our routines and life-styles to compensate, but back then was when things began to get worse. Everybody was talking about how bad the crime rate was and how much worse it might get. Our neighborhoods were beginning to deteriorate. Companies were abandoning the city; jobs were being lost. And, most troubling, middle-class families were fleeing the city because they feared the public schools were educationally inadequate and physically unsafe for their children.

Of course, the locus of much of this crime was in the city's minority population, as it is today. People didn't want to talk about that because they were afraid of being called racists, but that's just stupid. I have never been afraid to talk about it, even in 1973, and even at the risk of alienating some people, particularly the editorial boards of New York's daily newspapers. If you cannot identify and candidly discuss the problem, I maintained, then you cannot solve the problem. So I identified it. And I talked about it. I understood what was happening and, with my candor, the people understood me. They began to see me as the one candidate who was not afraid to speak out about crime and its root causes and was willing to defend himself against the unfair charges of racism that such honesty evoked. If I had been able to get my message across to the city, instead of only to those I was able to talk to personally, I would have generated much greater support. But that only comes with television commercials, which we could not afford.

One of my favorite stories from the 1973 campaign was a related anecdote involving a judge named Allen Murray

Myers, whom I had helped elect to the court. I worked the anecdote into some of my speeches, and it came to symbolize my position on crime. The story, as I later recounted it, occurred before a group of two hundred senior citizens at a Jewish senior center. I told them that a judge was mugged and later called a press conference to discuss the impact of his mugging with reporters. I told my audience that the judge had said, "This mugging would in no way affect my decision in matters of this kind," at which point an elderly lady stood up in the back of the room and shouted, "Then mug him again!"

With great common sense, this woman had tapped into the mood of the city: the judiciary was out of touch with reality; senior citizens felt like prisoners in their own homes. The judge's story always went over very well because it touched a nerve. It was also true. It crystallized my antiestablishment—what you might today call populist —position: the leadership of New York City had lost its common sense, while the people had maintained theirs.

I was running on common sense. People seemed to like the message, although I cannot say for certain how they felt about the messenger. Either way, I didn't have the money to stick around long enough to find out. We spent ourselves dry. There was nothing to do but withdraw and settle our accounts. On the morning after I formally exited the race, *The New York Times* very graciously acknowledged my aborted campaign on its editorial page, noting that I had abandoned my "long-shot quest with typical grace and good humor." I took their send-off as an unexpected high compliment. (*The New York Times* would continue in its kindness to me, even when I offended the genteel sensibilities of its editorial board with comments they thought rude, and I thought on the mark.) I am truly grateful.

With time, I realized the moment had not been right for me to make a mayoral run, and that I still had a political future. Maybe it would never lead me out of Washington, but I still had one. Until 1973, it seemed I always squeaked my way into office, then people got used to me. After that, they saw that I was quite good in my first term, and they reelected me with increasing majorities. But it didn't happen that way this time. I left the race quietly. I did not vow to return to seek the mayoralty in 1977, because that office had not been my long-held ambition. It seemed right at the time, but I had no idea how it would seem in the future.

However, in 1977 it seemed right again. I had persevered in Congress, winning reelection to a fourth and fifth term in 1974 and 1976, with increasing majorities, and I like to think I continued to have an impact there, but my dislike of the Washington scene had not diminished. Although, as most would agree, I could have made the Congressional seat mine forever, I still wanted to move on, and when the subsequent New York City mayoral election rolled around I was drawn to it a second time. This time out, the odds were again stacked against me. I entered the 1977 race with a recognition rating of about 4 percent among city voters.

According to the pundits, the voters outside my district had no idea who I was. I have never listened to the experts; they declared me an also-ran before the race even got under way. I thought I had as good a shot as any of the other Democratic candidates: Manhattan Borough President Percy Sutton, former Congresswoman Bella Abzug, Congressman Herman Badillo, businessman Joel Harnett, attorney and former Manhattan Democratic county leader Eddie Costikyan, and Abe Beame, the incumbent. Costikyan soon dropped out of the race and supported me, but he was replaced by New York Secretary of State Mario Cuomo, who rounded out the field after several weeks of public indecision. (Then, as now, Cuomo had some difficulty making up his mind.) Beame, Abzug, and Cuomo were generally regarded as the front-runners, with Harnett bringing up the rear; the rest of us were expected to finish somewhere in the middle, but far behind those in the lead.

It was, I knew, an uphill climb, and I looked immediately to David Garth, the media wizard introduced to me the previous year by my friend Bess Myerson, to help with my campaign. Understand, I had campaign managers in every one of my previous races, but they were always volunteers; I had never hired a top-notch media consultant to help me win an election. It had never been necessary. But I was smart enough to recognize that I needed one then, and even smarter to recognize David Garth as that one. At our first meeting (which, as I recall, was at a 1976 dinner party at Bess Myerson's home), David was admiring of my Congressional career, and he told me he'd be interested in managing my media campaign if I ever considered another run for mayor. So my first order of business was to call David and remind him of this conversation. I didn't have to prod too much. He remembered. And he was happy to sign on, provided his good friend Mario Cuomo, to whom he had already pledged his services (and support), would not be a candidate. David double-checked with Cuomo, who was firm in his resolve not to run, thereby marking perhaps the first time in Cuomo's political career that his indecision cost him an election.

Governor Hugh Carey, with whom I have had my share of problems over the years, was a friend and client of Garth's (David had been his campaign manager in the gubernatorial race), and he checked in early with his support. Like Cuomo, Carey was not the most decisive man in politics. He turned out to be a fair-weather political friend, rescinding his support as soon as Cuomo decided to run. Carey actually asked David to abandon my campaign and sign with Cuomo. I couldn't believe it. David refused to step down as my media adviser (Cuomo wound up hiring Jimmy Carter's image makers, Pat Caddell and Gerald Rafshoon), which provided me with the first of many reasons why David Garth and I will always be close friends.

Before deserting me publicly, Carey asked me to meet

him at the brownstone of former Mayor Robert F. Wagner, on East Sixty-second Street. David had briefed me on the governor's plan, and I decided to put him on the defensive immediately. "Governor," I said when I arrived, "before you tell me whatever it is you want to tell me, I just want you to know I will be supporting you next year. Now, what is it you want to tell me?"

"Well, Ed," he said, "it's like this. I really think you're the best candidate, but I don't think you can win. Mario wants to run and I think he can win. That's what it comes down to. We have to stop Bolla and Beame, and I think Mario is our best shot. I hope you understand."

I let him go on for about twenty minutes, without interruption, while he couched his jettisoning of me in every conceivable euphemism (and some inconceivable ones), trying desperately not to piss me off any more than he had to. When he was finished, I said, "What makes you so sure Mario Cuomo can win? The last time he ran for anything [for Lieutenant Governor in 1974 against Mary Anne Krupsak], he was beaten badly. I've won nine elections in fourteen years. As far as I'm concerned, Mario can run on my ticket for city council president."

"Actually," Carey said, "I was thinking about it the other way around."

"Governor," I said, with as much respect as I could muster, "I represent the most prestigious district in the Congress. For me, city council president would be a step down. For Mario, it would be a step up. He will not be elected mayor. I will. I am not withdrawing."

That was the last I heard from Governor Carey until the general election, but the heated exchange handicapped my candidacy from that point forward. Part of the party machine (that part controlled by Governor Carey and former Mayor Wagner), which would not have been behind me no matter what passed between me and the governor, was now working against me. And the regulars and the balance of the machine were backing Beame. Most people wrote me off as a ridiculous long shot, with no hope of even making a respectable showing. David Garth was out to change all that. He took total charge. He became my most trusted adviser, as well as my de facto campaign manager, media guru, and image consultant.

This last was very important to him. He didn't like my image. At least, he didn't care for the way I looked. He liked what I stood for, which I suppose was also a part of my image, but he focused on the packaging. He was on me constantly to lose weight, which I did, under his watchful eye. He told me it was to keep my energy up during the campaign, but I knew he also wanted me to cut a better figure. More, he had me discard my ultraconservative, three-button Brooks Brothers suits for the more modern Dunhill broader-shouldered, two-button variety. He actually sent me out to buy a new wardrobe of Dunhill suits, which back then cost fourteen hundred dollars apiece, off the rack. I was able to find comparable suits at a wholesaler for considerably less. My mother never would have understood spending fourteen hundred dollars on a suit, and neither could I.

(For City Hall fashion historians, I wore the two-button suits throughout my three terms as mayor, and returned to my three-button, natural-shouldered favorites after I left office.)

And, most difficult for me, David quashed my sense of humor. He really sat on it, or asked me to. I didn't agree with this part of his strategy at first, but I came to see the logic of it. David's thinking was that I had to fight against the perception that I was some kind of flake from Greenwich Village, that I was loose-lipped and out of control. He wanted to present me as someone who not only understood the mounting fiscal problems facing the city, but who was also able to cope with them—a serious statesman, if you will. As each succeeding candidate announced, David positioned me as the liberal with sanity that my record as a Congressman had shown me to be, but that the impression I first made perhaps did not.

To this end, David orchestrated a media campaign

along the high road. My television commercials were straightforward, on-target, and generally brilliant. The only problem with them, as far as I was concerned, was that they were entirely humorless. The standard line of the campaign—a dismissing reference to the incumbent Beame and his predecessor, Lindsay—offered just about our only indication of a lurking sense of humor: "After eight years of charisma, and four years of the clubhouse, let's try competence."

My greatest strength, according to David Garth, was my honesty. I wasn't about to argue with him. I rarely lie, because I find it so difficult. It's almost a compulsion with me to tell the truth. There are, I have said, only two acceptable lies: it is permissible (although not always advisable, as my personal experience has taught me) to tell a terminally ill patient he or she doesn't have cancer and will get well; it is also okay to protect what is left of the reputation of a fired employee by saying he resigned (except in cases of corruption, when the truth must be told). I have obviously told a few of those lies over the years. As a public official, though, on matters of substance, I have lied less than most others—not only less often, but also less convincingly. I never play poker. I could only lose.

David played to this strength wherever possible. If he could get the voters to hear me or see me, they would find a candid, undaunted, intelligent straight shooter, and our campaign would have a chance. So this was the message he tried to get out. He did it by crafting a series of high-minded radio and television spots, and by carefully monitoring my public appearances, encouraging me to stick with my prepared remarks. I knew he was succeeding when I was out stumping one afternoon, shortly before the September primary. It happened that I was accompanied on this stop by the journalist Murray Kempton, who had described me in one of his columns as very able, but with no chance of winning. I was handing out literature in a supermarket parking lot and shaking some hands, when a woman approached me. She accepted the literature, shook my hand, and without prompting on my part repeated my "eight years of charisma, four years of the clubhouse" line. Then she asked, "Why do I believe you?" She was asking herself as much as me: "Why do I believe you?" Then she told me that her husband caught her the night before, watching one of my commercials transfixed, and said, "What the hell is going on here? Do you have the hots for this guy?" Then she said she was going to vote for me, and that's when I knew I was going to win the primary.

I was overwhelmed by this woman's candor and support. "Would you give me a kiss for luck?" I asked her. Her name was Phyllis Vigilante—I will never forget it—and she did. And Murray Kempton was on hand to record the entire scene.

My one perceived political weakness as a mayoral candidate was my bachelorhood. I call it a perceived weakness because I did not see the fact that I was unmarried as any kind of liability. David Garth did, though, and he may have been right. Sure, there should be nothing wrong with being a single man at the age of fifty-two, or at any age for that matter, but if you happen to be seeking the mayoralty of New York City, then it becomes an issue. Most likely, it will be a question mark that will be seized upon by your opponents, their campaign managers, and their staffs. It had been an issue in my previous campaigns for city council and Congress, but it was to be magnified here. Of course, this was to be expected. When you're seeking the mayoralty of the greatest city on earth, the stakes are tremendous.

It mattered to David Garth because it made his job more difficult. Typically, a politician's family plays a key role in a campaign, helping to paint a well-rounded portrait of the candidate as a stable, conventional, and traditional member of the community. Moreover, family members—wives, children—can fan out to make secondary campaign appearances on their own, effectively placing a candidate in two or more places at the same time.

My father, brother, sister, and nephews were involved in my campaign. I was happy for their support and enthusiasm. They were all tremendously excited and proud, my father especially so. My father is as blunt as I am, and he loved to talk to reporters. He came up from Florida for the campaign, staying with Rose's son in Westchester. He traveled from Westchester to Far Rockaway for one of the events accompanied by Rose, an advance man, and a reporter for the *Soho Weekly News*. The advance man must have died many times on the way to the appearance.

"What do you think are the problems your son will have to face?" the reporter asked my father during the ride.

"The problems?" Dad responded. "You talk about the colored people. They're on relief, they don't want to work. They don't want to work."

He actually said this, to a reporter, during a formal interview scheduled to shed (preferably) favorable light on his son's candidacy.

And it got worse.

"Have you ever thought of running for office yourself?" the reporter asked.

"Yes," my father said. "I was thinking of mayor of my hometown in Florida. The guy we've got now is an Italian, a real racketeer."

Then the reporter gave my stepmother a chance to speak before thinking. "What did you do when you were younger, Mrs. Koch?" he asked.

"I was a milliner," Rose said. "I used to make these wonderful, beautiful hats. I made them for Gloria Swanson and for Adolf Hitler's girlfriend, a very nice girl."

I shudder to think what they would have said if it was a longer drive.

When I later learned of this exchange, I was mortified and filled with anxiety. I feared it would do our campaign tremendous damage, although it did not because the resulting story appeared after the election. Now I am merely amused by it. It represents the prejudices that people of my father's generation—white or black, Jew or Gentile—

had grown up with. I was different, and never felt the need to apologize for my father. He was what he was, and I loved him.

Let me sneak in a few words here on the subject of my never marrying, as long as we're on it. I assumed that I would marry, as a younger man, but I never found myself in a relationship where it felt comfortable to do so, and with each passing year the chances of that happening seemed more and more remote. I was always consumed by my work. My days and evenings were never lonely except when I was in Washington. Some of my critics, and even some of my supporters, have compared my lifelong bachelor status to that of a priest, who remains celibate to devote his life to his calling. The two situations are in no way analogous. I did not make any sort of political vow— to myself, or to anyone else—that in order to fully execute the duties of my various offices I would foreclose on the idea of marriage. Nonsense. In fact, whenever I was asked about it—whether by my mother, when she was alive (and before I ever sought elected office), or by a friendly or hostile reporter—I always said that I would welcome the idea. I really would have. Perhaps I avoided the prospect of an unhappy union after seeing how miserable my parents were in all their years together.

I have never regarded marriage as a bona fide political plus, although it clearly would have been an asset in the 1977 mayoral election. From a personal point of view, it would have been nice to have someone to come home to. It would have been even nicer to have children. While I don't regret that I never married, I do admit that there have been a great many times that I could have used the support, or the company, a good marriage would have offered. I have had a full, rich life; a family of my own would have made it even fuller. There is no question that my single status ultimately proved a plus for the citizens of New York City: my constituents got more work out of me than they would have if I'd had a family to run home to.

Nevertheless, in 1977, my all-but-confirmed bachelor-

My mother and father at 320 Ocean Parkway in the early 1940s.

My mother, my father, and me at a summer resort in the Catskills.

Above: With my sister, Pat, in front of 61 Milford Avenue, Newark, New Jersey. I am about thirteen; Pat is about six years old. *Above right:* On the right side of the picture is my brother, Harold, about thirteen years old, my sister, Pat, about three, and me, about ten. Alongside of me is our cousin, Seymour Bodner, probably about six. *Right:* On a bus in Newark, New Jersey. I am about fifteen years old.

Right: 1944. The 104th Infantry Division in France. *Below and bottom:* 1946. In Germany, leaving for the U.S., after being discharged.

Above: In front of 320 Ocean Parkway, Brooklyn, New York, with my dog Boxer. Taken about 1948. *Right:* Having taken guitar lessons at the Greenwich Village Music School on Barrow Street, I'm playing at a family circle gathering, 1956.

Above: Taken May 25, 1985, at the Vatican when I met with Pope John Paul at the elevation of Archbishop John J. O'Connor to Cardinal.
Left: Greeting then Archbishop O'Connor at St. Patrick's Cathedral during the Annual Solidarity Sunday for Soviet Jewry Parade.
(Odette Lupis)

Above: At City Hall in 1986.
Left: Here I am on Broadway in 1986 doing a walk-on, playing the role of a cop, in the production of *Singing in the Rain*.

Right: Governor Mario Cuomo and me at a political event. *(Lou Manna Studio)*

Here I am with Leonard Bernstein, This photo was taken at the van he was using in Central Park when he was conducting the Philharmonic. *(C. Zumwalt)*

Conducting a Circle Line cruise around the island of Manhattan.

hood gave rise to persistent rumors that I was homosexual. While I was running for office, I felt compelled to respond to reporters' questions concerning my sexual orientation. I am angry with myself for doing so. I should have said then what I say now: "It's none of your business." It isn't. I don't use my social life for political purposes, and I will no longer comment on my sexuality. There is nothing wrong in being either gay or straight. People are whatever God made them. If that doesn't satisfy anyone, he or she should vote for someone else.

Regrettably, I let my fear of losing the election get in the way of my better judgment; in seeking to reassure the voters, I allowed my private life to become a topic of discussion. It was a no-win situation. It bothered me a great deal that my sex life was considered fair game, simply because I had sought public office. In my twenty-five elections (counting primaries and runoffs), I have been called homosexual, heterosexual, bisexual, and asexual. As far as I know, no one has ever called me a transvestite, or accused me of pederasty or bestiality, so I suppose things could have been worse. Being called upon to deny being homosexual, or bisexual, is more than just offensive, because inherent in those denials is a subtle and cowardly put-down of those groups.

It is nobody's business what goes on behind closed bedroom doors between consenting adults, so long as no one is engaging in scandalous public conduct. Homosexuality is not scandalous. I wish I had had the guts to tell off every slimy reporter, columnist, or television interviewer who over the years tried to get me to admit to one sexual leaning or another, with a simple "Fuck off!" They rarely came right out and asked, "Are you gay?" or "Are you straight?" They usually danced around it, but it was always clear what they were after.

Therefore, let me use this book to finally speak my mind. Read my lips, as my former Congressional colleague used to say: whether I am straight, or gay, or bisexual is nobody's business but mine. It was an indignity that I was ever asked to respond to the question. Besides, people don't believe the answer you give if it doesn't conform to their preconceived opinion.

What's particularly interesting, and important, is that the vast number of voters out there don't really care about a candidate's sexuality, even if they might be titillated by the discussion. I am convinced that, in every one of my elections, substantial numbers of those who voted for me thought I was gay, others that I was straight, and that for still others my sexuality was never an issue. To all of them, my gratitude. To the unfair reporters, candidates, or campaign staffers who sought to use this issue against me, may you suffer the torment of conscience for the rest of your waking life.

In 1977, the discussion crossed the last lines of decency and fairness, and as far as my campaign people were ever able to determine, it was Mario Cuomo who pushed things too far. I don't know that he did this directly, but his silence and lack of control over his supporters in this matter contributed to the slander. Specifically, it was Cuomo's campaign manager, Michael Dowd, who orchestrated it. According to a *Village Voice* article which appeared the week of the general election, Dowd stooped to hiring a private eye to look into my sex life, while Cuomo's Brooklyn coordinator, Thomas Chardavoyne, engaged a security consultant to see if "there was a chance Koch had a few boyfriends."

Cuomo, when confronted by *Village Voice* reporter Geoffrey Stokes with the alleged smear tactics of his campaign staff, reportedly said, "Oh, Christ. Holy Mother of God. I'm so . . . I'm so . . . disappointed. . . . Asking questions like that about someone can injure his reputation. What if you hurt this fellow and he wins? What you've done is you've scarred the reputation of the mayor of the greatest city in the world."

I couldn't believe it. Cuomo didn't even have the decency to denounce those two evil henchmen, or to promise to look into the situation and take appropriate action.

The ethical response, the decent response, would have been to fire both of them on the spot. That's what I would have done, if the tables had somehow been turned. By his inaction, Cuomo allowed those smears to continue. Worse, he perpetuated them by referring pejoratively to legislation that I had supported, pending in the city council, to prohibit discrimination based on sexual orientation. He did this in interviews and in debate, and what was particularly galling was that Cuomo had in fact supported the same legislation. He only changed his position when he thought he could use it against me in the closing days of the campaign, making the issue an even more pointed one.

During the general election, after I defeated Cuomo in the primary and the ensuing runoff and was now opposing his Liberal Party candidacy, we started to see hand-lettered "Vote for Cuomo, Not the Homo" posters around the city. I saw them in Grand Central Station and on various lampposts; other people saw them on major boulevards, particularly in Queens. Cuomo did not do anything to repudiate those allegations, just as he had done nothing to stop the rumors earlier. His silence was despicable; and, even though we have maintained a good public relationship over the years, as we had to because it was in the best interests of the city and the state to do so, I have never forgiven him for it.

I wish I could say the slander ended there, but it did not. On the final weekend of the campaign, the Associated Press issued a story saying a police officer alleged he had once arrested me for soliciting male prostitutes on a city street. It was a totally fabricated story, and we had reason to believe, as I still do, that it was placed by one of Cuomo's campaign workers. This was a libel of huge dimensions, and for a while it seemed the story would do us in. By the time we could discredit the claim, the election would be over.

The story was sent out on the AP wire, where it was placed "on hold," which meant that subscribing newspaper editors were not supposed to run with it until the allegations were confirmed by the wire service.

David Garth responded immediately, and with great acumen. He put me on the phone with the AP editors, and I denied the story. I even tried to reason with them. "Look," I said, "this never happened. If you think about it, you'll see it just doesn't make sense. If it did happen, it would be reported by the cops in their daybooks. Have you demanded or seen the cop's daybook to verify if such an entry exists?"

Without confirmation, the wire story never made it into the papers, although the AP did provide a copy of the story to Cuomo for comment. According to *The New York Times* of November 10, 1977, when an AP reporter handed Cuomo the offending story after a television debate, my opponent said, "Let me take it back and read it."

"Somehow," the *Times* continued, in a comprehensive article entitled, "Smear Against Koch Attempted in Race," "copies of that story turned up all over town in the next day or so. . . . Could Mr. Cuomo's copy have been the source of the duplicates that were circulated? He said he did not know, that he had given the copy to an aide, Richard Starkey, in his headquarters at Four Times Square, and had no idea what might have happened to it."

In that same article, the *Times* also stated that a political reporter for the *New York Post* had been told about the AP story and its contents by Cuomo's press secretary, Harold Holzer. The article also reports additional conversations Holzer had with reporters from the *Times* and the *Post* on the same subject.

Holzer defended his actions to the *Times* with the following comment: "The AP may be able to embargo a story for publication, but not for conversation, especially when the AP was unprofessional enough to distribute advance copies of a potential story." (Holzer was later rewarded for his services and loyalty with a high-level position in the Cuomo administration, after Cuomo was elected governor in 1982.)

For all of this, and for a whole lot more, I hold Mario Cuomo responsible. And, for his extraordinary and successful handling of the smear campaign against me, I am forever indebted to David Garth. He really was at his best. You can find no better or more caring friend than David Garth when the chips are down, and I shall always be grateful to him. It would have been easy, in many of those moments of tension and anxiety, to break down and let the campaign falter. But I did not. We did not. We met the challenge.

While we did not anticipate scurrilous attacks from the Cuomo camp (indeed, when David signed on as my campaign manager, Cuomo was not even a candidate), we were concerned that my single status would be used against me. Strangely, our handling of the issue became controversial, after my election as mayor. Bess Myerson, the onetime Miss America and a veritable princess of the New York Jewish community (and the non-Jewish community as well), had been a good and faithful friend since she was appointed by Mayor Lindsay to serve as the city's commissioner for consumer affairs in 1969. She was one of my earliest and most active supporters. There were many in New York political circles who thought she would make a better candidate than I did. Bess had been widely mentioned for City Council President in 1973, but declined to run. She was happy to throw her lot in with me, and her support brought me a lot of attention at the beginning of my campaign. The people loved her, and when David realized that, he tried to direct some of that affection for Bess toward me. He was doing his job as a campaign manager.

It was a savvy response. Bess and I made a great many campaign appearances together, and we were photographed constantly. She was even standing at my side in the picture we used for my main campaign poster. In later years, some reporters hostile to me have charged that we used Bess Myerson as a beard, to cover up the fact of my bachelorhood and to silence the homosexuality rumors.

Perhaps, to some extent, we did. But Bess and I were good friends. We had gone to restaurants and movies together before the mayoral campaign. She had a close relationship with someone else at the time, but we enjoyed our friendship as well. The media seized on it and made it into more than it was. Some columnists even speculated that there was marriage on the horizon, casting Bess as the potential First Lady of New York. It was all a little overblown. There was never any truly romantic relationship between us. I was never her beau. I enjoyed her company, and I hope she enjoyed mine.

But people believe what they want to believe, and in 1977 what they wanted to believe was that the Congressman from the seventeenth district was romantically involved with the former Miss America. I understood that at the time, and even played to the possibility that the voters were more comfortable with a candidate who was part of a high-profile couple. Yes, Bess and I were photographed holding hands, but it wasn't staged; sometimes we held hands. We even kissed on occasion, and this, too, was not stage-managed. We had held hands and kissed before I ran for mayor.

Let me just finish up about Bess Myerson, before moving on. I don't want to get into a long account of her recent problems, because that's not what this book is about. That's her book, if she chooses to write one. I still think of her as a friend, and I was delighted that her trial exonerated her of the various allegations against her. She will be remembered as a lady who gave a lot of herself to the city, just as she may give a lot more in the future. And I will remember her as someone who was very important in getting me elected.

Back to the campaign. One of the most telling indications of my long-shot, outsider status was the difficulty we had in collecting the ten thousand signatures necessary to get on the party's primary ballot. Without the help of the various political organizations, and their up-to-date lists of registered party members, that can be very difficult. We were forced to collect most of our signatures on the street, clearly not the most effective way to go about it. Consider: A supporter who knocks on the door of someone's home is able to verify that person's name and address and determine if he or she is a registered Democrat, before even soliciting their support or signature. On the street, it's a crapshoot. In New York, most people think they're Democrats, even if they're not registered as such, so a candidate invariably winds up with a lot of worthless signatures.

The general rule of thumb, if supporters are going door to door, is to collect three times the number of required signatures, as a cushion against a challenge from an opponent or from the Democratic Party leaders. We were only able to collect about twenty-five thousand signatures (most of them in the street) during the allotted time, which left us exposed to a challenge. Abe Beame, by comparison, collected more than one hundred thousand signatures, while the others all checked in with about fifty thousand. We submitted our petitions, and crossed our fingers.

Remarkably, and happily, we were never challenged, and we pressed on. The major issue of this campaign, clearly, was the mismanagement of city affairs and finances under the Beame administration. The city was in desperate financial straits, and the more each candidate talked about the city's budget woes, the more Beame's candidacy seemed to erode. We whittled away at his front-runner status, each of us shaving off pieces of his support for ourselves. As the September primary approached, it seemed fairly certain there would be a runoff. The election laws stipulated that if a candidate did not emerge with at least 40 percent of the vote in the primary, then the top two candidates would compete in a runoff election ten days later to determine the nominee.

By summer's end, with invaluable assists from David Garth and Bess Myerson, I had clawed my way to the crowded middle rungs of the campaign; the polls showed the six of us bunched fairly tightly, with Harnett at the bottom. The primary was up for grabs; as many as 20 percent of the voters were still undecided, and their votes would determine which of the six would finish on top.

I campaigned as tirelessly as ever. I did not take a leave from my duties as Congressman, but I did spend more time in New York than in Washington. My thinking was that if I won I would have nothing to apologize for to the voters in my district; I was, after all, still serving them in their constituent needs, with my superb Congressional staff working on overdrive. If I lost, however, then I would have to make amends, but I wasn't planning on losing. Most mornings in New York, I was picked up at my apartment by the campaign's big mobile van, which we christened the Beastmobile. I usually left my apartment at six-thirty in the morning, pulling up at various subway and bus stops during the rush hours and at lunchtime spots at noon, so I could work the crowd in my usual way. This time out, though, I had the entire city to cover, so every moment was precious.

The campaign made steady gains. The turning point came in August, about three weeks before the September 8 primary. I can actually trace it to one phone call. It was seven o'clock in the morning. The Beastmobile had broken down, and I was in my apartment at 14 Washington Place waiting for it to be fixed, or for a new car to arrive, whichever came first. The phone rang. "Congressman," the caller said, after I picked up. "This is Rupert."

I thought to myself, I don't know any Rupert. Rupert is not a Jewish name. "Rupert," I said, even though I still had no idea who was on the other end of the phone.

"Yes," Rupert said, as his distinctive Australian accent came through. "I'm just calling to let you know we're endorsing you today. It will be on the front page of the *New York Post*. I hope that it helps."

Oh. *That* Rupert.

"Rupert," I said, now that I was on a first-name basis with the media magnate Rupert Murdoch, the *Post*'s publisher, "I can't tell you what this means. It means I'm going to win. I can't thank you enough."

"Well, Ed," he said, "we wanted to be the first newspaper to endorse you, and I wanted to be the one to tell you."

"I'm very appreciative," I said. "You won't be sorry. You picked the best guy running."

The *Daily News* unexpectedly followed with my second endorsement from the city's three major newspapers (*The New York Times* had earlier come out for Cuomo), but the *Post* was the first, and therefore the more significant. Campaign contributions, which had been coming in slowly, poured into our offices after the endorsements from the two tabloids, enabling us to make an all-important, last-minute push with our television commercials.

On primary day, I received 21 percent of the vote, just a shade over Cuomo's 20 percent. Beame finished third, less than 1 percentage point behind Cuomo; Abzug was fourth; Sutton, fifth; Badillo, sixth; and Harnett, seventh. In a city of over seven million people, the top six candidates each tallied between 100,000 and 180,000 votes. It was an extremely tight race.

As anticipated, a runoff election was scheduled to be held ten days later, leaving Cuomo and me to jockey for the support of our fallen opposition. Beame, despite our differences, threw his support to me, mainly because he was not about to endorse Carey's candidate; he hated Carey with a passion for not supporting him, and still does.

Abzug lined up behind Cuomo. This was expected. I had had an adversarial relationship with my former Congressional colleague, dating from when I first ran for Congress and she opposed my candidacy. Over the years, I began to take a sporting interest in our run-ins. In 1976, for example, when Bella was running for Senate, I received a letter from a woman's group opposed to the sending of jets to Israel. Bella's name was on the letterhead as one of the group's directors. I was, of course, in favor of the jets, so I placed a copy of the letter, and my response to it, into the *Congressional Record*. I also sent copies of the correspondence to every Jewish group I could find. I didn't say a word about Bella Abzug. I didn't have to. Her name was right there on the group's letterhead, and it said enough.

A couple of days later, Bella cornered me and said, "What are you trying to do, destroy me?"

I played dumb. "What are you talking about, Bella?" I said, sweetly.

She told me she was receiving outraged, middle-of-the-night phone calls from rabbis and Jewish leaders, denouncing her for her position on the jets. These people were waking her up and screaming at her, and Bella seemed a little frayed around the edges.

After a great deal of back-and-forthing (she even sent Sid Yates, the dean of the Jewish delegation in Congress, to intercede on her behalf), Bella demanded the list of people and organizations to whom I had sent copies of her group's letter. She wanted to accurately state her position on the jets, and undo the damage I had done to her credibility in the Jewish community. I refused to turn over my mailing list. More, I refused to let her use the frank—our free mailing privilege—to make what was clearly a political statement. Instead, I offered (quite reasonably, I thought) to send out Bella's rebuttal statement to the groups and individuals on my list, provided she pay for the postage.

Understand, I had sent out only a hundred or so copies of that extract from the *Congressional Record*. I knew the true figure wouldn't be upsetting enough to Bella, so I padded. When she asked me how many copies I had sent out I said, "Oh, hundreds of thousands."

That was the last I heard from her on this matter.

A small digression: Bella Abzug was one of the most bullying members of Congress that I recall. She had enormous energy, was highly intelligent, and brooked no dissent, particularly if her dissenters were from New York.

Members of Congress took her on very carefully, if they took her on at all. She was quite formidable. I took her on, many times.

My favorite Bella Abzug story, though, happened when someone else tangled with her. Ron Dellums, the black Congressman from California, was the only other colleague I can remember standing up to her. She approached him one day on the floor of the House, after he voted against what she thought to be the politically correct position on some issue that I no longer recall; she began to berate him. Dellums just looked at her, waiting for her to finish. When she did, he said, "Don't you ever talk to me that way again, you white motherfucker."

Nobody talked that way to Bella Abzug, but Ron Dellums did, and she behaved herself around him from that day on.

Herman Badillo also decided to support me, which gave me a key advantage in the Hispanic community. The real key to the runoff, though, was not so much gaining the separate endorsements of the losers' campaigns as it was that of the Democratic Party leadership. Both Cuomo and I had made it a point to distance ourselves from the machine during the primary campaign, and I think we were both uncertain about pursuing party support at this late date. I know I was. Still, we did not want the other guy to win the endorsement of the party establishment, even though we were reluctant to embrace it for ourselves.

It was a kind of political Catch-22, which is why I was confounded when Meade Esposito, the Brooklyn Democratic leader then a real force in party politics, reached out to let me know he would support me over Cuomo, if I wanted him to. I was delighted, but also confused. After spending the past six months denouncing the county leaders, the banks, and the landlords, I couldn't do an abrupt about-face and welcome Esposito's endorsement. On the other hand, I could not ignore his offer to help. He represented a substantial base in one of the largest outer boroughs, where Cuomo would be formidable.

I drove out to Brooklyn with David Garth and John LoCicero, my campaign managers, to meet with Esposito at his home in Canarsie. We got lost on the way. We must have been more than an hour late for the meeting. Nobody had any idea how to get there. I couldn't believe we didn't have the proper directions for such an important meeting. You don't keep a county leader waiting, not when he wants to help you. David was absolutely livid. I was more bemused by the whole adventure, but nevertheless concerned. When we finally made it to Esposito's home, he could not have been more solicitous. He offered to do anything we wanted him to do. What we wanted him to do, essentially, was nothing, at least nothing public. We needed to know that he would not endorse Cuomo. I welcomed his support behind the scenes, but I did not want him to support me in any public way. I worried it would backfire. He understood. At the house in Canarsie was Meade's close friend, Milton Mollen, presiding justice of the Appellate Division, Second Department. While the judge was there throughout our meeting, Mollen did not offer any comments on the potential situation.

Cuomo, meanwhile, had received the support of the Liberal Party, so he knew he would be on the ballot for the general election, whether or not he defeated me in the primary runoff. For me, the runoff was do or die. For him, it was the second of three chances. This time around, I beat Cuomo by a decisive margin—nearly eighty thousand votes. But even this was not enough. Now I had beaten him twice in less than two weeks, and yet I found myself having to do it again! It was like a horror movie: The Thing That Wouldn't Die.

I began the general campaign as the favorite in the polls, but my support eroded as Cuomo used his genuine outsider status as a Liberal candidate to attack what he saw to be my anointment as the party's standard-bearer. Of course, he had sought that same standing in the primary and runoff elections. He was a masterful speaker and rhetorician, even if it was more poetry than prose.

Listening to Mario Cuomo, then and now, is a lot like listening to a Japanese haiku: it sounds inexplicable, wonderful, yet without substance, at least to a westerner's ear. But however unfounded his attacks against me were in the general campaign, they were also quite effective. He began to gain in the polls, and I began to slide.

Cuomo's bastion of strength, clearly, was the city's Italian community, and it was difficult to cut significantly into his support there. Still, we tried. I remember one campaign stop at Arthur Avenue in the Bronx, a heavily Italian area. Bess Myerson was with me on that trip, along with my friend Dan Wolf. Mario Biaggi, the hero cop and local Congressman, was also there to introduce me. He had supported Cuomo throughout the primaries, but as a loyal Democrat he threw his support to me when I won the nomination. I appreciated this a great deal, but his mostly Italian constituency did not. A huge crowd turned out, but they were not there to cheer me. Really, it was the most vicious crowd I ever encountered. They booed Biaggi off the truck when he tried to introduce me. "Faggot!" they yelled as I took the microphone. "Jew!" "Queer!" "Kike!" The insults showered down on me like rocks.

I wasn't about to run from this battle, so I jumped from the truck down into the crowd. I was determined to shake hands, even if those people hated me. The only way to deal with their name-calling, I felt, was to ignore them and continue on. I tried to shut them out of my mind, but of course this was impossible. A few people shook hands. Most did not, and I wound up working my way through the mean-spirited crowd as quickly as I could. Later, when the campaign car was buzzed by a carload of locals screaming, "Faggot! Queer!" Bess leaned out the window, yelled "Fuck you!" and gave those urban rednecks the finger. She was wonderful.

My Republican opponent in the general election was State Senator Roy Goodman, but he was never given a serious chance. Of course, I have never taken any political opponent for granted, even if the temptation to do so was certainly there. Obviously, most of my energies were directed against Cuomo, but I did engage Goodman, as well as Barry Farber, the Conservative Party candidate, in debate. Farber also used the innuendo about homosexuality during the debate. He was despicable.

On November 8, 1977, I received about 50 percent of the vote in the four-way race, to become the 105th mayor of New York City. Cuomo gave me a good run, collecting 41 percent of the votes tallied. The people had spoken, and I was thrilled. A lot of people have since asked me if I didn't feel somewhat intimidated on election night, after it became clear I had won—if the goal, now attained, did not suddenly seem overwhelming. It honestly did not. I suppose it would be easy to be intimidated by the prospect of leading 7.5 million New Yorkers into a new era, but I wasn't built that way. I said to myself, There are a lot of people out there who are smarter than you, Koch, who could do this job better, but they didn't offer themselves up for it; they were afraid, or otherwise engaged, or uninterested; and those who did offer themselves, the people decided, were not as good as you; you were judged to be the best available candidate. That little internal speech became a great comfort over the next twelve years, whenever things got tough.

David Brown was in charge of my transitional staff, as he was when I was first elected to Congress, and what I recall best about the several weeks between my election and inauguration was how deferential everyone was to me. It was unlike anything I had ever experienced before. I was the outsider, let in to suddenly become the ultimate insider. I could have made an E. F. Hutton commercial: people stopped whatever they were doing to listen to what I had to say.

A lot of this deferential treatment, I quickly realized, came from the Beame appointees who were concerned for their jobs, but our strategy was to let one administration ease into the next. I saw no reason to fire every Beame appointee simply because I had not hired them. I knew I would need the experience and seasoned judgment of as many good people as I could find, if there was to be a smooth transition.

Twelve years later, I feel compelled to mention, my successor approached his new office somewhat differently. David Dinkins fired almost everybody, and not only at the top levels. It was foolish of him, really. Most of my appointees were not political. Some were. But Dinkins didn't realize that. He was so concerned with cleaning house and bringing in his gorgeous mosaic of blacks and Hispanics and others that I think he sacrificed competence for color, on several occasions. This is not a racist remark, although I recognize there are those who will see it as such. I don't mean to convey that there are not enough people of color out there to do the various jobs. Of course there are. But Dinkins didn't find them. In examining the agencies under Dinkins, it's clear that many people were fired because they were white, to be replaced with people who were black or Hispanic, or some other ethnicity. One of the best (or worst) examples of this was Dinkins's appointment of Dr. Emilio Carrillo to head the city's Health and Hospitals Corporation; Carrillo wasn't qualified to do the job and left the fifteen city hospitals under his jurisdiction in disarray when he resigned in October 1991. Clearly, Carrillo was hired because he was Hispanic, not because he was the best candidate. And, to keep his mosaic gorgeous, Dinkins's search committee sought another Hispanic to replace him but couldn't find one.

But I'm getting ahead of myself. January 1, 1978, the date of my inauguration, was a cold winter Sunday, somewhat overcast, and as I remember it, I was the only one there who didn't wear a coat. We were out on the steps of City Hall, and I was freezing. My nose and fingers were numb. But I had an image I wanted to project, and I wouldn't surrender to the cold. I wanted people to see me and think of strength, confidence. I wanted to stand in marked contrast to the tired and aging persona of Abe

Beame. If I was going to breathe new life into this ailing city, I should at least look the part. I also thought, This is the way Kennedy did it. I remembered JFK didn't wear a coat to his inauguration. He may have, but in my head he didn't. That's the look I wanted, the zest, the spirit. The city was in such a low mood that I wanted to do everything in my power, and some things not in my power, to lift up every New Yorker. I didn't even wear thermal underwear.

"New York is not a problem," I said in my prepared inaugural remarks penned by my speechwriter, Clark Whelton, whose always brilliant prose almost always fell victim to my ad-libs. "New York is a stroke of genius. From its early days, this city has been a lifeboat for the homeless, a larder for the hungry, a living library for the intellectually starved, a refuge not only for the oppressed but also for the creative. New York is, and has been, the most open city in the world. That is its greatness. And that is why, in large part, it faces monumental problems to-day."

As I spoke, the sun came out. It was like a cue. I took it as a kind of portent for the future, even though the sun often appears at such formal moments, if only in memory. In fact, it did that for Pope John Paul, when he visited New York City in 1980. I went to Kennedy Airport to welcome him, and it was pouring rain. When the Pope stepped out of the cabin and onto the stairs, the rain suddenly stopped and the sun came out. As the sun smiled on the arriving Pontiff, Bob McGuire, my police commissioner, overheard one cop say to another, "That's the kind of guy you like to make a golf date with."

So the sun came out for me too. God was smiling. Good things were to come.

"But government cannot do what the people will not do," I continued. "In calling upon the people of New York City to join with me in the hard work needed to bring this city back to the top again, I call upon the only people who can do the job. These have been hard times. We have been tested by fire . . . we have been inundated by problems, we have been shaken by troubles that would have destroyed any other city. But we are not any other city. We are the city of New York, and New York in adversity still towers above any other city in the world. . . .

"Today, we begin a new year and a new administration. The mistakes of the past are past. We have been tested and the testing will continue. But we have survived. And soon we will begin to flourish."

7

Gracie Mansion

BEING MAYOR OF NEW YORK CITY is like no other job in the world, just as New York is like no other city in the world. I suppose I always knew those things, on some level, but I never thought about them, and if I did, I didn't really appreciate them fully until after I was elected.

I appreciated them soon enough, though. With my election, my public persona was transformed almost overnight. It was a complete makeover. My private life, which I was able to quietly maintain as a Congressman, was suddenly a memory. As mayor, my time was no longer my own. I couldn't go anywhere without a phalanx of aides and security guards alongside me. And if I was attending an event on my public schedule, there would be reporters as well. People began to stop me on the street. Everyone, it seemed, had something they wanted to say to the mayor; sometimes they wanted to call me to task over some issue or other, but most times it was just to give a friendly hello, or to chat. I was, for a time, the city's most recognizable citizen, at home and abroad. Even small children knew my name. While their parents would call me "Mr. Mayor," the children would often shout out "Koch," not "Mayor," not "Mr.," and not "Ed." It was, "Hey, Koch!"

I never minded the notoriety, even if I never deliberately sought it. In fact, I came to like my new status. In restaurants, I believe I received larger portions than the others at the table; I never asked for them and, regrettably, I never left anything on my plate, always mindful of my mother's reference to "the starving children in China." Whenever I entered a room in any official capacity, I was the center of attention. Whenever I went someplace in an unofficial capacity, people would gravitate to my side of the room.

The special treatment was most conspicuous among my peers. The best example of this came early on in my first term, when I attended a business and labor breakfast hosted by David Rockefeller, then chairman of Chase Manhattan Bank, and Harry Van Arsdale, who was president of the New York City Central Labor Council, AFL-CIO. I have told this story before, but I'll tell it again here to illustrate the sudden turnabout in the way I was perceived, and the significance placed on my new position. There were about thirty bankers and labor leaders in the Chase boardroom when I arrived. Every single one of them stood up when I entered the room, and they remained standing until I sat down. It was really quite an extraordinary reception, made more so by the fact that many of these people had never liked me before I became mayor. Indeed, many actively opposed my campaign. After I was seated between the two hosts, Rockefeller went to get me a cup of coffee, and Van Arsdale went to get me a Danish. Neither one of these guys especially liked me either, but I was the new sun in the sky, around which they and their separate interests would now revolve. When United States Senator Jacob Javits walked into the room a short time later, no one stood to greet him, and a waiter was dispatched for his coffee and Danish. The contrast was a revelation and a source of private satisfaction. In the eyes of these bankers and labor leaders, the new mayor was more important than the old senator who had served them and their city so well.

Two years later, I should mention, I tried to assist the ailing Javits in his reelection campaign. He had done many good things for New York City, and when he ran his final race for the Senate, I wanted to return the favor. Javits, who at seventy-six was in failing health at the time of the campaign, was defeated in the 1980 Republican primary by Al D'Amato, and he was running in the general election on the Liberal Party line. (Ms. Hostility, Liz Holtzman, was the Democratic candidate, having beaten Bess Myerson in their primary.)

One of the biggest issues of the campaign, naturally, was Javits's health. The voters knew he was suffering from amyotrophic lateral sclerosis, the degenerative illness also known as Lou Gehrig's disease; even his supporters worried he would die before his term expired. I approached his campaign people and encouraged the Senator to confront the issue head-on. The direct approach is always best. I even offered an interesting slogan, which I said the Senator was free to use in his campaign: "One year with Javits is better than six with D'Amato."

He never used it. Who knows? It might have won him the election.

But let me get back to those first days of my first term. The constant press attention was the only real, nagging side effect of my new position. I just couldn't get used to it. Reporters followed me wherever I went. They even followed me to the bathroom door. Of course, they waited outside for me to come out, but it was still unnerving. It was also a little embarrassing at first because I have a weak bladder, and so whenever I left a conference or a meeting to go to the bathroom, a sizable number of those in the room would leave with me, and then do it again. It was an odd scene. This kind of attention diminished with the passage of time, but it never ended.

I was like the Pied Piper to these reporters, and to others as well. I had brought attention back to City Hall, which had not been the center of attention when Abe Beame was there. It would have been easy, as the expression goes, to "buy my own act," but I never did. I believe that at no time during my twelve years as mayor did I ever think of myself differently than I did before I was elected. I was never overcome by the power, privilege, and prestige of my position. I knew I would be in office for a limited time, although not as limited as some might have thought. I said early on and publicly that I needed twelve years to turn the city around. Some, I'm sure, thought such a comment arrogant on my part, and never believed I'd make it past one term.

No matter what my critics would like to think, I came to the mayoralty without any baggage. I owed nothing to the political system. I had no commitments. I was absolutely my own man. I'm very proud of that. My only commitment was to the people of New York City to do the right thing, and part of that pledge was to be the same person I was when they elected me their mayor. I had sold them on me, and I had to deliver. I couldn't let the office make me over. My personality was too large a part of my character. I wanted what the average New Yorker wanted, which is why I acted the way the average New Yorker would have acted if he or she were the mayor. I was, as the magazine editor Clay Felker (who has never been my supporter) would refer to me ten years later, "the quintessential New Yorker."

Nothing in my experience as an elected public official, three years as councilman and nine as Congressman, could have prepared me for my new position. There is a majesty to the mayoralty in the city of New York, a special aura. This was true for every mayor who preceded me, and will remain so for every one to succeed me. No mayor is ever prepared. Now that I've left office extra attention is still shown to me. It's taken a slightly different turn for the better, at least in some ways. People are less formal now, more direct. They say what they mean, and expect me to respond in kind. I'm the uncle in the family, and happy in the role.

In writing about my twelve years as mayor, I am faced with something of a problem. My administration has been exhaustively chronicled—in books, magazines, and newspaper articles. Indeed, I have done some of the chronicling myself. My first two books, *Mayor* and *Politics,* covered many aspects of my first two terms in considerable detail; my fourth book, *All the Best: Letters From a Feisty Mayor,* examined some additional particulars, up to and including my third term, also in considerable detail; somewhere in the middle, my third book, *His Eminence and Hizzoner,* written with John Cardinal O'Connor, archbishop of New York, explored some of the more pressing social issues facing the city during my administration. Moreover, in New York, Sunday morning television talk shows have rehashed my every move, at every opportunity; after I left office, they put my administration under the microscope again. (As a local Sunday morning television talk-show host myself, for a year after I left office, I contributed to the reassessing.)

By my own tally, my name appeared every single day in one of the daily newspapers, or on television or radio, and many times in or on all the media on the same day, throughout every year, almost always attached to a significant story on a substantive issue. I don't set this out to brag but to make a point. Every official act and statement during my twelve years in City Hall has long been a matter of public record; even some of my unofficial acts are well known. I don't want to repeat myself here, or to offer up a stale recounting of events and issues already recorded by some of the same reporters who used to follow me to the bathroom. To go over this same territory here would, I think, alter the focus of this book. It would also be boring. A great many disagreeable people have said many terrible things about me over the years, but few have ever called me boring.

Therefore, I will use these pages to address some of the more personal aspects of my life as mayor, to offer up some of the sidelights that never made it into the newspapers, or onto the nightly news, and to confront for the first time certain aspects of my administration that have until now escaped my own intimate assessment, such as the

Parking Violations Bureau scandal that tormented me throughout my final term, and beyond. I will also cover such personal and transition episodes as my emotional leave-taking, after an unsuccessful bid to become the only four-term mayor in the recent history of New York City.

I'll start at the beginning. I resigned from Congress after my election. There was no ceremony attached to this. I simply signed and filed the appropriate papers and closed that chapter in my life. Formally, I resigned on December 31, 1977, which marked nine full years representing New York's Silk-stocking District. If I had completed my fifth term, it would have been ten years. I am proud of those nine years, during which I was voted by the New York City Congressional Delegation as its most effective member. This was high praise indeed, especially considering that the members undoubtedly voted themselves number one in the secret balloting, as did I. I was almost everybody's number two, plus my own number one, and that elected me.

I was happy to be leaving Washington, although I moved into Gracie Mansion almost reluctantly. I wasn't exactly kicking and screaming, but I did not like the idea of giving up my Greenwich Village apartment. In fact, I did not give it up at all, thinking I would return to the Village some weekends after taking office, and knowing that an inexpensive rent-controlled apartment in a nice building would be hard to replace once I left office. As it turned out, I used the apartment less and less as the months went by, but I kept it throughout my three terms. Friends and relatives stayed there on occasion, but for the most part, after the first year or two, it remained empty.

Gracie Mansion, my new place, was tastefully furnished by some of the previous tenants. It was nice enough, but it wasn't entirely comfortable. I like to be comfortable. The library, or study, became the center of the house, and it was where I spent most of my private evenings at home. It was the only room not furnished in a style consistent with the grand history of the house—just some very comfortable modern furniture, and a television with a VCR.

The grand history of the house is worth a few paragraphs here. It was built in 1799 by Archibald Gracie, at Eighty-eighth Street overlooking the East River, which in those days was considered upstate New York. The house was later taken over by the city after subsequent owners failed to pay their real-estate taxes, and for a while was operated as a concession stand (with public toilets in the basement) for the patrons of adjacent Carl Schurz Park. In 1934, Parks Commissioner Robert Moses offered the home to Mayor Fiorello LaGuardia, to be used as the official residence of the mayor of New York City. LaGuardia considered the offer for seven years and moved in, in 1942. Up until that time, the city's mayors lived in their own homes. In fact, it was a tradition for the city to place a special street lamp in front of each mayor's home. There is still one on display at 4 St. Luke's Place, in the Village, where former Mayor Jimmy Walker lived.

Gracie Mansion actually backs onto East End Avenue; the front door is at the back of the house facing the East River. The floor in the entrance hall is the original wood plank, although during a $5.5 million restoration in 1984 it was repainted in the old style, to make the wood look like marble. To the right of the foyer stands the living room, which is decorated in Victorian style; to the left, the library, which I have already described. I often had my dinners there, at the coffee table. Immediately behind the library is a formal dining room, which can seat more than twenty people. Beyond the dining room is the Susan E. Wagner Wing, which was added in 1966 to accommodate public receptions and dinners, and named for Mayor Wagner's first wife. On numerous occasions throughout my three terms, I hosted lunch or dinner receptions for as many as 175 guests, who included the Presidents and prime ministers of China, Israel, and Italy, and the mayors of Paris, Madrid, and Tokyo.

The bedrooms are on the second floor. The oldest piece

of furniture in the house—a Dutch cabinet of rough pine wood, dating from the New Amsterdam period—rests at the top of the stairs. The larger of the two guest bedrooms is furnished in faux bamboo, on permanent loan from the Metropolitan Museum of Art. The smaller guest room has twin beds dating from the Federal period. The beds may be of historic value, but they are quite uncomfortable; they have no springs, and are held together with rope. The mayor's bedroom is also on the second floor; it is customary for the mayor to bring his own bed, and I did. The most spectacular thing about my bedroom was the view, facing the East River, and the way the morning sun bathed the room with each new day.

The mansion was so magnificent, it was almost intimidating. I was dwarfed by it, in many ways, and it took a while to feel at home there. I used to pull into the circular drive and think I was entering onto palace grounds. Each night when I was in Washington, and I saw the dome of the Capitol in the moonlight, I had a special sensation of history; sometimes, I was even moved to tears. The mansion never had the same sensation of history for me, although I did feel by being there that I had become a special part of the history of New York City.

I got used to Gracie Mansion soon enough. I came to relish its elegance, its charm, and its history. I even opened the mansion up to public tours. I was the first mayor to do that, and, at the height of the tours' popularity (which dovetailed neatly with the height of my own popularity), some twenty thousand or more visitors passed through the mansion's gates each year. The entire mansion was on view, every nook and cranny, save for my bedroom on the second floor. I was inclined to let the people in to see where their mayor slept, but I was cautioned against it for security reasons.

One of the most charming things about the mansion was the way it was absorbed into the neighborhood surrounding it, almost without ostentation. To illustrate, I was having dinner in the mansion's library one night with Allen Schwartz, when there was a knock on the front door. No one moved to answer it (the household security staff was downstairs eating, I later found out), so I proceeded to the front door myself, on the other side of which I found a disheveled young man, who asked, "Does Mrs. Rose Feigenbaum live here?"

"Who?" I said.

"Rose Feigenbaum," he said again. "Is she at this address?"

"No," I said, thinking, I want to get off this porch as quickly as I can and get this door between him and me as soon as possible. I thought, where is the security guard, and when he didn't appear, I wondered, Isn't this what happened to Abe Lincoln?

"Are you sure?" the man tried again.

"Well," I fumbled, "now that you mention it, maybe she is inside. If you'll excuse me a moment, I'll go in and take a look."

I closed the door and called for the security guard, who came upstairs and took over. As it turned out, my disheveled visitor was a cab driver who announced he was here to pick up a fare and was waved through the gate. And, in fact, there was a Rose Feigenbaum living across the street.

On occasion, I was host to some rather prominent overnight guests. One of these occasions came about shortly after Egyptian President Anwar Sadat and Israeli Prime Minister Menachem Begin signed their historic Camp David accords. I sent a letter to both in care of their embassies, inviting each to stay at Gracie Mansion for as long as he'd like, the next time he was in New York. The Egyptians responded that they would consider the invitation, should the president be planning a visit. (Sadat later did visit New York but did not take me up on my offer.) The Israelis asked to inspect Gracie Mansion, to see if the accommodations would be suitable for the prime minister. I told them that whatever they wanted to do was fine with me.

Well, it happened that Begin was to arrive in New York

shortly thereafter, and the Israelis called my chief of staff, Diane Coffey, to arrange a tour of the premises. They sent some security people. A few days later they called back with their decision: the prime minister would be pleased to stay at Gracie Mansion, provided that the mayor moved out during the prime minister's visit.

I was shocked, and furious. *That* was chutzpah! I told Diane to tell them to shove it, and she cleaned up my message and passed it along. We figured that would be the end of it. But sure enough, the Israelis called back. Okay, they said. The mayor can stay.

So Begin arrived with his wife, and I put them in the major guest bedroom. We must have bought the entire appetizers department of a kosher deli, or received it free, in anticipation of their visit. Mrs. Begin was really quite lovely, and most solicitous of her husband. The prime minister was tired when he arrived. He had just gotten off the plane. We had a pleasant dinner, after which, at about eight o'clock, he said he was ready to retire for the evening.

"That's fine, Mr. Prime Minister," I said. "I have to go out on my rounds, anyway." Eight o'clock was far too early in the evening for me to retire. And, as mayor, there was always some function or event at which my presence was requested.

When I returned home, at around midnight, the mansion was quiet. I came in the front door, which faces the river, and climbed the grand staircase to the second floor. There, at the top of the stairs, I was rushed by two menacing-looking guys, with Uzi machine guns pointed directly at me. I was petrified, but immediately realized what was going on. These were the prime minister's guards, posted at his bedroom door.

"Don't shoot!" I cried out, holding up my arms in mock surrender. "It's only me, Ed Koch. I live here!"

The guards lowered their guns and smiled.

Once we got our comings and goings sorted out, we actually had a wonderful visit. The prime minister was a delightfully charming man, very genteel, very courtly. I thought it was rather sweet that he and his wife retired to their room on the Sabbath. We sent them up a huge samovar, for tea, which was their only sustenance. They didn't come down until well after sundown the next day. I don't know what they did up there all day long, and I didn't ask.

Another prominent visitor was Sir Laurence Olivier, who was being honored by the city at a public ceremony. Prior to the formal ceremony, Olivier and his wife, Joan Plowright, joined a small gathering at the mansion. It was really quite a special moment. This was shortly before Olivier's death in September 1989, and he was a physical wreck, in constant pain. His wife asked that we position someone alongside him following the ceremony to ensure that no one would try to shake the actor's hand. He was in such tremendous pain, and his body so sensitive to touch, that it was agonizing for him even to shake hands. I'll never forget that.

As we chatted in the living room prior to the ceremony, it became clear to me that my guest was uncomfortable. I tried some small talk, to perhaps distract him from his discomfort. I asked how I should address him. "Is it My Lord," I inquired, "or Sir Laurence?"

"Please," he said, in that magical voice of his, "call me Larry." Even in frailty, his voice brought back memories of Heathcliff. It rang with its familiar lilt and chill. Olivier always had a way of sounding somber and amused at the same time, and he managed it even on this night. "Mr. Mayor," he said, "I am so sorry to inconvenience you, but my ankles are very swollen, and I have to raise my legs. Would it be possible to locate a box on which I could rest them?"

"Larry," I said, gesturing to the coffee table at his feet, "this table would be honored to have your legs placed upon it."

"Oh, Mr. Mayor," he said, "I couldn't do that. This is your home. It would not be right."

"Please, Larry," I insisted. "Honor us, and the table."

And he did.

Throughout my twelve years, I tried my best to separate my personal household expenses from legitimate city expenditures wherever possible. Sometimes, though, the lines between city and personal business became blurred. For example, I used to host regular private dinner parties as mayor, a practice I have continued to this day. I would invite my guests from all walks of life, from the worlds of arts and letters, media, big business, and national government. I usually invited about sixteen to eighteen people, some of whom I had known for many years but most of whom I had first met as mayor. I tried always to have a diverse guest list and to lead the dinner table conversation along substantive lines.

I worked hard to make these dinners successful, but they didn't always come off as planned. Once, when I invited the celebrated musician and conductor Leonard Bernstein to be my guest of honor, he called back at just about the last moment and asked if he could bring about seven of his friends. This upset the planned mix, more than a little. After all, I couldn't comfortably seat more than twenty guests, and now nearly half of these seats would be filled by my guest of honor and his party. A part of me wanted to refuse Bernstein's request, because it wasn't what I had in mind for the evening, but I was convinced by members of my staff that it would be discourteous of me to do so.

Bernstein was very flamboyant when he arrived. He was a little inebriated, and he drank a lot while he was there, which made him even more flamboyant and too often obnoxious by the time he left. Still, I couldn't help wondering why he had accepted my invitation in the first place. If he wanted to spend an evening with seven of his close friends, why didn't he just invite them to his own home, or take them out to a nice restaurant? I know he was a genius, but it was clear that night he had bought his own act and could do anything he wanted, no matter how rude.

Nevertheless, I thought *Candide* and *West Side Story* made it all worthwhile.

Gracie Mansion offered such a wonderful and stately setting, it would have been a shame not to put it to constructive social use. It is probably the most famous public house in the nation, after the White House. I saw these evenings as an extension of my role as mayor, to set a tone, to bring together some of the sharpest minds from various segments of our city, or our society at large, and to debate the various issues of the day. The evenings were always capped by some musical performance. Most times, we were entertained by a chamber music quartet, but on occasion folksingers came to the mansion to do the honors. The folksingers were a mistake, even though I love folk songs; our folksingers generally sang their own self-composed songs, which generally didn't sound too good; I longed for the oldies.

The city paid for these functions, because I always saw them as serving its interests. True, they were essentially social gatherings, but they were helpful in one way or another. We always discussed the problems facing the city, and what to do about them, and the guest list always represented a cross-section of New Yorkers. Besides, the household staff was in place and paid for, and the food never amounted to more than a few hundred dollars for any one evening. The entertainment was provided free, generally by the Mannes School of Music or Affiliated Artists, except of course for the folksingers.

The police department wanted me to keep a gun in my living quarters. It was simply a matter of additional security to them; to me, a gun made no sense, and served mostly as a troubling reminder that I had traded my heretofore quiet, private life for a more public life, with the danger of being taken hostage, shot, or assaulted by kooks or criminals. There were cops stationed at the mansion, of course, but I was told this was not enough. There was a locked closet in my private bathroom in Gracie Mansion, which was just off my bedroom, and the police department wanted me to keep the gun there. As I indicated, I wasn't crazy about the idea. What did I need a gun for? So I could kill myself trying to use it on someone else? I knew that many people who kept them for their own protection wound up having their own weapon seized by their attacker. Or the gun is found by others and one innocent child kills another. I just didn't want one around. It would have made me too nervous, knowing it was there. In any event, I jokingly argued with the police, did anyone seriously think I would remember the combination for the closet lock if people were banging down the door to take me hostage?

I prevailed after a few weeks, and the gun was removed. But Bob McGuire, the police commissioner, won the point on police protection for the few weekends I spent away from Gracie Mansion at my house in Greenwich Village. He didn't win it at first, though; it took a small scare to bring me around to his way of thinking. On a Saturday in the first few months of the first year, I left my apartment at 14 Washington Place at about seven o'clock in the morning, to get a newspaper. I was walking on University Place. The street was empty. All of a sudden, I noticed a disheveled-looking guy in his mid-thirties. He crossed the street, headed toward me. I was all alone, and I was thinking, Oh, shit, Bob McGuire was right! I'm gonna get killed!

"You're the mayor," the young black man said as he approached. There was almost no tone to his voice, but what tone he had did not suggest that he was happy to see me. He came alongside and started to jostle me. I kept walking. I didn't know what else to do. He followed step for step, taunting and harassing me. I tried to pick up the pace.

About a block from the newspaper store I saw a familiar face from the neighborhood, a middle-aged man who is a folksinger and lived across the street from me. He was coming out of the store and with him was his big Alsatian dog. This guy was also black, and he looked toward me and saw I was in trouble. "Mayor!" he yelled. "Are you all right?"

"I am now," I yelled back, as the street guy took off.

I had police protection from that point on. I had resisted it at first, I think, because I wanted to lead as normal a life as possible. It was not normal to have two cops following me around all the time. (Later on, after several threats, there were five.) It was not normal for my every move to be manipulated by security concerns. But I decided to be cautious instead of normal, and for the rest of my administration, after I got used to the various peculiarities of having a team of security guards, I was able to move about with relative peace of mind concerning my own safety. I put their presence out of my mind.

I no longer have this total peace of mind, I should mention. I was forced to hire a private security detail, once I left office, to guard against the kooks and to escort me to the various public appearances I am called on to make. The city provided protection for me, when I first left office, but rescinded it after six months. I was of two minds about this. On the one hand, I could certainly understand the argument to eliminate police protection for a former mayor, because it did cost a lot of money, but I was angered at the way my particular case was handled. I don't blame David Dinkins for ending the protection, although I am sure he was involved in the decision. Most likely, he was informed by the police department, told that I presented no lingering security problems, and then he simply agreed with their recommendation to eliminate my protection. I can't imagine that he would have left me exposed if his advisers even suggested to him that I might be in some danger.

What troubled me was that they removed my protection on one day's notice, without consulting me directly. There have since been several incidents of aggressive behavior against me. Each of these has been readily defused, thanks to my security people. I never needed protection before I became a public official, and the only reason I need it now is because of some of the things I said and did as mayor. A part of me thinks it would be no imposition on the city, truly, to recognize a responsibility toward me, and to continue to protect me. And yet, if I had been consulted on the matter, told of the city's pressing fiscal concerns, and asked to do my bit to help out by liberating the police department from its unspoken obligation to protect me, of course I would have agreed. Fortunately, I can afford to pay for the protection myself, but it is costly.

One of my first official acts as mayor was to issue an executive order banning discrimination based on sexual orientation in city contracts, jobs, and housing, which had been one of my campaign promises. It was not my first executive order, as some have stated. It was actually the fourth. The first three were just regular orders necessary to keep city government functioning. For example, I had to reinstate all executive orders issued by Abe Beame, because executive orders die with each administration. I can't recall what the others were, but they were pro forma. The discrimination order, though, was the first meaningful act of my administration. A lot of people thought it was too controversial, and that I wouldn't go through with it, but I never wavered. Why would I not keep my promise? The order was responsible and fair. Still, a great many reporters and others were shocked when I did it, but the sky didn't fall. Some years later, during my third term, I actually signed into law a bill prohibiting discrimination based on sexual orientation in the private sector. The executive order had applied only to government; this legislation was more far-reaching. Again, many people opposed the legislation, and again, the sky didn't fall.

There was a funny story tied to my first day in office. I was determined to devote every minute, including breakfasts, to solving the problems of the city. I wanted to do things differently than they had ever been done before, and one of the ways I planned to do this was in breakfast meetings scheduled in my office at City Hall. But I didn't want to serve coffee and cake with paper cups and plates, as others had done. I wanted to use china, because people react differently if you treat them nicely, and elegantly. It sets a special tone.

So we brought down a very nice porcelain tea set from the mansion, and on the first day I had my first breakfast meeting. I honestly don't remember who was there, but it was probably one or two of my commissioners, and one or two of my deputy mayors. It was about seven-thirty in the morning. We had our coffee and cake, and conducted our business, and that was that. When my guests left, I took the dishes and stacked them in the sink in the small kitchen which was right off the office.

The next morning, I came in to find the dishes still in the sink, still unwashed. I thought, Okay, this is new, nobody's done this before, nobody knows what they're doing yet. No big deal. So I washed the dishes myself and dried them, and set them out again for my second breakfast meeting, after which I once again stacked the dirty dishes in the sink.

On the third morning, sure enough, the dishes were still in the sink, still unwashed. This happened three days in a row, and on the fourth day I was pissed. So I called in Diane Coffey and asked her to look into this little housekeeping problem. And she did. Later that day, I got a report that the cleaning lady said she doesn't do dishes. She was a District 37 cleaning lady, Victor Gotbaum was her union leader, and she was refusing to do those lousy dishes. It was ridiculous. After all, as I said to Diane, it's not like I asked her to do windows.

So I sent a message to this cleaning lady, through Diane, that if those goddamn dishes were still in the sink the following morning, then I would get a new cleaning lady, who would be Ukrainian. At the time, most of the women who cleaned most of the commercial buildings in the city were Ukrainian, and they were, by reputation, very hardworking, cleaning in the early hours of the morning and going home by subway at 4:00 A.M. or later.

The dishes, from that day forward, were sparkling.

Now, I told that story on many occasions, and after a short while I was challenged on it by Victor Gotbaum. "That's a racist story," he said. I couldn't believe he would say such a thing. Why was it a racist story, in his mind? Because the cleaning lady happened to be black. It was such a lot of nonsense. There was nothing racist about it. I didn't care what color my cleaning lady was or what her ethnic background was, as long as she cleaned my dishes.

One of my first obligations, in my own head, was to review and reform the way judges were selected for appointment by the mayor. I promised to do this during the campaign, and I wanted to set my reforms in motion immediately. At his own discretion, the mayor appoints the city's Criminal and Family Court judges. They number a hundred and forty, in total, and each one of them serves for ten years. One of Abe Beame's last acts as mayor in December of 1977 was to fill ten vacancies. Even though he had a committee to review qualifications, these appointments were almost all condemned by the New York City Bar Association as unqualified. Nevertheless, he officially appointed them, ignoring criticism by the city bar and by the editorial boards of the city's newspapers. And no one could stop him.

I quickly created the first merit system for the selection of judges in New York City. Before me, there had been committees of lawyers to pass on the qualifications of the various judicial candidates sent to them by the mayor, but Lindsay, Beame, and even Wagner had appointed people to the bench whom their own committees had found unqualified. So I created a new selection system. The new committee became known as the Mayor's Committee on the Judiciary, and was composed of twenty-seven people, most of whom were lawyers. As mayor, I selected twelve members; the two presiding justices of the Appellate Division, First and Second Departments, each selected six; and the deans of three law schools each selected one. We set it up this way so the mayor never had a majority subject to his pressure on the committee.

I also directed that the committee send three qualified candidates for each vacancy to me, after which I would interview all three and make the final designation. My designee would then face a public hearing and be subject to approval by the Bar Association of the City of New York, to which I granted veto power. The public hearings on occasion produced witnesses with a personal vendetta against the designee, but that never caused me to withdraw a candidate.

To his credit, Mayor Dinkins has kept this system in place. Of all the things I have done in government, this change in judicial selection is probably the most salutary and lasting. Most of the judges I appointed will sit for twenty or thirty years; many have gone on to the higher courts of the state, and many more will do so in the future.

The key reason for the success of this system is that it is based on merit, not fueled by politics or racial quotas. One of the reasons I had trouble with many black leaders, as well as white leaders, was that their so-called progressive agendas included political reward and racial quotas in personnel appointments and vendor contracts. I was absolutely opposed to both, as I am today. *The New York Times*'s and other editorial boards of the dailies, with the exception of the *New York Post*, support racial quotas. They will often camouflage their support by referring to goals, but the goals they refer to are for equal outcome, not equal opportunity.

As mayor, I was constantly challenged by the black leadership, including members of the city council, who complained that not enough city contracts were being awarded to black businesses. This was true, but there was a reason for it. The city, when buying merchandise or entering into construction contracts, was usually required to accept the lowest bid, and minorities often couldn't compete in price, having small companies or being unable to procure construction bonds. I asked our people to come up with a procedure that would compensate for these differences, and to seek to involve black, Hispanic, and female vendors and construction companies.

At the time, all other systems used in the country provided set-asides in contracts, which often meant that 10 percent of the contracts were open for bidding only by blacks, Hispanics, and women. My new system changed that and provided set-asides on the basis of the capitalization of the firm (modest), and business location (depressed areas); of qualifying companies, at least 25 percent of the work force had to have a history of long-term unemployment. The effect of these and other requirements was that blacks, Hispanics, and women received 45 percent of the set-asides, running into millions annually. The balance went to the small, white-owned firms, which also needed the same help. And no quotas—racial, ethnic, religious, or gender—were involved.

When the United States Supreme Court ultimately struck down the racially oriented set-asides that had been in effect in Richmond, Virginia, and other cities such as Atlanta, where the quota was 30 percent of all contracts, my system was lauded by the American Civil Liberties Union as a model for cities seeking to preserve set-asides that would help minorities.

Regrettably, this progress has now been undone in every sector of our society, with the enactment of the 1991 Civil Rights Act. This legislation, foolishly signed by President Bush, will encourage quota hiring, no matter that he now says it won't. The law, simply put, requires that the employer's employee profile, in the private sector as well as in government, reflect the demographic profile of the applicant work pool. If it does not statistically do so—on the basis of race, ethnicity, religion, and gender, at every level of employment—there is a rebuttable presumption of discrimination, which the employer must overcome with proof, or risk owing substantial money damages to any plaintiff alleging discrimination. It is not enough for an employer to show that he took the best applicant, if he rejected someone fitting the profile who was minimally qualified to do the job. In a 1988 poll, before the enactment of the legislation, 18 percent of all Fortune 500 corporations were already admitting to practices of quota hiring. You can be sure, under the new civil rights act, that percentage will now increase dramatically.

Mayor Dinkins has said on a number of occasions that he supports racial quotas, and I believe his appointments in government show that to be true. I was always meeting people who thought they could do a better job than every commissioner I appointed, so it is clear to me that the new law will encourage lawsuits against government to ensure that quota hiring by government becomes the standard. It is also clear that many employees appointed by David Dinkins on a quota basis, but not covered by civil service protections, will remain in their jobs under any new mayor. Any attempt to remove them, even though they are provisionals or exempts, will be fought as discrimination, and it is nearly impossible to prove incompetence in government sufficient for removal.

The argument for racial quotas can be reduced to the absurd by suggesting that our professional sports teams also be subject to these restrictions. So what if a particular male Jew is only five feet ten and can't compete with a six-foot-ten black male? Isn't he entitled to be on the team to reflect the applicant pool? True, the purpose of team sports is to field the best possible team, and to win, but isn't the purpose of business to be successful and achieve the largest profit margin? What's the difference? Sports are a business, too. Try this argument out on a quota supporter. It will get you nowhere.

I have been opposed to all forms of discrimination, bigotry, racism, and anti-Semitism, throughout my adult life, and this opposition naturally extends itself to racial quotas and reverse discrimination. Even as a young man, my opposition took the form of action. As I wrote earlier, I was moved to fisticuffs to battle anti-Semitism the very first time I recognized it, back in basic training. In 1964, I went to Mississippi to defend a group of mostly black civil rights workers engaged in a voter registration drive, even though the trip, and my work there, put me in great personal danger. I think you have to put yourself on the line for what you believe, and I have. Blacks and whites who support racial quotas and preferential treatment have not only disagreed with me, but have falsely accused me of racism because I did not agree with their philosophy. I have always fought them publicly in defense of my position. False charges of racism, which those of us who take this position are often subject to, are as evil as racism itself.

Another priority, in those first weeks of my first term, was to reclaim the public school, transportation, and hospital systems from the unions and special-interest groups that had long dominated those state authorities, which were paid for by city tax dollars. My predecessors had distanced themselves to the point where the city Board of Education, the Metropolitan Transportation Authority, and the Health and Hospitals Corporation were actually being run as though they were totally independent of the mayor, using city funds but at the same time not accountable to the city. This was unacceptable to me. How could a mayor allow such vital public services to slip away from his involvement and responsibility? I vowed during the campaign to happily accept responsibility for our schools, subways, buses, and hospitals, and the services they deliver, if I could retrieve sufficient power to affect the policics of those authorities.

Filling this campaign promise was not as easy as I had thought, but I was determined. That I was able to partially succeed in this area and in so many others resulted in small measure from my persistence, and in large part from the unwavering dedication and general excellence of my staff. My administration was made up of the best people ever to work in government. Many of them had been a part of the Lindsay administration. Lindsay had picked a lot of good people. I wanted the best I could find, whether or not they had worked for Lindsay, whom I did not like. I always said that government was not for my friends. That didn't mean that my friends could not be in government, but I treated them exactly the way I treated everyone else. If they couldn't hack it, I didn't want them.

I didn't have to look very far to assemble the core of my immediate staff. I found it on my Congressional payroll. David Brown, Ronay (Arlt) Menschel, Diane Coffey, Victor Botnick, and Jim Capalino all came with me to City Hall. Almost everyone else I had never met before. I established expert search committees in ten different areas, and I interviewed those they recommended. In this way, I appointed some terrific people. I like to say that I hired the two best police commissioners the city has ever seen, and I'd never met either of them before they were recommended to me. Both in jest and seriously, I have said Bob McGuire was the best white police commissioner and Ben Ward was the best black police commissioner. Ben, whom I first appointed as corrections commissioner toward the end of my first term, was also the first black police commissioner, but he was truly great without regard to race.

There were two others who served as police commissioner during my administration, and they were also outstanding professionals. One of them was Bill Devine, who was dying of brain cancer. He had been McGuire's first deputy. To honor him, I appointed him, if only for two days, before he was hospitalized. Richard Condon was the other, and he followed Ben Ward, when he retired.

Stan Brezenoff, who ultimately became my first deputy mayor, also came to me in this way. He was recommended for a minor commissionership, where a tough guy was needed to administer poverty funds and programs. He quickly proved himself the best administrator in government. Before making him my first deputy, I appointed him head of the Human Resources Administration and later president of the Health and Hospitals Corporation. These were among the toughest and most important jobs in government.

My administration got off to an unusual start. Some

would even call it a slow start. I prefer unusual. I was hobbled, I think, by my decision to appoint seven deputy mayors. In the past there had been three. I was top-heavy with my own gorgeous mosaic: Basil Paterson, black; Herman Badillo, Puerto Rican; David Brown, WASP; Ronay Menschel, female WASP; Phil Toia, Italian Catholic; Herbert Sturz, Jewish; and Robert Milano, Italian Catholic. Diane Coffey, Irish Catholic, was my chief of staff. New Yorkers did not really know me at the time of my election, and I thought a "rainbow" of deputy mayors would help me reach into the various communities. The city was facing bankruptcy and I thought I could assemble a strong, demographically based coalition with these appointments.

Seven deputy mayors seemed like a good idea, but they ultimately became unmanageable. I delegated enormous responsibility to these people, in areas such as capital planning, operations, social services, economic development, finance, and policy, and it wasn't too long before things started to fall through the cracks. It was too unwieldy. I realized that what I had done was create a monster; more accurately, I had created seven fiefdoms, which were being run autonomously. I was losing touch.

My plan was to be my own first deputy. I didn't need a first deputy mayor in charge of all the others. But I couldn't handle seven different deputy mayors, nor could they effectively sort out their various jurisdictions. They got in each other's way. And I never knew exactly what they were doing from one day to the next. I felt the power of command slipping away from me. And the attempt at demographic representation in government had no impact on anything, including race relations.

So, a year and a half after I took office, I decided to pare things down. This was a fairly messy business. After all, some of my deputy mayors had been my friends. All of them were good, well-intentioned people, and here I was very publicly stripping them of their titles. It was painful, for all of us, but there was no other way around it. Indeed, I emerged with a leaner, more efficient administration. I reduced the deputy mayors to three, and changed the titles and responsibilities of the others who remained in my administration. Nathan Leventhal, who was then the commissioner of Housing Preservation and Development, came on as deputy mayor for operations; Robert F. Wagner, Jr., chairman of the city planning commission, came on as deputy for policy; and Peter Solomon came on as deputy mayor of economic development. Now we had two Jews, and one Irish Catholic.

I took full responsibility for the slow-footedness of my administration. It was my idea to try seven deputy mayors. No one tried to talk me out of it. I thought it was a good idea, but it turned out not to be, and when I realized things weren't working, I changed them. That's one of the attributes of a good leader—the willingness to admit his mistakes, and to correct them.

I had good press from the start. It is traditional for elected officials in high office to enjoy a honeymoon period with the reporters assigned to cover them, but in my case it lasted a lot longer than usual. It probably took me right up to the seven-year itch, and even a little bit beyond, to the beginning of my third term. I was fresh, unpredictable, and quotable. I had a strong opinion on virtually everything that was even tangentially related to the city, and I was always available for interviews, so most reporters were generally kind to me, some more than others. I made their jobs easier. I was good copy. And, as I had learned over nine years in Congress, honing my remarks for the one-minute hour, I gave good sound bites.

This good press relationship soured over the years, but there was a tremendous momentum to it at the beginning. There was a sense of camaraderie with the press. This was fueled, in part, by my spirited participation in the annual Inner Circle productions put on by the Room Nine reporters at City Hall. (Room Nine was the press room.) The Inner Circle is a lot like the Gridiron dinners hosted by the White House press corps. It is an opportunity for the press to turn the tables on its quarry, the mayor, and for the quarry to respond in song and dance. It's all in good fun. Sometimes, it's even in good taste. In my day, the Inner Circle productions were held at the Hilton Hotel and usually consisted of three acts, two of which were devoted to attacking the mayor and the city council, and one of which savaged the governor. Some reporter genius would rewrite the lyrics to a popular song, usually from a current Broadway score, and then the reporters (some with passable voices, some with no voices, and a few with spectacular voices) would sing out the insults.

We were roasted, mercilessly, although not always cleverly. The numbers were often quite sophomoric, but they always managed to entertain. Tom Poster of the *Daily News* offered hilarious impersonations of Bella Abzug and Herman Badillo. His turn as Abzug was savagely funny, with an exaggerated emphasis on her derriere. Abzug, watching in the audience, did not take it too well. She began to cry. I was quite touched by her distress, and moved to comfort her in the only way I knew how. "Bella," I said, "don't cry. As far as I'm concerned, you have the smallest tush in town."

I'm not sure I made any points with her.

Before Lindsay (Inner Circles have been going on as long as anyone can remember), the mayor's response to the lampooning was generally delivered in a prepared speech. But Lindsay was a showman, and he brought in professional songwriters and Broadway stars, and turned his response into a whole production. So this became the new tradition. Beame did it, and I did it, and now Dinkins is doing it, although Dinkins didn't do enough singing or dancing at his first three affairs.

I went beyond the call of duty. I did these shows to a fare-thee-well. Over the years, I worked with any number of Broadway stars, directors, and choreographers. The professionals were always very generous with their time and talent. One year, I did a vaudeville routine with Ann Miller and Mickey Rooney. Another year, I was part of a magic show. In another, Tommy Tune had me dress in a ridiculous gold lamé outfit, with a pigeon on top of my hat. I was nutty-looking, but this is what he wanted me to do, and I always did whatever the director wanted me to do. If they thought it would make a good show, then I was game. Tommy Tune was right about the pigeon on my head and the lamé suit; the audience roared.

At the end of this particular performance, with silly hat in hand, I thanked the professional performers for their assistance, and the audience for their indulgence. "I know my singing and dancing aren't so good," I ad-libbed at the close of the show, "but they remind me of the story of the dancing bear." Then I told the story: "There once was a circus, where the bear danced and the audience roared with pleasure and applause, as you have done. At the end of the show, one spectator turned to another and said, 'Why is everybody applauding the bear? He doesn't dance so good.' The companion responded, 'Don't you understand? It's a miracle he dances at all.' And that's me, a miracle."

There was no direct political benefit to my performing in the Inner Circle shows, except for the fact that I would catch hell from the reporters for an entire year if I did not. I might catch hell anyway, but I would have preferred to do so on the merits. So I played along. It was all part of the job of being mayor. Occasionally, though, I had second thoughts. For one production, we did a takeoff on the show *Ain't Misbehavin'*, the Fats Waller musical revue. Then one of Broadway's biggest hits, it featured an all-black cast, and someone got the idea of dressing up in an Afro wig. This was shaky ground, even for me, so I checked with the *Ain't Misbehavin'* cast members, who were helping us out with our routine, and they assured me that the wig was not offensive to blacks. Then I double-checked with David Jones, my community adviser on black affairs, and he too saw nothing wrong with the wig.

Again, the audience roared, although a few of them, it turned out, were roaring in protest. Charlie Rangel, the black Congressman and a former House colleague, denounced me for ridiculing the black community. This was typical of Rangel, who had once been a friend but who, like many of the city's black leaders, tended to see every issue along racial lines. His attack was political, and dressed in the hot charge of racism.

What was more troubling was an attack by Joe Bragg, one of the Room Nine reporters who organized the event. Bragg, who is black, worked for one of the local radio stations. He had one of the few good voices in the press section, and we had enjoyed a good relationship until this night. Bragg was livid at my appearance, and he denounced me in radio interviews and in print. This I could do something about. I was absolutely furious. These shows had originally been barred from press coverage by agreement, but in recent years photographers had been allowed to release still pictures from the show to the general public; later, even television cameras were let in. Still, I certainly never expected my choice of material to be judged in such a public way, by what was to have been an essentially private audience.

"I will never participate in this show again," I told the Room Nine representatives. "This is supposed to be fun and games. You take terrible swipes at people every year. Do I get upset when you dress up in caftans and black hats and *peyes* (earlocks)? No, because that's part of the fun. I'm not gonna let you embarrass me because of something I did to please you." I closed my volley vowing never to return to their Inner Circle stage again.

Well, the reporters practically fell to their knees in apology. I think even Joe Bragg apologized. After all, I was the show's major draw. They were charging a few hundred dollars a ticket. Ostensibly, the money went to charity, but as far as my staff was ever able to determine, most of it went to subsidize the food and drink at press parties preparing for the show; years later, the practice changed, and the money now overwhelmingly goes to charity. The trouble was, the press segment of the show was so amateurish, with rare exception, that no one was about to shell out that kind of money to see a bunch of reporters try to sing and dance. People wanted to see the mayor try. More, they wanted to see a professional show. We put on a professional show. We agonized over it; I sweated through the rehearsals. It was supposed to be fun for me, but the only part I enjoyed was the performance; once I was on, I was on, but I suffered great anxiety during the long hours of rehearsals and immediately before the show went on; there was enormous tension in preparing for each performance. All of that took me away from more pressing matters. What did I need it for? So the reporters could turn around and condemn me for doing something they all agreed was very funny? To hell with it, I thought. To hell with them.

Ultimately, I accepted Bragg's apology in time for the next year's show. I still thought his attack outrageous, but some of the more clear-thinking members of my administration convinced me that if I did not participate, the Room Nine reporters would take it out on us over the coming year. As I said, I only want to be criticized on the merits, so I relented.

I recognized early that the office of mayor opened a great many doors to me. I think I went through most of them in my twelve years. One of them even led me to Pope John Paul II. In the middle of my first term, I made a trip to the Vatican during a European vacation. I wanted to do my share to urge the Pope to recognize the state of Israel, which the Vatican had not done, and still has not done in any formal way. So I requested an audience with the Pope, and was granted a half-hour.

I wanted to use this short time to full advantage, so I did some homework. I was searching for a way to communicate with the Pope on a personal level, in the hope of somehow influencing his position on the Jewish nation, which was, and obviously still is, a very personal issue to me. My good friend Victor Botnick helped me to find just the way. He brought to my attention a story he had unearthed in an old magazine. In it, we read of a four-year-old Jewish boy in Warsaw being placed by his mother in the care of a Christian Polish woman, just before Poland was occupied by the Nazis during the Second World War. The Christian woman swore to the mother to care for her little boy and, after the war, to send him to live with his uncle in Connecticut, where he could be raised as a Jew. The mother, it turned out, was imprisoned by the Nazis and died in a concentration camp. Four years later, when the Nazis retreated, the Christian woman wanted to adopt the child, and raise him as her own, but her promise weighed heavily on her. She had cared for the boy for four years, had saved his life, and had him baptized. Because she was an honorable and religious woman, she went to see her parish priest, seeking counsel. That's where the Pope came in, as a young parish priest. I'll get to that part in a moment.

After discovering the article, my staff was able to locate the boy, now a man, still living in Connecticut, and I called him up to corroborate the story; it checked out, and I planned to tell it to the Pope because I thought it would help me to connect with him on a personal level.

The other thing I did in preparation for my audience with the Pope was to buy souvenirs for my staff. Whenever I traveled, I tried to bring back gifts for the fifty or so people I had a special relationship with at City Hall— deputy mayors, cops, secretaries, aides, interns. On this trip to the Vatican, I purchased rosaries and other religious items for the Catholics on my gift list. My plan was to ask the Pope to bless them for me. I knew that anything that had been blessed by the Pope would be of special significance to a Catholic.

When I entered the Pope's quarters, I was carrying these items in a small bag, but I knew this wouldn't do. It didn't look nice. As I sat there, and waited for my appointment, I was thinking to myself, How in the world can I take all this stuff in there without seeming crass and ridiculous? Just then, a priest came by lugging two shopping bags, which I could see were filled with religious items. It was clear to me he was going to get them blessed. Why else would he have them there? So, I determined, if this priest can do it, then I can too. Even so, I decided a shopping bag was bad form, so I stuffed my jacket pockets with a few dozen rosaries, and whatever other items I was able to fit. And then I went in.

The two of us sat alone at a desk in a special room where the Pope received his visitors. The room was sparsely furnished, and without ostentation. There was no interpreter. The Pontiff didn't need one. His English was fluent. Slow, but fluent. He understood everything I was saying, and he spoke clearly. We talked about a number of things—the condition of the world, the condition of the United States, the condition of New York City—until I shifted the conversation to the first of two agenda items.

"Your Holiness," I said, preparing to state the obvious, "I'm Jewish." He knew this, of course; the Vatican knows everything about you when you come in, but I wanted to put it on the record. I will paraphrase the rest of my plea, although I think it's pretty close to the original: "I'm Jewish, and I want to urge you to recognize the state of Israel. This is particularly important now because you recently received Yasir Arafat at the Vatican, and you embraced him. The Jews in New York City were very upset about this, but I explained to them there is nothing wrong with your doing that. Your religiousness requires you to embrace every sinner.

"In fact, Your Holiness, you did something which I tell people nobody else would do. You went into the cell of the Turk who tried to assassinate you. And you forgave him. Most people wouldn't do that. I couldn't do that. So I am not distressed with the fact that you embraced Arafat."

"Mr. Mayor," the Pope interrupted, and again I'm paraphrasing, although I am almost certain he addressed me in this way, "I understand your concern, and the concern of the Jewish people. Let me reassure you, I have been very supportive, in every possible way, and I will continue to be so in the future."

"Your Holiness," I said, "the best way you could reassure Jews of your affection and support is to recognize the state of Israel."

"Well," he said, "we do have relations with them. They're not formal, but we certainly do meet with representatives of the state of Israel."

"It's not the same, Your Holiness."

"Perhaps not, but what you seek is difficult. It will happen someday, but it can't happen now. I have a responsibility to the Catholics who live in the Koranic lands and who would be in danger if we recognized Israel."

"Your Holiness," I tried, "you are revered throughout the world. It's inconceivable to me that anyone would seek revenge if the Church took such a position."

And then, to illustrate just how highly regarded he was, I related the story Victor Botnick had found in the magazine. I thought it would redirect our conversation so that the Pontiff might see things on a more personal level. I also knew our appointed time was running out, and I didn't want to leave without telling him the story. I reached the part where the Polish Christian woman went to her priest for advice. "She had made this promise to the Jewish woman," I told him, "but now she had baptized this boy. She loved this boy. This boy was her son now. She saved him. She wanted to be released by the parish priest from the promise she had made to the boy's natural mother. But the parish priest told her she could not do that. She had made a promise, he said, and she must carry it out. The priest said the only thing she could do was to send the boy to his uncle in Connecticut."

I ended the story with: "And, Your Holiness, that parish priest was you."

"It was?" the Pope said, genuinely surprised and apparently pleased at the tie. Of course, he could not have been expected to remember every encounter with his parishioners, over so many years.

"Yes, Your Holiness, it was."

"You have made your point, Mr. Mayor," the Pope said, closing the matter. Then he stood, signaling that the one-to-one portion of our meeting was coming to an end; he had earlier agreed to spend a few minutes with my traveling party.

I still had another item on my personal agenda: the rosaries. I moved quickly. I didn't want to pursue this matter in front of the others. "Your Holiness," I said, "I'm taking back some rosaries as gifts for my staff, and it would mean something very special if you would bless them." I didn't want to trouble him by taking time to empty my pockets, so I simply held out my coat; the pockets were nearly overflowing.

And then the Pope blessed my gifts. It was really rather sweet. Clearly, he was pleased to do it. And my staff, when I returned home, was delighted at the significance of their gifts.

As mayor of New York City, I was welcomed in cities half a world away. Not only was I welcomed, but I was usually also given a red-carpet treatment and granted an audience with whomever I wanted to see. I doubt that mayors of other large American cities were ever greeted so grandly in their travels abroad. Of course, there were some times when things didn't go entirely my way. When I visited Poland in 1986, for example, the Polish government rejected my first application for a visa because I wanted to meet with both Prime Minister Wojciech Jaruzelski and Solidarity leader Lech Walesa. The authorities, in finally granting my visa, said I could meet with one but not both. Walesa, who was living in Gdansk at the time, was considered to be a major pain in the ass by the Polish government, even though he was seen as a courageous and charismatic leader by most of the rest of the world. I was issued a thinly veiled ultimatum, to which I was not required to respond until my arrival: simply put, if I wanted to see the Prime Minister, then I could not go to Gdansk.

"This is so foolish of you," I said to the Polish official assigned to handle the matter, when I arrived with my traveling party. "It's like asking an American visiting India at the time of the British raj to choose between a meeting with the Queen's Governor-General or a meeting with Gandhi. Who do you think they would pick? And in my case, do you think I can go home and say that, given a choice between meeting Lech Walesa and Prime Minister Jaruzelski, I picked Jaruzelski? I'm going to Gdansk."

Well, the Polish government was very upset with me, but there was little they could do at this point without causing an international incident. Still, they did their best to keep me from Walesa. Their best was actually quite childish. On the day I was to leave for Gdansk, I was meeting with a Jewish group in Warsaw when I was interrupted by a government official. "The Prime Minister will see you now," he said, "but you must come right away."

It was almost silly. Surely, they knew that my plane to Gdansk was leaving in a half-hour, and that if I missed it there would not be another to take me without upsetting the rest of my itinerary.

"I'm sorry," I said, "but I guess that means I won't be able to see the Prime Minister. I'm going to Gdansk."

They couldn't believe it.

There were about six of us in my party, and we flew to Gdansk. We were accompanied on the plane by two armed Polish soldiers, who stood for the entire trip. We were not allowed to leave our seats to go to the bathroom without raising our hands and explaining our needs to one of the soldiers. For some reason, they were afraid of a skyjacking.

In Gdansk, we were received in the home of a priest, who had been Walesa's benefactor. Our hosts could not have been nicer. I spent a long time with Walesa in the rectory, drinking vodka to keep warm, and talking about the shipyard where the Solidarity movement had its start. After a hearty lunch, we toured the two Gdansk churches the priest was rebuilding. It was an incredibly lively and interesting afternoon, and I was impressed by the hope and promise of Solidarity.

At the residence before lunch, I turned to our host and said, through our translator, "Lech, I am going back to America shortly. What should I tell the American people? What is your message?" At that point, we were on a first-name basis.

He proceeded to talk, also through an interpreter, and what he said didn't make any sense. It was amorphous, without substance, and essentially unintelligible. I thought maybe I was missing something, so I said, "Lech, I want to make sure I get this right. Would you mind repeating it?" So he repeated himself, and it was unintelligible a second time.

Finally, I turned to my friend David Margolis, who was with me on this trip, and I said, "David, am I missing something? Did you understand any of that?"

"Not a word," he said.

I came away from that meeting with the feeling that Lech Walesa was indeed charismatic, courageous, and charming, but he was no rocket scientist. There was nothing there. At least, there was nothing there that I could see. When it came to articulating his philosophy or ideology in real terms, he seemed completely lost. I was astonished. Of course, he is now the President of Poland, and a huge success, and I'm sure far more informed than he was then.

When I returned home, I offered up my impressions of Walesa to all who were interested, and they were as stunned as I was. Some were convinced that I was mistaken. I told the story to the great dancer Mikhail Baryshnikov, for one, a few years before Walesa was elected President. Baryshnikov was a guest at one of my Gracie Mansion dinners, along with the actress Jessica Lange, and he insisted that something must have been lost on the translation.

"You are wrong about Walesa," Baryshnikov said. "He

is a very smart man. He could not have done what he has done if he were not smart."

Maybe so. After all, Walesa did lead a revolution, and he did get elected president. He has a great deal of authority. He succeeded over all odds, he must be smart. But I did not see it in our meeting. Maybe I was the dummy.

I also visited the German concentration camp at Auschwitz, and it was probably the most memorable event in my life. It was a kind of odyssey for me, and it moved me on many levels. My father had lost a brother and other relatives in the concentration camps, so there was a deeply personal reason for my wanting to go there. I had never known that uncle, but I knew his children, who survived the war. Of course, Auschwitz was not the only site of the Nazi atrocities committed against more than six million Jews, but I had come to see it as the symbol for the mass slaughter. And, as symbol, it came to represent the Nazi terror that America and the world had fought against during the war, and the particular losses suffered by my family. I had to go there.

I had been to Dachau, the camp outside of Munich, many years earlier in 1961, but it did not register in quite the same way, and it did not prepare me for what I would find, or feel, in Auschwitz. What was most disconcerting about the camp was the way the horrors there were hidden, diluted. It was set up like a museum. As we walked through the gates, we were greeted by the message, "Arbeit Macht Frei," wrought into the bars and gate: "Work will make you free." In fact, Auschwitz was specifically created as a death camp for Jews.

It was a bitter cold winter day when we visited there. I was bundled up in sweaters and a heavy leather coat, but I was still freezing. Even inside the barracks, I was numb; then, as now, the barracks were unheated, and I shuddered to realize that the prisoners had been kept in pajamas, even in the dead of winter. They were even called out into the snow in various states of undress, to be counted. I imagine that a summer visit to the place would not convey the same sense of what happened nearly fifty years ago, or what I felt on this visit. In the summer there are open green fields, and trees, and flowers. In the summer, there is life; in the winter, there is nothing—only death.

In the barracks, behind glass partitions, there were rows of suitcases, with name tags still attached. There was a display of thousands of pairs of eyeglasses. In another room, there was the shaven hair of the female prisoners and in another the shoes of children. All of it was laid out, with simple explanations. The information provided was meager and did not convey the tragedy of what had happened. That, perhaps, was one of the most unsettling things about Auschwitz: that the Russian authorities concealed the fact that the years-ago inhumanities had been carried out overwhelmingly against Jews. For example, they labeled the barrack buildings, by country, to indicate where the prisoners from each had been housed: Belgium, Poland, Austria, France. But they were overwhelmingly Jewish! Belgian Jews, Polish Jews, Austrian Jews, French Jews, and so on. At least 75 percent of those killed at Auschwitz were Jewish. And yet, the word *Jew* never appears, except on one barrack building. The camp was a killing ground for Jews, but no one would know it on an uninformed, unguided tour. I am told this has since been changed, and visitors are now offered a fuller explanation.

I saw where the gassing took place, and where the crematoria were located. I saw the infamous wall, against which the prisoners were shot for their various infractions. I saw the ovens. I wept. It's easy to cry in a place like Auschwitz. I was even physically ill. I have heard people say there is a certain smell of death, still, in the ovens, but I couldn't smell anything. It was too cold.

What I could sense was an indomitable human spirit and courage. This sobering visit to one of the most brutal of the German death camps reinforced for me how strong the survivors needed to be, just to survive. The will to live is unique. If you lose it, even in simple sickness, you can die. But the survivors had the will to live. They knew that, sooner or later, this particular persecution would be over. There might be another to take its place, but this one would pass. It took a long, long time to pass, during which a great many suffered unspeakable torment, but this, too, did pass.

Each year, in New York, I attend a ceremony to commemorate the Warsaw uprising, and I am struck by the appearance of the survivors. I am overwhelmed mainly by the frail, usually tiny women who come to light candles for the six million Jews who died in the Holocaust. Some of them are still beautiful, but all are now quite old, and every year there are fewer. And these are the survivors! They nearly died, and yet they had that special will to live. Something kept them going. They are small miracles to me, those tiny, frail, elderly women. They come with their children, or their grandchildren, or sometimes their great-grandchildren, and they remember.

At Auschwitz, I remembered, and wept.

Some of my most memorable encounters with world leaders and foreign dignitaries came on my home turf. Occasionally, I would even rub elbows with royalty. In June 1981, the Prince of Wales, heir to the British throne, made an unofficial visit to New York City. At first, we were scheduled to meet at City Hall, but I had been openly critical over the previous weeks of England's continued presence in Ireland, and I was told that Prime Minister Margaret Thatcher urged the Prince to cancel our meeting.

He did cancel, although I cannot say for certain that it was as a direct result of the prime minister's urging—it may very well have been for security reasons. However, I was invited to meet with the Prince on board Malcolm Forbes's yacht, the *Highlander,* for a lunchtime cruise around Manhattan with about fifty other guests, including the First Lady, Nancy Reagan. I found the Prince to be a gracious fellow—a nice chap, as they say in England—and we talked at length about a number of issues. He allowed that he was sympathetic to the plight of the Irish Catholics in Northern Ireland, but reiterated that it was unfair to refer to the British presence there as colonization, because he maintained that a majority of those who live there, the Protestant community, favor the tie to England.

He seemed anxious to redirect the conversation to another topic, so he asked me how I solved the city's fiscal crisis. "Very simple," I replied. "We don't spend money we don't have."

After the luncheon cruise, I was asked by reporters for my impression of the Prince, and for a recounting of our conversation. Happily, I obliged, as I always try to do. In this instance, though, I was almost too obliging. I related the Prince's position on Ireland, and stated that I did not associate the position of the British monarchy with that of the Thatcher government. And then I went too far. "I'll let you in on something," I told the press, in an aside. "He's going bald. I'm an expert on this, and I detected the beginning of the end. Right now, it's just a small, quarter-size bald spot, at the top of his head. I don't think he'll end up looking like a billiard ball, but he is losing his hair."

Later that afternoon, Tom Goldstein, my press secretary, took a call from an incensed Patrick Nixon of the British Information Services, based in New York. "Mr. Goldstein," Nixon began. "Is the mayor not aware that all royal conversations are privileged?"

"No, sir, he is not," Tom replied.

"Well, they are," Nixon continued, rather emphatically, "and I should like it if you would call the press and withdraw the mayor's comments."

Obviously, Patrick Nixon was not well versed in the manners of the American press. (There *are* no manners in the American press.) I don't know how he manages to control the British media, but if the mayor of New York City tried to withdraw any comments made at an informal press briefing, then there would be a second scandalous story to go along with whatever the first one was. I suspected that the royal house was more upset about my

balding comments than they were about my disclosures of
our conversation.

I did apologize for not honoring the royal privilege, in
my own way, at my press briefing the following morning.
"Nobody told me about it," I said. "I don't hang around
with princes, so I don't know the protocol."

Sometimes, my home field advantage left me at a disad-
vantage in dealing with out-of-town guests. When President Ceausescu of Romania checked into the Waldorf
Astoria for a weekend stay, he was greeted by pickets denouncing him for his country's persecution of the Hungarian minority living in Transylvania, which had once
been part of Hungary. In a roundabout way, I was made to
apologize for the behavior of my constituents. Of course,
it was such a roundabout way that I found myself joining
in the chorus of protest, but I'm getting ahead of the story.

After going to the Romanian mission for dinner,
Ceausescu thought he could not get past the picket line
and back into his hotel. He was threatening to leave the
country in a huff, which would have been an embarrassing
diplomatic incident. I received an urgent phone call
shortly after midnight, from a State Department official.
Could I help ease the situation? the caller wanted to
know. I promised to rouse the police commissioner, and
arrange for the President to be personally escorted back
to his hotel. Then I called Bob McGuire and explained the
situation to him.

Two hours later, Bob called back and said everything
had worked out. He got the President's limo through the
picket lines and into the hotel garage, and there was only
one egg thrown at the car. Nobody was hurt.

The one egg cost me a couple of hours' sleep. Still later
that night, I took another call from the State Department
official, who told me that Ceausescu was absolutely livid at
the indignity of the picket line and the egg-throwing.
Could I come up to the hotel in the morning to try and
smooth things over, perhaps even apologize, in order to
avoid an international incident?

At eight-thirty the following morning, Bob McGuire and I arrived at the President's suite at the Waldorf. As I recall, he was on the twenty-ninth floor. The anteroom was filled with Romanian goons with guns. I was escorted into the living room, where I met Ambassador William Luers of the State Department for the first time. (Luers is now president of the Metropolitan Museum of Art, and a good friend.)

The President was raging, still.

"Mr. President," I said, gingerly, "I hope everything is okay."

"No," he said, through an interpreter. "It is not. I have never been so insulted. It is outrageous that there should be pickets permitted against me. I wasn't able to sleep because of all their screaming."

"Mr. President," I countered, "you're on the twenty-ninth floor. They're across the street. I hardly imagine you could have heard them, no matter how loudly they screamed. Besides, you should also know that in this country picketing is protected by our Constitution. Actually, you should feel complimented. We only picket very important people."

He did not appreciate the joke. "If you cannot control the picketing," he said, "then allow me to send in my people. They will."

"Thank you very much, Mr. President," I responded, as it dawned on me that I was getting nowhere with this man, "but that is not possible."

Clearly, Ceausescu was in a foul mood, and there was nothing I could do to talk him out of it. I changed the subject. "Mr. President," I tried, "as long as I'm here, may I speak frankly?"

(I often use this tack in broaching a sensitive topic with an important visitor, and I have never met anyone who said no. How could they?)

"Mr. President," I continued, upon his assent, "why are you persecuting the Hungarian minority in Romania?" As a Congressman, I had taken up the cause of the Hungarian minority and had been briefed on the subject many times, so I listed some of the persecutions being visited on these people.

Ceausescu was absolutely outraged, but I continued on. When I finally decided he had had enough, I stood up and said, "Now, Mr. President, can I take you to or recommend a good Romanian restaurant for lunch?"

When he didn't take up the offer, I left.

Many years later, in a BBC documentary on Ceausescu's rise and fall, I was gratified to hear a remark by my friend Bill Luers. Of all the people he knew who spoke to Ceausescu, he said, only one did not fawn on him and tell him how wonderful he was. That one person was me. I was surprised at the mention.

As mayor, one of the happier obligations of the office was to greet the various consuls general on their arrival to the city. Foreign ambassadors reported to the President; the consuls general reported to me, and at one point New York City was home to ninety-three of them. Our sessions were really just a brief formality, but I always tried to make the ten or fifteen minutes engaging, for me and for my visitors. They presented me with their credentials, I welcomed them to the city, and that was usually that.

Sometimes things got interesting, at least from where I was sitting. Once, in a meeting with the consul general of Burundi, I tired to impress my visitor with my knowledge of his country's history. Burundi is a small African nation in the middle of the continent. Its neighbor is Rwanda, and the two tiny nations were often at war with each other. Both had been Belgian colonies. For many years, the dominant tribe ruling both countries had been the Watusi; they were a very tall people, almost giants. The other, less powerful tribe was the Buhutu; they were a very small people—not midgets, but not at all tall. The Buhutu were enslaved by the Watusi, until there was a revolution; now, the Buhutu were in charge.

I wasn't briefed for this meeting, but for some reason I happened to know these things. I figured I might as well use them to some playful advantage, so I turned to the consul general when he sat down and said, "Have you stopped killing the Watusis?"

"We're not killing the Watusis!" he said, somewhat affronted by my remark.

"Well, you did kill the Watusis," I continued. "Lots of them." I don't know why, but I was just trying to egg him on a little, to have some fun. Even mayors are entitled to a little fun sometimes.

Apparently, my visitor from Burundi did not agree with me. He became very upset at my questions. "We did not kill the Watusis," he insisted. "They're just like anybody else."

"You mean there are Watusis in your government?" I said, continuing in the same vein.

"Yes, and they're treated like anybody else." At this point, the consul general appeared to have caught on to my sparring, and now he wanted to play along. He looked at me, smiled, and said, "You could be a Watusi."

I don't know how he meant it—size, perhaps?—but he said it with a mischievous smile. And then he stood, leaving me with a bag of Burundi coffee, as a parting gift. As I remember it, the coffee was quite good.

Another time, I shamed the Israeli consul general, Paul Kadar, into paying his country's long-overdue parking tickets, which had accumulated to over twenty thousand dollars in fines. I got tremendous satisfaction from this, and one of the most gratifying things about it was the way I surprised my visitor with my firm stance. He was not at all prepared for me to pounce on him for these outstanding parking violations, because he knew me, as everyone did, as a friend and supporter of Israel. He walked into my office with a big smile on his face, expecting to be greeted warmly.

"So," I said as we sat down. "When is Israel going to pay its traffic tickets?" It was just about the first thing out of my mouth. I said it playfully, but I also meant it.

He was enraged. "How dare you talk to me in that way!" he fumed. "I thought we were friends."

"We are," I said, "but that does not excuse your behavior. Next to the Soviet Union, Israel is the worst offender when it comes to parking tickets. Your people park wherever they want, whenever they want, and we can't make you pay your fines. I think it's terrible for your reputation."

Within the next several weeks, at the direction of their foreign minister, Moshe Dayan, Israel paid off every one of its outstanding parking violations, and I am proud that I was able to get them to do it.

I had to strong-arm our foreign visitors more often than some people might think. For example, when Gillian Sorenson, my commissioner to the United Nations, briefed me before a visit with President Mobutu of Zaire that the Zaire mission had failed to pay more than thirty thousand dollars owed to American vendors, we agreed to raise the delicate matter with the President in my office.

President Mobutu arrived at City Hall with his leopard cap, his fertility stick, his U.N. Ambassador, and about ten thugs, who all looked like they were packing weapons. After we went through the normal pleasantries, I turned to Mobutu and said, "Mr. President, may I be candid with you?"

"Oui," he said, which even I understood.

"Mr. President," I cautioned, "what I have to discuss is a very private matter, and I suggest that everyone be excused except for Ms. Sorenson, you, and me."

The Zaire Ambassador, who was primarily responsible for the failure to make payments, became very excited at this point, and insisted on staying.

"That is up to you, Mr. President," I said when Mobutu looked to me for approval.

"Oui," he said.

"But your security people," I said, "I prefer that they leave."

"Oui," he said.

After they left, I asked Gillian to explain the problem to the President. She did, in fluent and fiery French, denouncing the Ambassador for his failure to pay the bills. Mobutu listened quietly and at the end said, "The bills will be paid." He asked that Gillian accompany him to his hotel after this visit, to conclude the matter.

I considered the issue closed, but Gillian Sorenson still wound up with a story to tell. Afraid to return to the President's hotel by herself, she took along my special assistant for the black community, David Jones. There is, after all, safety in numbers. The two of them went to the President's hotel, whereupon a very surly member of Mobutu's staff kept them waiting in an empty room for nearly an hour. Finally, another staffer came in and said, again in a surly tone, "Follow me."

Gillian and David followed the man to another empty room. Inside, the aide opened a shoe box stuffed with dollar bills. I don't recall the denominations, but he counted out thirty thousand dollars, for which Gillian gave him a receipt. She had the money, but she was uneasy. She worried that this was a trap, and that when they got into the elevator they would be held up and robbed. So, quite intelligently, she requested a police escort from the Mission back to City Hall. The thirty thousand dollars was later distributed to the vendors.

For the most part, though, my official foreign visits nearly always concerned more significant matters. Often, the dialogue I pursued with these visiting dignitaries was related to the state of Israel. I will never go to live in Israel, but I still think of myself as a Zionist. The modern definition of a Zionist, for me, is someone who supports the Jewish nation. I do. Vigorously. The fact that I do not choose to live there does not diminish or in any way change my support, just as Americans of Italian, French, African, or whatever descent can continue to support the lands of their ancestors wholeheartedly without having to return to them. No one would ever think of telling an American Irishman that his commitment to Ireland was inadequate or divisive because he wishes to live in America; but if you're Jewish and publicly committed to the Jewish nation, you are sometimes made to defend your decisions and actions in support of Israel. Strange.

I have always seized every occasion to stand up for the state of Israel—before, during, and after my tenure as mayor. If I encountered a world leader whose country had not yet recognized Israel, or who behaved in a way that was inimical to it, or that I saw as inappropriate, then I said something about it. And, because I was mayor of New York City, they listened. They didn't necessarily follow my wishes, but they listened, as the Pope had done on my visit to the Vatican. For whatever it was worth, I made myself heard.

Two good illustrations of just how loudly I made myself heard come readily to mind. The first concerned Spain. Felipe Gonzalez, the Prime Minister, was in New York on his first official visit, and I was asked to attend a luncheon in his honor. We were seated next to each other at the Waldorf Astoria, and he impressed me as a rather charming and able young man, very engaging and intelligent. At some opportune point during the meal, I turned to him and said, "Felipe, you ran on a promise that you were going to recognize Israel. When are you going to do it?" He seemed somewhat surprised by my directness, but there is really no better way to initiate these conversations.

"It will take time," he said in measured response. "It will take time, but I will do it."

Time for what? I wondered, as I let him slither his way out of it and on to another subject. I would normally have pressed the matter with him, but there were other people present and I didn't want to cause him any embarrassment.

I next saw the Prime Minister some months later, in Spain, and I picked up right where I had left off. "Felipe," I tried again, "you still haven't recognized the state of

Israel. What's going on?" This time, I didn't mind if I embarrassed him. We were in his office.

"Well," he said, "I know I promised to do so, but I didn't promise I would do it immediately. I still intend to do it before I leave office."

"You're going to be in office for life, Felipe," I challenged. "That's not what the people expected. That's not what they understood."

We went back and forth on this for a while, until he confided in me the real reason for his delay. "The truth," he said, "is that the King is against recognizing Israel. I need some time to work on him."

Now, I had met King Juan Carlos on a previous occasion in New York City, and it had been a friendly visit, so I naturally decided to take the matter up with him. Conveniently, the King and Queen were due back in New York shortly after this second encounter with Felipe Gonzalez, so I drove out to Kennedy Airport with my protocol commissioner, Barbara Margolis, to greet them. It was pouring rain when their plane arrived, but still I stood out on the tarmac, waiting. The King noticed me as soon as he stepped onto the exit staircase with his wife, Queen Sofia.

"So good of you to come out here," he said, when he reached the bottom. "But it was not necessary."

"I wanted very much to greet you, Your Majesty," I said. "And I also wanted to take up a very important matter with you. May I see you at your hotel?"

"Yes," he said. "Of course."

(When you're mayor, they always say, "Yes, of course.")

He made time for me right away. We went back to his hotel in separate cars. The King and Queen received Barbara Margolis and me in their suite. They sat in easy chairs. We sat on the couch. "Your Majesty," I began, once again preparing to state the obvious, "I'm Jewish, and I want to talk to you about something that's very important to me, Israel, and something that's very distressing to me, which is that Spain does not have diplomatic relations with Israel."

"Oh, but we will, Mayor," he assured. "We will."

"Forgive me, Your Majesty," I said, "but that's not what your Prime Minister tells me. I spoke to Felipe just recently, and he tells me he would like to recognize Israel now. He tells me you're opposed to it."

Before I could continue, the Queen interrupted. "I must tell you, Mayor," she said. "You should know that some of my best friends are Jewish." So help me God, she said that. I could see she was trying to be sweet and nice. That was just her way.

The entire meeting lasted no more than twenty minutes, and I left knowing there was nothing more I could do. Spain opened up diplomatic relations with Israel not long after, and I don't pretend to think my discussions with the King and Prime Minister were responsible for the turnabout, but maybe they helped. They surely didn't hurt.

The second example illustrates a different approach on this issue. This time, it concerned Portugal, and this time, I did not broach the subject at all, because it wasn't necessary. Still, it came up. I received the Portuguese Prime Minister, Mario Soares, in my office at City Hall. He was in town on an official visit, and I wanted to greet him. We had met once before, in 1974, when I visited Portugal with a Congressional delegation. At that time, the United States was opposed to Soares's Socialist Party, but his rise to power caused a shift in our position. I liked him even when my government didn't. In our first meeting, he struck me as extremely thoughtful and passionate. When I explained to him that a picture of the two of us together might be helpful in my reelection campaign, he reached into his desk and produced a handful of eight-by-ten glossies, which he dutifully signed for me and my colleagues.

I liked Soares even more after our second meeting, after he had become Prime Minister and I had become mayor. The subject of Israel did not come up at all during our talk. We reminisced a little about our earlier meeting and marveled at the changes that had taken place in his country, and in both our lives. All of this was done through an interpreter. When it came time to leave, I walked the Prime Minister outside. I always walked my important visitors outside after our meetings. That is, if I especially liked them. If I didn't, I simply walked them to my office door. Soares, I liked very much, so I saw him outside.

"Mr. Mayor," he said, as we shook hands in parting on the steps of City Hall, "you didn't ask me about my position on Israel. I have a very good position on Israel."

Clearly, the Prime Minister had been briefed. Someone must have told him: this jerk, the mayor, the first thing he'll want to talk about will be Israel.

"Mr. Prime Minister," I responded, "I know your position on Israel, and I'm happy with it, so there was no reason to ask you about it."

My reputation had preceded me.

One of the unhappy obligations of the office were the too-frequent visits I was called on to make to city police officers and fire fighters who were injured in the line of duty. I made it a practice to go to the hospital on the very night of the incident, no matter how many stops I had to make on my rounds, no matter how late. Don't misunderstand me, I was happy to call on these good men and women, and to thank them for their bravery on behalf of the city; I just hated to have so many opportunities to do so. It got to the point where my reputation preceded me in this matter as well.

One night, to illustrate, six fire fighters were injured at Macy's, and they had all been sent to different hospitals. The fire had occurred toward the end of the day, and by the time I had seen five of them, it was about eleven o'clock at night. I trudged into St. Vincent's, my last stop, and was met by the sister in charge. It was so late, I asked her not to wake the last fire fighter, but she said he had left orders that no matter how late I came, I was to go into his room. She took me there and turned on the light. When I walked in, the fire fighter sat up in bed and said, sternly, "Where have you been?" We both laughed, but the fact was that every fire fighter and cop knew they could count on me, and I would be there.

As I write this, I realize for the first time that my first two terms as mayor have bled into each other with the years. I have now, in hindsight, begun to look on those first eight years in office as one long run, and it is difficult for me to place certain incidents in one term or another. (I look back on my third term somewhat differently from my first two, for reasons I will explain.) Of course, there were certain defining moments from each term, but these too have begun to blur with the passage of time.

One of the few significant episodes that I am able to date accurately is the death of my father, in January 1986, less than two weeks into my second term. His passing resonates in a way quite unlike the death of my mother, because they each died under such different circumstances. My mother was a young woman. She suffered a great deal, and for a long period of time. My father was eighty-seven years old. He died quickly, from a heart attack, and he suffered very little. He had a history of heart trouble late in life, but he remained active and relatively free of pain up until his very last day.

I got the news by phone, at the mansion, while I was entertaining the mayor of Cairo. My father was in Florida at the time of his death; he had retired there with his second wife, Rose. I honestly can't recall how I reacted when I put down the phone, or what I did next. Clearly, I was upset, but I was also relieved that he went quickly and without pain. My father lived a long, full life. I am forever grateful that he lived long enough to see me to City Hall. He took tremendous pride in my accomplishments. He used to introduce my brother by saying, "This is my son, Harold, not the mayor." Harold never minded, or if he did, he got used to it. This was just my father's sense of humor, and his enormous pride in my success. He had a wonderful sense of humor, and it was one of the many gifts he passed on to me.

Papa really loved the fact that I was the mayor. He got a similar kick out of my being a Congressman, but it was not quite the same thing. When I became mayor, he achieved a certain celebrity; as my name became well known, so did his, and he seemed to relish his notoriety. I don't blame him. After all, it wasn't every Polish Jewish immigrant who struggled from a childhood of poverty, through the worst of the Depression, and who raised a son who went on to become mayor of New York City. I'm happy I had the chance to give him that, which I considered small repayment for everything he had given me. I often think of my parents, and my brother and sister and I talk about them regularly. Warts and all, they were wonderful, and we were lucky to have them.

But beyond personal milestones such as these, those first eight years did blur together. A great many unsorted memories come racing to mind when I think back to that period. Some of them, I'm sure, even run over into my third term, but the happier recollections, or at least the most benign ones, I tend to place in the first two. Let me therefore use this opportunity to deliver a few parting shots at some of the more prominent New Yorkers, and out-of-towners, with whom I crossed paths, or words.

I'll begin with Donald Trump. What a supreme, egotistical lightweight! This was clear to me from our very first meeting. To be fair, he did build some good-quality buildings, but he was such a blowhard. The best comment I ever heard about Trump came from Alair Townsend, my deputy mayor for economic development, who said she wouldn't believe Donald Trump if his tongue were notarized. I think the line itself was not original with her, but she found its perfect target.

I thought it was rather disingenuous of Trump to crow that he single-handedly resurrected the ice-skating rink in Central Park in a miraculous way. I'll explain. The Wollman Rink had been under reconstruction for more than ten years. Plans for its renovation were under way before my term as mayor. The construction was a major disaster.

My first parks commissioner, Gordon Davis, decided to use cutting-edge technology to make the ice, and the damn thing didn't work. There were more than twenty miles of pipes running under the rink, and the freon was leaking throughout the entire length. No matter what he tried, he couldn't get the ice to freeze. It was a disaster and a public embarrassment. The city had spent millions, and the people still had no place to skate.

Enter Trump, who held himself out as a white knight to the ice skaters of New York City. I will do for the city what the city cannot do for itself, he said, in so many words, and I will do it because I am such a nice guy. To his credit, Trump made good on his claim. He didn't renovate the rink himself; he subcontracted the work to others. The city could not do this. The city is restricted by the regular municipal building process, which requires that work under contract be given to the lowest bidder. In construction, the lowest bidder is not always the best contractor. With Trump, we were able to liberate the project from these restrictions, because he was a private developer, and he then contracted the job to a Canadian firm that was well known for its skating rinks.

When he was finished, Trump actually asked me to name the rink after him, in honor of what he had done for the city. I thought to myself, I so dislike him, but I also thought, Well, the city is strapped for money, and if I can get him to pay for the renovation (which cost $3 million), it might be worth putting his name on the rink. Foolishly, he rejected my offer. On reflection, I'm delighted that he did. He said he would consider paying for the project at some later date, but he did not want his contribution to be linked to the naming. Knowing him, I would never have put the city in that position. We would never have seen the money. Now, at least, we don't have to see his name on the Wollman Rink.

George Steinbrenner was another tough man to do business with. I had a very bad experience with him. The city went to him to try to renegotiate the long-term lease on Yankee Stadium, which had been entered into under Mayor Lindsay. It was a lousy lease for the city. It was so badly drawn against us that, on occasion, we actually owed the Yankees money at the end of the year. Under Lindsay, the city had spent $125 million to renovate the stadium in the 1970s (a project that was to have originally cost $24 million), and we were hardly making any return on our investment. I believe it was money well spent, even though I am not a sports fan. The Yankees are good for the city, and good for the Bronx. It was important to refurbish Yankee Stadium to keep them there. But that didn't mean we shouldn't negotiate a fairer lease, under terms more favorable to the city.

Steinbrenner wanted the city to build luxury sky boxes at the stadium, which we had done at Shea Stadium for Fred Wilpon and the Mets. Fred Wilpon was a gentleman, and the city got a fair deal on the renegotiated Shea Stadium lease, and so did the Mets. The city wanted to extend the length of the Yankees' lease, and improve some of the terms; we also wanted a greater share of the team's lucrative cable-television revenues, which had not been fully anticipated when the deal was first signed in the 1970s. All of these things were fair and reasonable, but the negotiations were still tough. They dragged on for months.

Finally, I went up to the Bronx with our negotiators to conclude the deal. The only thing left was for Steinbrenner to choose from among several agreed-upon options created at his insistence. A memo of understanding was signed between the city and the Yankees. We did not anticipate any problems. Of course, we should have. We later learned that Steinbrenner had been secretly negotiating a $500 million cable television deal, and when he came to terms on that deal he reneged on his still-unsigned agreement with the city. He did not want to share what was suddenly a $500 million pie and withdrew from the negotiations.

I was outraged. Our deal, of course, was not enforceable, since the contract had not yet been executed. I never forgave Steinbrenner for this, and vowed to take the hardest possible line in all future dealings with him. Steinbrenner, for his part, acted as if he had done nothing wrong. He still wanted his sky boxes, but I refused to give them to him.

On the other hand, Steinbrenner fielded a championship Yankee team, which he did three times during my administration—in 1978, when the Yankees won the World Series; in 1980, when they won the American League Eastern Division; and in 1981, when they were the American League champs. The city dutifully hosted a ticker-tape parade for the victorious Yankees. I was thrilled for the players, and for the fans and the city, and then even felt good about George.

The Mets were another story. When the Mets won the World Series in 1986, I was among their loudest cheerleaders. Normally, when I went to a baseball game as mayor, I left after the first inning or two. I never cared much for professional sports, and attended these events mostly for the sake of appearance. In 1986, though, I was caught up in it. Mostly, I was caught up in the idea of getting doused with champagne in the locker room after the game. I had a vivid image of Mayor Lindsay getting similarly soaked after the Mets' 1969 World Series victory, an event credited for his reelection victory that year, and I figured if he could be showered with champagne, then why not me?

Of course, this meant that I had to stay until the end of the game, because they don't break out the champagne after the first or second inning. I went out to Shea Stadium in an old suit, preparing for the inevitable. After the game, I went down to the locker room to congratulate the players, and all the while I was thinking, Okay, pour, give me your best shot. Everybody was pouring champagne over everybody else's head. Finally, they got to me. Let me tell you, champagne is actually very clammy, when it's poured over your head. Sticky. I've heard people say it stings the eyes, but I didn't find that to be the case. It was pretty uncomfortable, though. As soon as I could, I removed myself from the happy scene and raced home to Gracie Mansion to take a shower.

Later that year, when the New York Giants won the Super Bowl, I could not have cared less. Like I said, I was never much for professional sports, but the Giants didn't even play their games in New York. They were a New Jersey team, as far as I was concerned, so when they won the Super Bowl I decided that there would be no ticker-tape parade to honor them. "Let them have a parade in East Rutherford or in Moonachie where they hang out," I told reporters, when I was asked why there was no parade.

As mayor, I had special opportunities to meet all manner of celebrities. I danced with Liza Minnelli at a fundraiser, and I must tell you, she has never looked better as a dancer than when she was doing the fox-trot with me. We looked terrific. I'm actually a terrific fox-trotter. For anything else, I have two left feet, but I can fox-trot with the best of them. I must say, Liza was also terrific.

On one occasion, I introduced Paul Simon and Art Garfunkel to a huge crowd on the Great Lawn at Central Park, when the singers performed their free concert there. You can actually hear my introduction on the live recording issued shortly after the event. On the advice of friends, I kept my remarks short, and to the point: "Ladies and gentlemen, Simon and Garfunkel."

I also attended Diana Ross's legendary free concert in Central Park. The concert itself was memorable because most of the show was held during a downpour, but the violent aftermath was what got all the headlines the next morning. Diana Ross attracted a dangerous, unruly crowd, through no fault of her own. When the crowd dispersed, after the storm forced the show to end prematurely, a number of the frenzied concert-goers poured out of the park and dispersed throughout the nearby neighborhoods on a series of "wilding" rampages—breaking windows, looting, snatching purses, and harassing and assaulting many who happened to cross their paths. There were a number of incidents of violence. Ross drew a broad mix of people to her performance, but the culprits here were mostly black youths. It was truly a horror show, and for the balance of my administration I instructed the parks commissioner to avoid booking any acts that might attract similar crowds bent on violence, such as rap groups. We need only look to the tragic December 1991 trampling deaths of eight City College undergraduates attending an open-seating celebrity basketball game, featuring several rap stars in a campus gymnasium, and to these earlier "wilding" incidents, to understand why there will probably never be a free rap concert in Central Park under David Dinkins, or any other mayor, white, black, or Hispanic. Is this a racist attitude? I don't think so. Those same youths would be welcome at a Paul Simon concert, as they were in the summer of 1991, after which they dispersed without incident.

One special thrill came during my third term, when Woody Allen asked me to appear as myself in a cameo in his segment of the movie trilogy *New York Stories*; the other two segments were directed by Martin Scorcese and Francis Ford Coppola, who did not have the good casting sense of their colleague. I was quite good in the role. When I delivered my lines, acting out a press conference at Gracie Mansion, I had no idea what the plot was. The way Woody Allen works is he only shows the actors the portions of the script that are relevant to their scenes. I only had to preside over a pretend press conference, so everything else was irrelevant. I was as surprised as anyone in the audience when I finally saw what the movie was about.

There was a funny scene between Woody and me some months after the filming, but before the movie was released. I ran into him at Elaine's, the celebrity hangout on the Upper East Side. I approached him as though I were an extra going to see Flo Ziegfeld. "Mr. Allen," I said jocularly. "Do you remember me?" I was still mayor at the time.

He looked at me, and flashed what I took to be a wry smile. We shook hands. I continued: "Did I end up on the cutting-room floor?"

"No," he said, "you're in the movie. Actually, you were very good."

I took it as a high compliment.

I had a number of encounters over the years with Joseph Papp, the theater producer. They were more like run-ins than encounters. As a theater producer, Papp was without parallel, even if on occasion some of his productions were boring. He made a huge and vital contribution to the city. His Shakespeare-in-the-Park productions have become an institution; *A Chorus Line* was a historic production and stands around the world as a glorious billboard for the New York stage. But there were other aspects to his personality. Once, when he was trying to stop construction of the Marriott Hotel, in Times Square, he came to City Hall seeking a permit to park a flatbed truck on Forty-third Street. He planned to have well-known theater people stand on the flatbed and protest the demolition of the Helen Hayes Theater, which stood on the hotel site.

"We won't be denouncing you, Mr. Mayor," he assured, "we simply want to give the theatrical community a chance to speak out against the project." I didn't ask for his assurance, but he offered it.

He got the permit. Sure enough, Papp and his people spent the entire day ripping me apart. He set me up as an enemy of the cultural community, when in truth I had done more for the arts in this city than any mayor before me. New York City's budget for the arts doubled under me, and was second in size to the federal arts budget.

By now you know I'm not the most forgiving person in the world. But it was easy to forgive Papp each year because I knew he would find some new way to piss me off in the new year. Each year on Rosh Hashannah, I forgave him, and each year we got right back into it. (Incidentally, Papp had a religious conviction that surely was unknown to the public, which I appreciated; he was one of the few members of the Park East Synagogue, which we both attended, who wore rubber-soled sneakers on Yom Kippur, when you're not supposed to wear leather soles.)

Our last argument was over the Public Theater. He wanted the city to extend the lease on it to ninety-nine years. I thought that was too long, and agreed only to a twenty-five year lease. "How do we know what will happen after you're dead?" I joked.

Sadly, the city now has a chance to find out. Shortly before Papp's death in 1991, David Dinkins bent to the producer's pressure and extended the lease to a longer term. So now we'll see what happens.

And I entertained the Democratic Presidential hopefuls in 1980, 1984, and 1988, as they passed through town on the campaign trail. I'll get to the 1988 campaign a little later on in these pages, but there is a story from the 1984 primary season I want to find room for here. Former California Governor Jerry Brown was making his second try for the White House that year, and he stopped by to see me at the mansion. He's a small man, and he was so overweight that his buttons were bursting and his shirt gaped, exposing his belly. He took off his jacket and folded it over his arms, covering his belly in what I took to be embarrassment.

He told me that he was going to win the party's nomination and the White House. "I will win," he insisted, "because I am the most conservative and the most liberal of all the candidates."

I thought to myself, Well, anyone who is both cannot possibly be either. I also thought that anyone who aspired to both should not be trusted to lead the country.

Brown sensed I was having trouble with this concept, so he explained himself. At least he tried to, but here, too, he wasn't making much sense.

When he finished, I asked him why he was in New York.

"I am here to see the Jews," he announced.

"You are?" I said. "Which Jews?"

Actually, I was interested to see who was on his list, which an aide handed to Brown and Brown handed to me. There was not a name on that list that I recognized, which was pretty strange. I think it's fair to say that I was probably the head Jew in New York City at that time, and if I didn't know who these people were, then Jerry Brown was in trouble.

I thought, These people are nuts, and it turned out I was right.

Each day as mayor was scheduled to the fullest. Even on days when we didn't make headlines, we were busy. Every meal, it seemed, had a meeting attached to it. Even my nights were frequently interrupted—by police and fire emergencies, or simply by the unrelenting responsibilities of the office. There was never enough time to pause, to adequately consider where my administration had been, or where we were going.

The obvious times to consider our accomplishments were in planning for my reelection, which I did three times during my term in office, twice successfully. In 1981, I looked back over my first four years with a tremendous sense of accomplishment, and also with a new image of myself. The office had not changed me, as I had vowed not to let it; I was the same person, with the same beliefs and positions, and the same demeanor. What was new was the way I thought of myself and my job. I liked being mayor, and I thought I was quite good at it. There were times when I convinced myself that I was born for the job and could not imagine myself holding any other office. There must have also been times when I convinced others I was born for the mayoralty as well. That's the only way I can explain the election results from that year. I was returned to office with an astonishing 75 percent of the vote, due in large measure to the unusual endorsement of the Republican Party. I became the only mayor in the history of the city to receive the designation, after contested primaries in both parties, of the Democrats and the Republicans.

Shortly after the beginning of my second term, I made an ill-advised and ill-fated decision to enter New York's 1982 gubernatorial campaign. This was another time for taking stock and measuring my impact in office. Once again, I came away pleased at my accomplishments and grateful for the renewed opportunity, although for some reason I chose to let my reach exceed my grasp. I really don't know why I entered the race, now that I've had ten years to think about it. It was, I suppose, a decision born of equal parts hubris and chutzpah. After all, New Yorkers had just given me the biggest majority in the city's history. How could I possibly abandon them? Why would I want to? And, how could anyone ever again take me seriously after my much-discussed pledge—made at the Western Wall in Jerusalem, no less—that I would never seek higher office? What in the world got into me?

In my defense, I should point out that the seeds of the idea actually took root without me. I was out of the country, in mid-January 1982, vacationing in Spain with David Garth, Dan Wolf, and David and Barbara Margolis, when the *New York Post* began a coupon campaign to draft me for governor. Soon, other papers and pundits began to kick the idea around. The coincidental fact that I was out of the country, with David Garth and other close advisers, just two days after Governor Hugh Carey announced his decision not to seek reelection, simply fueled the speculation, and by the time I returned home to Kennedy Airport, my party and I were met in the lounge by a crowd of reporters, eager to know my intentions. I had no intentions, not at that point anyway, but I was by this time a seasoned politician, so I kept my options open. Why not? Privately, I was flattered at what I saw as a draft-Koch movement, and I wanted to see where it would take me.

I have written about my race for governor before, and others have second-guessed and dissected my campaign endlessly, so I won't dwell on it here. Let the record simply show that I was beaten in the September 23, 1982, Democratic primary by Lieutenant Governor Mario

Cuomo, in a race decided by less than 6 percentage points. Let the record also show that I made some foolish mistakes prior to the campaign—such as telling *Playboy* magazine, with foot in mouth, that living in the suburbs was "sterile," and that rural living was "a joke," when the majority of the state population lived in rural or suburban areas—and that I was made to suffer for those remarks, personally and politically. Further, let the record show that the Cuomo camp once again returned to the smear tactics first used in 1977, reviving the covert "Vote for Cuomo, Not the Homo" campaign against me. (Bernard Ryan, Cuomo's northeastern campaign coordinator, rekindled the slander in an appearance at an upstate college; true to form, Cuomo did not admonish or fire him.) And finally, let the record also show that I conceded the close primary to my supporters with grace and good cheer: "First, don't shed a tear," my concession speech began. "It is better to win than to lose. But if we have done everything we can and the people decided otherwise, that is the nature of the democratic system, and so I have no regrets. And I'm still the mayor. And that's not bad. In fact, it's good."

Indeed, it was. And it would be so for the balance of my second term. It wasn't until January 1986—just two months after I was reelected to a third term as mayor with 78 percent of the vote, and just two weeks after my third term officially began—that things began to sour.

The honeymoon was finally over.

8

Queens

MY THIRD TERM AS MAYOR was marked by a major political crisis, and I don't think I'm overstating the case to admit that the corruption crisis aged me, affected my health, and probably contributed to my having a stroke. For a while, it certainly diminished my reputation, my effectiveness, and my usual enthusiasm. At a certain point, it almost cost me my life. I'll explain.

On Friday, January 10, 1986, just ten days into my third term, I was awakened by a 3 A.M. phone call from a police officer. Queens Borough President and Democratic Party county leader Donald Manes had been found in his car, on a Queens highway near Shea Stadium, bleeding to death from knife wounds to his wrist and ankle. It was a shocking and disturbing call, but that was all the officer knew. I immediately dressed, and left Gracie Mansion for the emergency room at Booth Memorial Medical Center, in Flushing, Queens, where Manes had been taken.

I learned on the way that the police were baffled by the circumstances of the incident. There was no evidence of foul play, and yet there was no clear indication of what had happened to Donald, who had been seriously hurt. Manes, conscious at the time he was found but not entirely lucid, supplied no explanation for his condition. When I arrived at the hospital, he was still in no shape to talk. The doctors told me he had lost a third of his blood.

In fact, he wound up losing half of his blood. I offered to donate some of mine, but I was told they had an adequate supply.

Over the next several days, Manes gave several explanations for the mysterious incident. At first he claimed not to know what had happened. Later, he said he had been kidnapped by two black men, who were hiding in his car. Bizarrely, he said, one of them had a black face and white hands. Ben Ward, the police commissioner, said, "This man will not be hard to find." Finally, he admitted that he had attempted suicide, for what he claimed were "personal reasons."

Manes's suicide attempt was front page news in the city, and elsewhere in the country; the events that drove him to try to take his own life remained on the front page for the next several months. And it didn't take long for me, as the mayor and his friend, to be dragged onto the front page with them.

It developed, of course, that Manes's suicide attempt was not made for personal reasons, although it took several days for the true reasons to emerge. As he recovered in his hospital bed, and as I visited him a second time (and hugged him, and kissed him on the brow, and told him everything would be okay), details of the corruption scandal that drove Manes to this desperate act began to surface.

The unraveling disgrace at the Parking Violations Bureau, the subunit of the New York City Department of Transportation charged with the collection of parking fines, turned on the involvement of the corrupt PVB director, Geoffrey Lindenauer, an obese crook who was one of Donald Manes's closest friends. Lindenauer positioned his own company, Citisource, Inc., in which Manes and Bronx county leader Stanley Friedman also had an interest, as the low bidder for a city contract to produce a hand-held computer intended to help police and traffic agents instantly learn the ticketing history of any vehicle simply by entering in a valid license-plate number. At the time of the bidding, Citisource had no assets or engineers. They had no apparent physical plant. They didn't even have a working prototype. Their ability to produce more than one thousand of these computers for the city was alleged solely by Lindenauer. That was enough for the PVB to award the company a contract for $22.7 million.

Further, it was revealed that Manes had received thirty-six thousand dollars, over a period of eighteen months, from a Queens attorney whom I knew from the Cuomo mayoral campaign staff of 1977. The attorney was none other than Michael Dowd. He had served as Cuomo's campaign manager in that 1977 mayoralty race, and had engineered the smear campaign against me. Once again, I was reminded how small a city like New York can sometimes be. Dowd claimed he regularly paid off Manes in order to win valuable PVB contracts for his collection agency. This, evidently, was standard operating procedure. At the time, there were nearly a dozen collection agencies regularly employed by the PVB to collect unpaid parking fines, a service for which the agencies received as much as several million dollars each in commissions. I was not surprised that Dowd had sunk so low as to pay bribes for lucrative contracts—after all, he didn't have that far to go—but I was astonished to learn of Manes's corruption, as was everyone, including his critics in government and in the news media.

The related scams revealed themselves quite by accident. Investigators on a similar case in Chicago happened to intercept a telephone conversation suggesting the corruption in New York's PVB, and the matter was referred to the U.S. Attorney in the Southern District, Rudolph Giuliani, for further investigation. Until this chance revelation, no law enforcement agency—city, state, or federal—or investigative reporters had detected that corruption.

When the depths of the scandal became known, I accepted full political responsibility. It happened on my watch. I had never met Lindenauer, who had been appointed to the PVB in 1977 before I was mayor. Manes was an independently elected official. He had been borough president for four years before I became mayor. Stanley Friedman did not serve in my government. He was the elected Democratic county leader in the Bronx. He had served as Abe Beame's deputy mayor and had been appointed by Beame to a lifetime sinecure on the city's Water Board, which early in my administration I got the legislature to abolish as unnecessary, depriving him of that position. But the incident did take place on my watch, and I was quick to acknowledge that. As an administrator, this was my problem, even if it was not my doing. Regrettably, with more than three hundred thousand city employees, most of them civil servants, it was inevitable that a relatively small number turned out to be dishonest. Wherever there is money and opportunity, weak people will succumb to temptation. That's just human nature, and even government is not immune to human nature. Indeed, every year, the Department of Investigation of the City of New York, our in-house investigatory body, looked for instances of corruption and turned them over to the U.S. Attorney or the District Attorney. Hundreds of people were prosecuted each year during my administration, although most of them were low-level inspectors or functionaries. This, as it played out, was something else entirely.

I was embarrassed, chagrined, and mortified that such high-level corruption could have existed and that I did not know of it. I had considered Donald Manes a good and trusted friend. We had served together in the city council in the 1960s. He was a bright and able borough president. The people of Queens apparently shared my opinion of him. They reelected him four times, the last time with 85 percent of the vote. He received the editorial endorsement of every newspaper in the city that weighed in with an opinion. Insiders speculated about his political future, which might have included a run for mayor, or United States Senator. I would have made him executor of my estate, and rested easily in my grave.

But I was wrong in my judgment, as were others. In the end, Donald Manes betrayed all of us. To my mind, there is no greater betrayal than that of the public trust. Manes also betrayed my personal trust; his actions, and those of Stanley Friedman, did more to undermine the stature of public service than anything else that happened during my three terms. They also undermined my first eight years in office, and my credibility, and I had to fight like hell to get things back to where they had been. One of the ways I chose to do this, in the early, uncertain days of the investigation, was to confront Manes in a very public and direct way, urging him to come clean with a full disclosure of his involvement. He did not do this, so I pressed on.

By Saturday, January 25, 1986, as the allegations against him mounted, I called for Manes's resignation. "I believe if he does not step aside in the next day or two," I told a reporter from United Press International, "then he will have to be removed by due process, and that process is called impeachment."

Manes, recuperating at home from his self-inflicted wounds, and an ensuing heart attack, did not respond to press inquiries, or my own. He did not issue a statement admitting or denying the charges against him. His only public response came the following Tuesday, when he took a temporary leave from his post and handed over the borough presidency to Claire Shulman, later elected borough president of Queens in her own right. By the end of the week, I was telling reporters that Manes's temporary leave was not good enough; I was determined to drive him out of office permanently, and I was infuriated that he had yet to make a public statement on the matter. "He can't stay in his house forever," I told reporters.

When Manes finally did surface, he said little. He attacked me for calling him a crook. He even called me a Nazi. And he tried to suggest that some of the allegations against him should perhaps be redirected toward me. On February 11, he finally resigned as borough president and county leader. Privately, his friends worried about

Manes's mounting depression, and that the case against him was building to where he might seek to take his life again. (There was a history of suicide in his family.) My only concern was to see him tried, and hopefully convicted, along with Friedman and Lindenauer and all the others.

Now the press sought to implicate me. I couldn't open a newspaper, or turn on the television or radio, without learning of some new attack against my integrity. The message—sometimes subtle, sometimes not—was always the same: Koch must have known. When did he know? What did he know? What did he do about it? These were the questions asked about Richard Nixon, after Watergate, and the same ones that would be asked about Ronald Reagan, when the Iran-Contra scandal surfaced later in 1986.

The *Daily News* editorial board was then in the control of an editor for whom I had only contempt, Michael Pakenham; he was uninformed and lacked the judgment needed for his powerful position, but he became the leader of the pack against me. He was joined by everyone else whom I had injured by an insulting remark or with my moderate, middle-class approach to government, particularly reporters and politicians on the radical left—white, black, and Hispanic.

Jimmy Breslin was one of my more formidable attackers. Unfortunately, Breslin is a terrific writer. I say this is unfortunate because often what he writes is fiction, and he's so good at what he does that people mistake it for the truth. Breslin had always been very critical of me, which was indeed his privilege, but I thought he was grossly unfair. At the beginning of this scandal, he predicted on "Larry King Live!" that I would be out of office in six months. He meant that I would resign or be removed. I was only a few months into my third term, having been reelected with an overwhelming majority, and here he was predicting I would be judged unfit to remain in office.

I thought to myself, You dog! You're one of the most

intellectually dishonest reporters in the country. I was furious, and determined to respond in kind.

You have to understand, Breslin was a close friend of Donald Manes. Manes was corrupt. He was a close friend of Michael Dowd. Dowd was corrupt. Breslin had another friend, an attorney referred to in his columns by the pseudonym Klein the lawyer, who was also found to be corrupt. He was a close friend of City Marshall Chevlowe, who was corrupt. Breslin was an investigative reporter. If four of his close friends were involved in the scandal, and he didn't know about it, then how should I have known?

I responded at the first real opportunity, which happened to come on a subsequent Larry King show. When King asked about Breslin's comments I dismissed them, and him, with these words: "I will deliver the eulogy at his funeral." It was undoubtedly a harsh statement, even for me, and I took a lot of criticism for it, but I wanted to make clear that I would outlast him, and outlive him.

I understood these attacks against me, on a rational level, but I could not bear them. After all, I was the big fish, the mayor of the city of New York; it was only natural that they came after me. On an irrational level, though, I was scared to death. Really, I was petrified. I knew that under the rules of evidence in a federal court, corroboration isn't needed to make a case. All that's required is for the jury to decide who is telling the truth. Indictments were being handed down right and left. Who was to say they wouldn't indict me? I never knew when someone like Geoffrey Lindenauer, Manes's bagman, might falsely accuse me, or when one of the others would perjure themselves and implicate me in exchange for a lesser sentence, even though I wasn't involved at all. I was frightened, and I was alone. This was one of those times when a wife and children would have been of special comfort, to help diffuse the tension and anxiety of this ordeal, to offer a safe haven, and common sense. But I had no one. I had a lot of friends and supporters, and a loyal staff, but it was not the same thing.

Alone, I became irrational in my fear. I found it hard to get to sleep each night, and harder to get up each morning. It was like being in a Kafka novel. I mean, I hadn't done anything corrupt. I didn't appoint Geoffrey Lindenauer. (Not only did I not appoint him, but my administration had prevented his promotion, on the merits, as well.) I didn't elect Donald Manes and Stanley Friedman. I didn't know those things were going on. But none of that mattered to my accusers, who were growing in number. Every day, it seemed, there was another column or editorial attacking me. And they were all excoriating. Maybe I was reading more into them than was really there, but I don't think so.

Manes, meanwhile, sank further into his depression. He hired an attorney to represent him in his defense. He spoke to some reporters, mostly to criticize me for calling him a crook. He appeared to be cooperating in the investigation, at least on the surface. Then, he once again retreated from the public glare, and once again fell silent.

On Thursday, March 13th, I was hosting a reception and dinner at Gracie Mansion for the New York State Assembly, when I took a call at about ten o'clock from Police Commissioner Ben Ward.

"Donald Manes has stabbed himself in the heart and has been taken to the hospital," Ward said.

"How bad is it?" I said.

"It doesn't look good," Ward replied, "but they are keeping him alive on machines."

I decided it would be better not to go to the hospital until I had a clearer picture of Manes's condition. About a half-hour later, the point became moot. Ward called back to say that Manes was dead. He also related the circumstances of his suicide: Manes, in a state of agitation after a telephone conversation with his psychiatrist, and in the presence of his twenty-five-year-old daughter, Lauren, took out a kitchen knife and stabbed himself in the heart. The daughter apparently saw her father playing with the knife, then turned away momentarily; when she turned back, she saw her father with the knife in his chest. Marlene Manes heard Lauren's screams and came rushing into the kitchen, where she found her husband lying face up on the floor. She removed the knife from her husband's chest and flung it to the side. Then she passed out.

What a horror story. What a tragedy.

I decided I should go to the funeral, even though I knew I might not be welcomed by the Manes family, and though it was probably not in my best political interests to be there. I agonized over this decision. There were many city leaders, I knew, who would not be in attendance, and I did not think that was right. After all, despite his recent troubles, Donald Manes had, in many ways, served the city well for a great many years. We had worked together and enjoyed a friendly relationship. Nevertheless, I had been extremely critical of Manes in the past two months, as the extent of his corruption became known, and I did not want to go against the wishes of his family.

I wanted to do the right thing, but I didn't know what that was, so I called Claire Shulman the next morning and asked her to intercede on my behalf. "I would like to be there," I told her, "but not if it's an embarrassment to Marlene. I don't want an incident. Would you call her for me and find out if she would like me to be there?"

A few hours later, Shulman called back. "Marlene said it is okay with her if you come," she said, "but this is not an invitation."

I thought to myself, Not only is this less than an invitation, it's a rejection. Perhaps I should stay away. But I wanted to be sure, so I had a letter hand-delivered to Manes's widow, expressing my condolences and my desire to attend the funeral. She responded with a telephone call, which I was not in to receive.

I finally reached her on the car phone. "Marlene," I said, "this is Ed."

"Ed," she said, "I got your letter. Thank you. I would very much like for you to come."

"I'm so glad," I said. "I want us to be friends."

"Of course," she said.

So I went. I kissed Marlene and shook hands with her two daughters, and with her son. I then sat in the first pew, where I was joined by Governor Cuomo and his wife, Matilda. The service was brief. There were two speakers: Rabbi Israel Moskowitz and Assemblyman Alan Hevesi, who was a close friend of Manes's. Neither speech was terribly uplifting, but how could they be?

I made a foolish mistake outside the chapel. As I walked outside, I was met by a handful of reporters. I have never shied away from the press, and even on this somber occasion I saw no reason not to stop and answer their questions. Cuomo just walked right past these reporters, without comment, but I could never do that. My mistake was in allowing my advance man, Peter Kohlmann, to set up the microphone stand, which he always carried in his car. He kept one handy as an aid to the reporters. A microphone stand allows the reporters to make a larger circle; without it, they have to crowd around and muscle in to ask their questions. The problem was, though, that it looked like I was holding a prepared press conference. To the press it looked premeditated, as if I was using the funeral as a platform, an opportunity to advance my own innocence, and that was not what I'd intended. I should have anticipated that.

Even with Manes gone, the corruption crisis continued. In fact, it kicked up a notch. In death, Manes became a ready symbol for all that was wrong with city government. My public approval rating sank to an all-time low. I had flown so high, and now my critics took great delight in bringing me down. Each day held a new attack against me. Before all of this, I used to spring out of bed, go to the gym, and then to the office. I was an upbeat person. I looked forward to each day and what it promised. Now I worried about what each new day would bring. There was a great weight on my shoulders. I was so weary. I was overwhelmed by the shame of it all. There were times—alone at night, or behind a closed office door—when I wept. How could this be happening to me? I despaired. I'm an honest guy in a world where that is not the coin of the realm.

My integrity was the most important thing to me; my good name meant more to me than anything else I had. I couldn't stand the thought that the people of New York City had turned on me, that when I stepped out into a crowd there would be those who thought I was a crook. It was unbearable. I never minded if people disliked me for the positions I took, or for the things I said, but I simply could not accept that people might think I was dishonest.

I suffered enormously. The newspapers were hectoring me every day. It was difficult to get out of bed in the morning, knowing not only that I would have to read the papers and all the terrible things being said about me, but also that those writing the stories knew I was honest and set out to attack me anyway. Their job was to sell papers, no matter the cost. I didn't think there was any letter I could send, or correction I could demand, that would ameliorate the damage to my reputation.

In August, under these clouds, I attended a Special Olympics event in the Bronx, which I hoped would distract me from the swirl of negative publicity. The activities were run by volunteers, many from the Archdiocese of New York. One of the key figures involved in the event was Father John J. Kowsky, who was the police department chaplain. I knew him very well, through our too-frequent meetings at the hospital bedsides or funerals of our fallen police officers. I really liked him, and I knew that he liked me as well.

I took the helicopter from the Sixty-third Street heliport to the Bronx, and we landed near the field where the track meet was to take place. Even though this was to be a nice outing, celebrating the abilities of our physically and mentally handicapped children, I didn't feel particularly happy. The horrendous news reporting was wearing me down.

Father Kowsky waved to me as I got out of the helicopter. "Mayor," he said, "can I be frank with you?"

Oh, God, I thought, he's going to lecture me. So I steeled myself and said, "Of course, Father."

"I mean really candid?" he said.

I steeled myself even more and said, "Yes, Father."

"Fuck 'em," he said.

He didn't need to elaborate. He knew my pain, and he found precisely the right tone and phrase to make the difference. I was so grateful.

I have another Father Kowsky story, which I will slip in here. When I ran for my third term as mayor, he volunteered to work on my campaign. He said he thought he should do some phone work, since it might not look right for a priest in a collar to be handing out literature on my behalf. So he was put in one of the phone banks. He told those in charge of the phone bank that he thought his name sounded Jewish (he was Polish) and suggested that he call the Jewish voters. They agreed, and handed him the phone lists for our Jewish neighborhoods. His spiel went something like this:

"Hello, my name is Kowsky. I am calling you to urge you to vote to reelect Ed Koch. He's been a great mayor, and he's one of ours!"

I couldn't believe my ears. He was amazing. I felt like hugging him. He had a heart condition and wasn't supposed to continue with all of the activities he was involved in, but he never stopped ministering to the cops. When he died, I went to his funeral and wept. He was a special man, and a special friend.

There were good friends who sustained me during this trying period—Allen Schwartz, most of all, but also Stan Brezenoff, Dan Wolf, Diane Coffey, Pat Mulhearn, John LoCicero, and a few others—but even their attempts at consolation were not enough. It was a very painful time. There were even moments when I thought seriously of killing myself. I really did. I thought about it in tactical terms, and I thought about it in spiritual terms. I thought about Donald Manes, about how he was free, in a way, from all the pain and turmoil now confronting me. Of course, I knew, I could not kill myself in quite that way, but I did play out the scenario in my head. I ran through a bunch of ways, and came up with reasons for discounting each. I could cut my wrists and sit in the bathtub, I thought, but that would be messy, and painful, and unpleasant. I could take a whole bottle of aspirins, but with my luck they probably wouldn't kill me. I would come out a vegetable. I didn't have a car, or a closed garage, so exhaust fumes were out. I couldn't jump out my window—Gracie Mansion is only two stories high, and I could never get to an open high-rise window without attracting too much attention. I was always in the presence of my security detectives protecting me from others.

If only I had a gun . . .

Thank God I had convinced Bob McGuire to remove that gun from my bathroom safe all those years ago. If I had had it, at that vulnerable point, I really think I might have used it. A gun would have done the job nicely, cleanly, quickly. I think it's entirely possible that if I had had a gun nearby, in the spring and summer of 1986, I would not be here today. I don't know that I would have willfully held the thing to my head and fired, but I might have taken it out and played with it, contemplating my next move. I might have accidentally pulled the trigger without really meaning to. Or—who knows?—in my weakest moment, I might have just determined to get the whole ordeal over with.

I was in absolute, unrelenting agony. I knew my family would be distraught if I took my life in any of these ways, but I was so dispirited I sometimes saw no other way around it. I felt that my brother and sister would be better equipped to handle the mess I left behind than I was able to deal with the pain I was suffering.

I don't know how I came through this period whole and sane, but somehow I did. The swirl of negative publicity surrounding those scandals almost killed me, in more ways than I have just described. I believe that my anxious and depressed state of mind was a contributing factor in my 1987 stroke, but I'll get to that.

Let me first tie up the loose ends on the PVB corruption crisis. In November, Lindenauer, Friedman, and the lesser players were all found guilty on all major counts against them. The city also sought to sue the estate of Donald Manes, claiming that his ill-gotten monies should be returned. (A settlement with his widow was ultimately reached.)

"These convictions are a frightening example of what greed can do to people who have somehow lost their moral bearings," I said in a prepared statement following the verdict. "All of these men had achieved degrees of success, but for them that was not enough. As a result, they undermined not only their own lives, but they destroyed those lives and severely injured the body politic. They made tangible the cynicism with which too many people unfairly view government and politics. We do not live in a pure society, but believe me, this government will continue to make every effort and strain every resource at our command to root out corruption wherever it exists. I promise you that."

Michael Dowd became a witness for the prosecution and received immunity from prosecutor Rudolph Giuliani for his cooperation in the case. Of course, Giuliani could not protect the corrupt attorney from disciplinary action, which was taken by the Disciplinary Committee of the Appellate Division. Dowd was suspended from the practice of law for five years. But then, in one of the most infuriating twists of my entire political career, Governor Cuomo rescued Dowd from professional oblivion by appointing him director of special projects and advocacy for the Office of Domestic Violence, at a salary of sixty thousand dollars. Such a reward from the governor, for a man who had so sullied himself, who had admitted to his role in the corruption but avoided an indictment by testifying against a principal accessory, was incomprehensible and reprehensible, both. With this appointment, the governor demonstrated the same insensitivity to the people of New York City that he had shown to me and my campaign nearly ten years earlier.

My unexpected public supporter was the prosecutor, Rudolph Giuliani. He, more than anyone else, helped to restore the public trust in me, and in my administration. I have problems with a lot of things Giuliani did as U.S. Attorney. I have problems with a lot of the positions he took during the 1989 mayoral campaign. But, on this important occasion for me, Giuliani was a mensch. Regrettably, when he ran for mayor several years later he was not as honorable in his comments.

Even after the trial, there were continuing whispers and speculation in and around City Hall that I had somehow been involved in the corruption scandal, that I had dodged a bullet. People still believed that I knew something, at some point, on some level, no matter that the evidence or testimony had proved otherwise. It was in this climate that Giuliani voluntarily came to my defense. At a public meeting one night, he responded to a question about my involvement in the scam, saying, "I think I know as much about these investigations as anyone knows, including a lot of confidential material, and there's not a single shred of evidence or suggestion that Major Koch knew of crimes that were being committed by several of the Democratic leaders and the borough presidents, or had any involvement in those crimes or would have done anything other than turn them in if he had found out about them." Only one newspaper carried his statement: *New York Newsday*. Even when I'm otherwise angry with them, I remember that important and decent action with thanks.

I was deeply moved by Giuliani's expression of faith in my integrity, and I called him at his office to thank him. "Rudy," I said, "I don't want to embarrass you, but I want to tell you I appreciate what you said about me."

"Mr. Mayor," he said, "please don't thank me. There is no reason to thank me, and I'll tell you why. When I was a young lawyer, I was trying a case before Judge Edward Weinfeld [an esteemed federal judge]. I made a motion and he granted it. And I thanked him. Well, the judge called me aside and said to me, 'Young man, never, ever in this court say thank you to me again. Whatever I do, I do on the merits.' And what I'm saying to you, Mr. Mayor, is you don't have to thank me. I said what I said about you because it was true."

Giuliani's unsolicited defense was a very important and ethical act on his part, and I was reminded of it about two years later, in the fall of 1988, after my friend Bess Myerson, her boyfriend Andy Capasso, and Justice Hortense W. Gabel were acquitted of federal corruption charges. The press was really on Giuliani's case, attacking him following the verdict. The charges against Bess and her codefendants were based on testimony from Sukhreet Gabel, the justice's somewhat bizarre daughter. Giuliani's case rested on the assumption that Bess had given Sukhreet Gabel a job in return for Justice Gabel's favoring Capasso in his divorce proceedings. As such, many people thought it was an unprovable case and should never have been brought to trial.

After the verdict, a number of reporters called me for comment; they were probably expecting me to blast Giuliani because of my friendship with Bess, and because it was widely rumored that the U.S. Attorney was planning to run for the Republican nomination for mayor, which would have pitted the two of us against each other in the general election, provided each of us won our respective primaries. (In my case, this turned out otherwise.) The reporters smelled a good story. I told them I was delighted with Bess's acquittal, but surprised them by supporting Giuliani's decision to bring the case to trial. He had an obligation to do so, I said. The government had a prima facie case against the defendants, and when the grand jury issued its indictments, the prosecutor had no choice but to go forward.

A few weeks later, I happened to be at midnight mass at

St. Patrick's Cathedral, on Christmas Eve. Giuliani was there with his wife, Donna, and their son. "Mr. Mayor," he said, approaching me. "I want to thank you for your comments. My staff and I have been under attack, our morale was very low, and what you said meant a lot to all of us, especially to me."

"Rudy, what I said was on the merits," I replied, thinking of Judge Weinfeld. "So don't thank me for saying what I believe to be true."

But back in the fall of 1986, even Giuliani's public absolution was not enough to lift the clouds that would follow me throughout most of my third term. It was a long, arduous three years before I was able to put the corruption crisis behind me. In the interim, I immersed myself in my work. There, I was able to distract myself from my critics, and from adversarial reporters. One of the richest, most fulfilling distractions took me far outside the boundaries of New York City. In November 1987, I made an eye-opening trip to Central America, as part of the Central American Peace and Democracy Watch, put together by former Virginia Governor, now Senator, Charles Robb. Our New York delegation, which I organized, was charged with helping to monitor compliance of the Esquipulas Accords, or Arias Peace Plan, which had been signed by five Central American nations the previous summer.

I was delighted at the opportunity to help carry out and assist U.S. policy in that all-important region, even in this small way. I also welcomed the chance to put some distance between myself and the reporters at City Hall, even if it was only for a few days, although many denizens of Room Nine accompanied us. I was familiar with the issues, having, in the 1970s, led the fight in Congress, along with Representative Don Fraser, to cut off military aid to the Somoza regime, so I was no doubt tabbed by Robb as a knowledgeable person who was interested in events in the region.

Our delegation included Ted Sorenson; the president of Hostos College, Isuara Santiago; the executive director of the Urban League, Harriet Michel; the former public official Richard Ravitch, who was later to run for mayor against me; the president of WMCA, Peter Strauss; and labor leader Charlie Hughes, among others. We met with the author of the peace accord, President Oscar Arias of Costa Rica, and with Presidents Cerezo of Guatemala, Ascona of Honduras, and Duarte of El Salvador, all involved and able leaders. The most impressive of the five leaders was President Daniel Ortega of Nicaragua, who was the youngest and most charismatic leader in the region. Head of the Sandinista revolution, a Marxist-Leninist, he and I had met before. As a Congressman, I had supported the Sandinistas in their ultimately successful efforts to overthrow the corrupt regime of Somoza.

Years later, after I had been elected mayor, Ortega came to New York with Miguel DeScoto, the foreign minister of Nicaragua. The two men attended a West Side fund-raiser for their country, hosted by my former law partner Victor Kovner, and his wife, Sarah. At one point during the evening, DeScoto turned to Kovner and said, "You know, there was a Congressman who helped us against Somoza. His name was Koch. Whatever happened to him?"

Of course, when the Sandinistas betrayed the revolution and turned their government into one that was, in their own description, "Marxist-Leninist," I left them and supported their opponents, the new revolutionaries known as the Contras. But on that night in Managua's central square, Ortega singled me out before an estimated one hundred thousand of his supporters, departing from his speech to tell the crowd that I had helped the Sandinistas by leading the fight to cut off aid to Somoza. He called me a friend of the Sandinistas, and said that I was safer here in Managua than I was in my own city of New York. This, after Ortega led the crowd in the chant, "Allí, Allá, Yanqui Moridá!" ("Here, there, Yankees will die!")

But despite Ortega's public charm, intended for our public benefit, we were denied our private meeting. At least it appeared that way. On our last full day in Nicaragua, we were told that we would be unable to meet with the President, but that the Vice President, Sergio Ramirez, would be made available. This was unacceptable. I had met with the other four signatories to the peace accord, and I expected an audience with Ortega. We decided that if we agreed to see the Vice President, then we would never see Ortega, so we declined the invitation.

By five o'clock in the afternoon of our last day, we were told there would be a meeting with Ortega, but we were not told where or when it would take place. We were running out of time. By nine-thirty in the evening, we had still not heard anything. We were told by Ortega's advance people that they did not know when the President would be through with his appointments.

Finally, at about eleven o'clock at night, we were notified at our hotel that Ortega was ready to receive our delegation at his home. We climbed into our tour bus and drove to an opulent section of Managua that resembled Great Neck, Long Island—manicured lawns, lavish homes. We had not seen this part of town on our official tour, and it stood in marked contrast to other, impoverished sections of the city. Managua had been decimated by an earthquake several years earlier and never rebuilt.

When we arrived at his home, Ortega came outside to greet us. He was dressed in military fatigues. He had a very warm handshake. We went through the usual formalities and pleasantries, during which I presented him with two New York Yankees baseball jerseys, which Yankee owner George Steinbrenner had given to me for this purpose. I also gave him six Yankees baseball caps, and six Mets caps.

"I like the Yankees," Ortega said, in English, with a broad smile.

"You didn't last night, Mr. President," I replied, referring to the "Yanqui Moridá" chants from the night before.

He laughed, pointed to one of the jerseys, and said,

"These Yankees, I like." He understands English, but rarely speaks it.

The formal portion of our meeting took place in an open-air atrium, Spanish style. I sat next to Ortega. It was late, and I did not want the President to take up all of our time with a prepared speech, so I suggested that we begin the session with questions from delegation members, to which Ortega could respond and tell us whatever it was he wanted us to know. He graciously agreed.

I began the questioning. "I want to talk to you about El Chipote," I said, referring to the infamous Nicaraguan prison and interrogation center, where the cells were said to be so narrow the prisoners were forced to sleep while standing. "The world believes, as I do, that it is a place in which people are tortured. Maybe it is not true. Maybe this is a libel against your government. But the fact remains that you have never allowed on-site inspection of the prison, and I have met people who have said that they were tortured there. Some said they were beaten, and some claimed they were deprived of food. One man told us that he was without food for twenty days. That is torture."

"We do not torture anyone there," he said. "I would not allow it." He responded through an interpreter. His English, we were told, was adequate, and in our small talk he spoke English, but he obviously wanted to use the language barrier to his advantage, giving him more time to reflect on his answers.

"Isn't it true, Mr. President," I challenged, "that you were in El Chipote and you were tortured under Somoza?"

He lifted his hand to his forehead, put a finger to a scar, and said, "That is true."

"Why don't we go out there tonight and see for ourselves?" I presumptuously suggested.

"No," he said, "that wouldn't make sense. Even if we did go, and found nothing, your people would say that I had called ahead."

"You are probably right," I said. "Then why don't you agree to have the International Red Cross, or Americas Watch, go in to see the prisoners?"

"I will consider it," he said.

I pressed him to make a decision on this matter within thirty days, and he said he would.

I then moved on to discuss the specific cases of four Nicaraguan prisoners, whose names had been given to us by their families, seeking clemency. I told the President we didn't know anything about the individual prisoners, but that we felt an obligation to present them for his consideration.

Ortega looked at our list of names, and almost immediately shook his head. "You wouldn't want this one released," he said, with sincerity, indicating the first name on our list. "He is a murderer. He has killed children."

"As I told you, we can not vouch for these people," I replied, "but I will tell you that his mother thinks he is a good boy."

"So did Adolf Hitler's mother," Ortega said.

I thought that was a superb response. I directed him to the other names on the list.

"One of these others looks okay," he said. "The other two I am not sure of."

"If I were Jesse Jackson," I joked, "you would give me all four," referring to an earlier visit Jackson had made to the region.

"Ah, but you are wrong, Mr. Mayor," he said, smiling again. "Jesse Jackson was here and I didn't give him any. But I may give you two."

At the time, many believed Ortega was being duplicitous in his effort to comply with the accords, but I did not share this opinion after our meeting. Rather, I found him to be sincerely interested in the prospects for democracy, and genuine in his desire for a lasting peace in Central America; he was charismatic and extremely convincing. I also recognized that there were other powerful Sandinistas, such as Tomas Borge, the minister of the Interior, who might seek to subvert Ortega's policy of complying with the accords.

When I returned to New York City, I offered my impressions of the man, and the region, to the Council on Foreign Relations, and resumed the more direct obligations of my office. In the years since our visit, there has been an enormous change in the region and Violeta Barrios de Chamorro and the Contras won a democratically run election against Ortega and the Sandinistas. Without the shedding of more blood, the reins of power were turned over to Mrs. Chamorro, who became president. I believe that our delegation, and others which followed, played a constructive role; the State Department, I am told, shared that view.

While I wanted Mrs. Chamorro to win, I still had a feeling that Ortega could one day peacefully resume power and carry out the original revolution, this time democratically. When Mrs. Chamorro visited City Hall the December before the election, few thought she stood a chance. In fact, her alliance was so strapped for funds that she arrived at City Hall by taxi, instead of by the customary limousine. When I heard this, I offered her the use of my city car, and my driver drove her and her party back to their hotel.

On a strictly personal level, there were other third-term distractions to divert me from the persistent charges of corruption. Chiefly, there was my stroke, on August 6, 1987, to which I referred earlier. I was speaking at the Sheraton Center Hotel at a *New York Post* forum on AIDS. Afterward, I went off to visit a welfare facility in Harlem. When we got to Seventy-third Street and Third Avenue, I realized that I wasn't listening to the commissioner of the Human Resources Agency, Bill Grinker, who was sitting beside me. That wasn't like me. When I tried to speak, the words didn't come out right. That wasn't like me, either. I knew instinctively that I was having a stroke.

I tapped the detective, Eddie Martinez, sitting in the front passenger seat and said, "Eddie, I'm having a stroke.

Take me to Lenox Hill Hospital," which was about six blocks away. Then for some reason, it occurred to me that the press would undoubtedly interview everyone in the car and ask, "What did he say before he died?" I didn't want the public to think I had no confidence in the municipal hospitals, so I added, "And if you can't get to Lenox quickly, take me to Bellevue." (This was hardly likely, since Bellevue was at least forty blocks away.)

When I got to Lenox Hill about two minutes later, there were several doctors waiting for me in the emergency room, and the press, I was later told, started arriving in droves. The stroke's grip came and went several times, affecting my eyesight and distorting my face. I was then placed in the intensive-care unit. My sister and brother and their families were the first to come and see me.

The next visitor was Rabbi Arthur Schneier of Park East Synagogue, of which I am a member. He said, "Ed, I'm not going to stay very long, you have to sleep, but I want you to say with me in Hebrew and English the prayer asking for God's intercession." The prayer is simple: "Heal me and I shall be healed, save me and I shall be saved." I repeated the prayer with the rabbi, and he left.

Ten minutes later, Cardinal John O'Connor came. The cardinal and I are friends. I have requested that when I die he participate in the funeral ceremony. He has agreed to do so. He said, when he entered the room, "Ed, I'm not going to stay very long. You have to sleep." Apparently, that's what everyone says when they enter the room of someone they think is dying. He went on: "I want you to know you are in my prayers, and if you would like, I'll pray for you in Hebrew."

"Your Eminence," I responded, "I've taken care of the Hebrew. Would you try a little Latin?"

Four days later, I left the hospital without any diminution in motor function or cerebral faculties. Most people agreed with the first premise, although the second was contested by some of my critics. The doctor said that I had to take a week off and rest. That's not so difficult to agree with when you're living at Gracie Mansion. I went home. The next Sunday, while I was sitting on the porch, the cop at the gate called on the telephone and said, "Mr. Mayor, a car just pulled up and there are four nuns in it, and one says she's Mother Teresa." It was about three o'clock on a hot August afternoon.

"That's hardly likely," I said. "I know Mother Teresa, so keep them there, and I'll be right down." When I approached the car, sure enough, it was Mother Teresa. "Mother," I said, "what are you doing here?"

"I knew you were ill, Ed," she said. "You are in my prayers, and I came to see how you're doing."

"Mother," I told her happily, "your prayers are working. I'm doing fine." I asked her to stay and sit with me awhile, so she got out of the car with the sisters. I took her by the hand, and we skipped up the path toward the porch overlooking the East River. The three nuns followed behind us, and I remember thinking it was just like a movie.

"Mother," I asked, as we sat on the porch, passing the time, "is the city providing you with any money for your work?"

"We don't take money from any government," she said.

"How do you raise the money you need to provide for the poor?"

"The Lord will always provide," she said.

"Mother, you do so much for all of us, is there anything I can do for you?"

"Yes," she responded, without hesitation. "I need two parking permits."

"Mother," I allowed, "that may be harder than getting money for you, but I'll see what I can do." Of course, I was able to arrange quickly for the two permits she needed, to park in front of the AIDS hospice she runs in Greenwich Village, where she cares for fourteen terminal patients. Even a saint has to park.

At that point, my chef came out with a pitcher of ice-cold lemonade and freshly baked chocolate-chip cookies. I poured the lemonade for Mother and the sisters, as well as for me. I thought mine was delicious, but Mother and the nuns did not drink.

"Mother," I said, "the lemonade is really good, and it's so hot outside. Why don't you drink it?"

"Ed," she explained, "my sisters and I work primarily in India, and if a poor family were to offer us the same there, it would cost them a week's wages. So we have a rule: we never eat or drink in the homes of the rich and powerful, so when we go into the homes of the poor and the hapless, they are not insulted because they know our rule."

How charming, I thought, and went on to say, "But Mother, these chocolate-chip cookies are the best ever baked."

"Wrap 'em up," she said. She is, after all, a practical saint.

When I took her to the car to see her off, I knew the chef had also thrown in a cheesecake he had made for dinner. I kissed her hands in admiration and love, and waved good-bye.

Governor Cuomo and his wife, Matilda, visited me at the hospital. After chatting, he said, "Is there anything I can do for you?"

"Well," I said, wanly and weakly, "yes." There was, at the time, a bill before him which would have increased pensions for city workers, another ripoff of the taxpayers. (New York City workers have much higher pensions than those provided by the state of New York to its employees.) "Veto the bill," I whispered.

Cuomo left when he spotted reporters, telling them, "He's crazy," and reporting on what I had asked him to do. He did, in fact, veto the bill, regrettably signing it into law a year later.

Andrew Stein, who as president of the city council stood to become interim mayor in the event I was unable to continue in office, also came to see me at the hospital. He was very solicitous. After our visit, he went downstairs to talk to the reporters. He told them he had noticed I was speaking very slowly, implying that my mental faculties had been somewhat impaired by the stroke.

David Garth, who was always a genius in responding to such matters, came up with a brilliant line in rebuttal. "What Andy Stein doesn't understand," he told reporters, "is that every time the mayor talks to Andy, he speaks slowly."

Every day I was recuperating at Gracie Mansion, I received visitors. Senator Al D'Amato came one afternoon. I like Al and am one of his supporters. It bothers me that he is constantly put down by *The New York Times* and the cognoscenti, who refer to him as Senator Pothole. What they're trying to convey is that he does too much constituent service. That's ridiculous. You can never do too much constituent service, as long as it's legitimate. But the *Times* and others prefer someone like Pat Moynihan, whom they regard, rightly, as more cerebral. As mayor, I was constantly taking calls from Moynihan, who complained almost every time I praised D'Amato without including him. Of course, the city needed Moynihan's help as much as D'Amato's, and I was a loyal Democrat, so I tried to include Moynihan in the praise.

I don't mean to denigrate Moynihan, who is brilliant in many areas. I've just never been able to figure him out. He is one of the few Democratic heavyweights who is never considered for the national ticket. He is, quite probably, a genius, but he's quixotic. You can't depend on him. And you can never be sure he's functioning at optimum level.

I think his spirit was broken with the publication of his controversial book, *Beyond the Melting Pot,* more than twenty years ago. In it, Moynihan presented himself as one of the first white academics who was not a racist, and used his often-quoted phrase "benign neglect" to say that blacks have to stop being professional victims and start taking responsibility for their own failures. He blamed the breakdown in family structure for most of their problems. It was a brave thing to say, and I applauded him for it, but the book produced such a heated reaction from blacks, who called it racist, that I don't think he ever recovered. I sat down with him once at my apartment at 14 Washington Place, when I was still a Congressman and he not yet a Senator, and we talked about it. He told me he would never again be so candid on that issue. Lately, to his credit, he has begun to speak his mind more candidly on a whole host of matters, including race.

But let me get back to D'Amato's visit. At the time of my stroke, the two of us had been working to create a wing at the Museum of Natural History to house the American Indian collection, but the Native Americans wanted their own facility. The trouble was, neither they nor we had the money to pay for it. There was a tremendous amount of bickering, and for a while it appeared we would lose the museum to Washington, D.C., where there were funds available. *Newsday* was constantly attacking D'Amato and me for our position. And we knew we couldn't prevail.

"Al," I said, as he sat down, "let's get off this goddamn thing."

"Fine with me," he said, "but what will we say?"

"What we'll do," I said, "is announce that we'll help the Indian museum raise money to keep the museum in their own building in New York." I was improvising as I went along: "We'll give every patron an honorary Indian chief name and form a committee, with the Governor, Pat Moynihan, and David Rockefeller, and each of us will take an honorary name."

"I know what I want to be called," D'Amato said, warming to the idea.

"What?"

"Tonto."

"Fine," I said. "You can be Tonto."

Then we called David Rockefeller, and he too liked the idea. He also had a name at the ready: "I'd like to be known as Chief Pocantico," he said. Pocantico was the name of his family estate, along the Hudson River.

Moynihan checked in with his enthusiasm, and with a

name of his own: Chief Oneonta, in honor of a county in upstate New York.

Cuomo also liked the idea, but he couldn't think of a name. I told him I would get a good one for him.

Next, I called the director of the American Indian Museum, Roland Force, to get some suggestions for names. I told him what we were up to.

"I don't think it's such a good idea," he said. "I think you're liable to upset lots of Native Americans by using their names in this way, even if it is for a good cause."

"Well, in the event that we do go forward with this, I will need two names, one for the governor and one for myself."

A half-hour later, he called back with a name for Cuomo—the Peace Maker, who was the major chief of the Iroquois confederation—and a name for me—Hiawatha, who was a New York Indian. I always thought he came from the Northwest, but I was happy to carry such a proud name.

"There is something else I should warn you about, Mayor," the director said, "if you're determined to go through with this."

"What's that?"

"Well," he said, "I think Senator D'Amato should consider taking another name. I don't think he'd be happy if he knew what 'Tonto' meant."

"What does it mean?"

"It means 'stupid' in Spanish," he said.

So, all those years, when the Lone Ranger was calling to his sidekick by name, he was really calling him "Stupid."

I called D'Amato right away. He was happy that I had discovered what would have been a terrible gaffe and agreed to take a different name. I think it was Chief Red Jacket. Then on reflection, recognizing that Force knew more than we, we scratched the whole idea.

In the wake of my stroke, I was forced to confront for the first time my own mortality. This wasn't as difficult as I had thought it might be. I even planned my own funeral, while I was recovering, and set these plans down on paper. It was sort of silly, both the plans I laid out and the fact that I thought to make them. I had it all figured out—the line of march along Fifth Avenue, where I wanted to be buried (in the garden at Gracie Mansion), even the hymn I wanted sung at my funeral (my favorite being a Catholic hymn, "Be Not Afraid," which I have heard so many times —indeed, too many times—at the services for our fallen police officers). In retrospect, my plans were much too grandiose, and I will undoubtedly be buried in New Jersey in the plot which holds my father and mother.

On a more serious level, and in a deep and profound way, I realized after my stroke that I was not afraid to die. I did not want to suffer, as my mother had, but I was not afraid to leave this world, if that was what the Lord had in mind. I had led a full, unique, and satisfying life. I had made a contribution to public service and the city of New York. I had left a legacy. I would be in the history books. I just wanted to go quickly and without pain, like my father five years earlier.

I don't mean to suggest that I was ready to pack it in, during the summer of 1987, after I recovered from the stroke. Not at all. In fact, quite the opposite was true. The crushing blows of the corruption crisis were finally easing, and I had survived these as well. I began to turn my thoughts to a fourth term. There was still a great deal I wanted to do, and eliminating the effects of the corruption crisis was at the top of my list. Indeed, there was much to distinguish my third-term administration: a $5.1 billion housing program, reductions in class sizes and dropout rates in the city's schools, all-day kindergartens, a strong antidrug program, measurable economic growth in all five boroughs, and much more. But if I were to single out my major contribution to the city's well-being, I would say it was bringing back fiscal stability, with ten consecutive, fully balanced budgets. And, just as important, I had returned to the city its spirit, personality, and pride.

There had never been a four-term mayor in modern

times in New York City. Fiorello LaGuardia and Robert Wagner were the only other three-term mayors of the modern era, in addition to myself. I was out to change that. My advisers were all telling me to quit while I was ahead and step down gracefully, to let Manhattan Borough President David Dinkins, Comptroller Harrison Goldin, and the others in the emerging Democratic field battle it out for the party's nomination, but I could not do this.

I ran for two reasons. The overriding reason, I'll admit, was my pride. I was not about to let my critics drive me out of office. If the voters wanted me out, that was another matter, but it was up to them to decide. The second, less tangible, reason was that I wanted to send a message to the people of New York City. I knew the city was facing some tough times ahead; the stock market crash of October 1987 and the resulting flattening of the city real-estate market were harbingers of that. I also knew that David Dinkins would emerge as my most likely successor. I did not want it to be said that Koch, and the whites, walked away from the city when it wasn't worth having, and only then gave it to the blacks. Obviously, this city, this job, will always be worth having. New York is a great city, and to be its mayor is an extraordinary honor and achievement. To be its mayor a fourth time would be unique.

So I went to see David Garth, to tell him of my decision. He had run every one of my mayoral campaigns, save for my try in 1973, which never really got off the ground. I could not hope to prevail without David's enthusiastic involvement in the campaign.

"You shouldn't run," he reiterated, and then he reminded me that my public approval rating had dropped to 17 percent, an all-time low for me, in January 1989.

I knew the figures. "I have to run," I said, "and you have to help me."

He did. David came to admit after I lost that I was right to run. "I was wrong," he confided to me, after we were defeated in the primary. "I tell everybody that. I'm glad you ran. It was important that you ran for the reasons you gave me. And it makes no difference that we lost."

When I formally declared my candidacy, I was very low in the polls, but slowly I began to creep up. Dinkins was well out in front, I was second, and Harrison Goldin and former MTA Board Chairman Richard Ravitch were bringing up the rear. I was somewhat surprised by the poor showings of Goldin and Ravitch, who wound up with about 6 percent of the vote between them at election time. Goldin had been the city's comptroller throughout my three terms, and under Beame for one term, and he and I never got along. He was one of the smartest people I ever met, with a great sense of humor, but we didn't get along. I didn't trust him. He didn't like me because he wanted to be mayor—and, undoubtedly, thought he could do a better job. Strangely, Ravitch came in ahead of him, a terrible personal defeat for Goldin.

Ravitch had been in politics for as long as I had been, although never in an elected position. He held appointed posts. His name was well known, as was Goldin's, but for some reason those guys were just floundering. Few voters were supporting them.

So it became clear that the vote was either going to Dinkins or to myself. Of course, I was determined that it would go to me. I didn't enter this primary race simply to make brownie points; I meant to win. Whenever I throw myself into anything, I do it wholeheartedly. In every election, I always believed I would win, even when it became apparent I might lose. How can you win, if in your heart you have already conceded? I cannot, therefore, say in any prescient way that I knew I was going to lose this election, but on reflection I should have, and perhaps even unconsciously, I saw it coming.

The turning point of the campaign, I think, was a horrible crime committed on August 23, 1989, on the streets of the predominantly white Brooklyn neighborhood of Bensonhurst. The tragic incident, in which a sixteen-year-old black youth, Yusef Hawkins, was killed in a racial attack, effectively changed the direction of the primary campaign. On that night, Hawkins had come to the neighborhood with four black friends, to inspect a used car one of them wanted to buy, when they were assaulted by a hateful mob of young white men, many of them toting baseball bats; one of them was carrying a gun. Amid cries of "Let's shoot one!" Hawkins was shot twice in the chest.

As mayor, I sought to quell the passionate racial tensions which flared in the wake of this outrage. I tried to discourage a group of militant black activists, led by Al Sharpton, from marching through Bensonhurst to protest the killing, to no avail. "There is nothing wrong or illegal about a protest march," I said. "The question is, do you want to be helpful in reducing the tensions, or do you want to escalate those tensions?"

My comments were not well received by the city's editorial writers and columnists, or by the black community, although I still believe this was the correct position for the mayor of New York City to take. As a candidate, perhaps, opposed as I was in this particular election by a formidable black opponent, my clear-headed position left the door open for David Dinkins. Brooklyn's black community, up until this time, was not united behind Dinkins. His core support came originally from the Harlem community. There were still some important inroads to be made in Brooklyn, and I might have been successful there. Indeed, in 1985, when I ran for mayor against Denny Farrell, another black candidate with a Harlem base, I carried the Bedford-Stuyvesant area with 38 percent of the black vote.

I don't mean to reduce the anguish of Yusef Hawkins's murder, and its aftermath, to pure political terms, but there is no denying their impact on this campaign. They provided the black leadership—much of which is militant, left-wing, and radical, in my judgment—with another reason to act demagogic and whip up the black electorate against me. Of course, many of those leaders never liked me before, but now they had another reason. They didn't like me before because I didn't pander to them, because I treated them like I treated white leaders and legislators: equally. Many don't believe in equal treatment without regard to race, religion, ethnicity, or gender. They want special, preferential treatment, and I wouldn't give it to them. David Dinkins, on the other hand, had publicly stated he was for racial quotas in hiring and contracts. He was clearly their man.

The incident also cost me Governor Cuomo's back-handed endorsement. Earlier in the campaign, he had told the press that he thought the city should stick with the old jalopy. I was the old jalopy. It wasn't the most attractive endorsement I had ever received, but everyone understood it for what it was.

After the Bensonhurst murder, though, Cuomo re-canted. It's interesting to note why. Both of us, separately, attended Yusef Hawkins's funeral. I went with Ben Ward, then police commissioner. When we arrived, we were booed by the crowd of a few hundred people assembled outside the church. Worse, we were kept waiting, outside in the hot sun, by the bully boys of the Muslim minister Louis Farrakhan, who had been brought in by Moses Stewart, Yusef Hawkins's father, to be in charge of security. I actually overheard one of the regular churchgoers lean over to one of Farrakhan's people and say, "That's the mayor and the police commissioner, don't you think you should let them in?" And the Farrakhan guy said, "We know who they are."

Finally, after a half-hour or so, they let us in. Meanwhile, Cuomo was still out there, sweating underneath the same sun and even worse curses, mostly directed at his Italian heritage. Throughout his political career, he had always enjoyed a major base of support in the black community. I think I did more for blacks in the city than he has done for blacks in the state, in employment and programs, but his rhetoric was always so magnificent. My rhetoric was apparently inadequate, and my deeds apparently didn't count. On this day, the blacks put him through the same mistreatment that I was subjected to, and for somewhat longer, until finally, he too was let in.

The very next time the governor was asked to take a position on the mayoralty race, he shifted gears. He was no longer sticking with the old jalopy. Now, suddenly, the city needed someone who could bring this town together. He didn't say whether he thought Dinkins or myself could best accomplish this, but the implication was clear: only a black mayor could do it. He joined Felix Rohatyn, head of the Municipal Assistance Corporation, who had endorsed David Dinkins earlier.

In the end, however, it was not Yusef Hawkins's death but my longevity that did me in. The corruption crisis was no longer a major issue. The Yusef Hawkins tragedy, coming just a few weeks before the September 12 primary, galvanized the black vote; white voters, particularly the Irish and Italian Catholics, were not really interested anymore and stayed home. I had worn out my welcome. I can even understand it. The voters had grown tired of me. They wanted to see if someone else could do the job, and that someone else, for better or worse, was David Dinkins. Cuomo, Rohatyn, columnists, and some editorial writers were promoting Dinkins as someone who would bring racial peace to New York.

On September 12, I went through my usual election day routine: I cast my vote, first thing in the morning, at the Loeb Student Center at New York University. Then I went back to my office to conduct city business. The campaign was over. There was nothing to do but wait. By early evening, I had joined my campaign staff at our Sheraton Centre Hotel headquarters, awaiting the returns. I was hopeful, but the mood of the room was tentative. The early numbers showed me with a slight lead, but this was deceptive. Historically, the city's white precincts filed before the black areas, so I was merely carrying the neighborhoods I was supposed to carry. And not by a big enough margin.

My brother and sister and their families were with me

on that night, along with hundreds of loyal friends and supporters. I began to realize the inevitable. When the outcome was clear, I tried to lift the spirits of the others in the room. In truth, I felt a tremendous weight lift from my own shoulders. I breathed a long, deep sigh. My life, I knew, would go on. Someone else would now have the daily burden of worrying about the welfare of 7.5 million New Yorkers.

I retired to one of the bedrooms in our hotel suite and conferred with my advisers—among them David Garth, Stan Brezenoff, Dan Wolf, Diane Coffey, and John LoCiccro—and we agreed to concede the election early, to give Dinkins the spotlight for the balance of the evening. It would be good for him, and for the party, to be on the eleven o'clock news.

I didn't think about what I would say in my concession speech until that moment, and when I did I naturally assumed that someone on my staff had thought to prepare a speech. I rarely read from a prepared speech, but it was always nice to have one handy to use as a kind of crutch, particularly on those occasions when I was likely to be distracted, or overwhelmed with emotion. This was one of those occasions, but there was no speech. None had been written for a win or a loss. I sat for a moment with David, Stan, and Diane, and we hastily went over a list of people to thank, and points to make, but for the most part I was going to have to wing it. As we were making our way down to the ballroom, where the television cameras and our campaign workers were waiting, I was still frantically searching my mind for something to say.

I spoke extemporaneously. "I just called David Dinkins and I wished him all success and I told him I am ready to serve, to help him to become the next mayor," I began. "He won the race, and he won it fairly and squarely and by a large margin. I think it's something like 42 to 50 percent. That's a substantial victory. This is my twenty-fifth election, and I've lost three, counting the one tonight, which means I've won twenty-two. So I know what it is both to win and to lose. And I'm not going to use the trite line because it's too trite. But the fact is that my concern, in all honesty, is more about you. I have had twelve glorious years as mayor. . . .

"I obviously would have preferred winning, but I'm not distressed to the extent that the supporters are, because you've given it everything and for nothing other than the satisfaction of seeing someone you believe in win. I want you not to feel sorry for me. Believe me, there is life after the mayoralty. . . ."

That's what I said, but now I had to figure what, exactly, that life would be.

9

Washington Square Park

I NEVER THOUGHT I WOULD HAVE a third career. To be honest, I never counted on a second, but there it was. And now, here I am, nearly three years into my new life as an attorney, radio talk-show host, newspaper columnist, television news commentator, syndicated movie reviewer, public speaker, university lecturer, commercial spokesperson, and author. That's nine jobs by my count, which suits an old workaholic like me just fine. Let me tell you, I'm having such a wonderful time, I sometimes wonder why it took me so long to get here.

Of course, I didn't beat a smooth path to where I am now right after my primary defeat. First, I took a European vacation to relax. In London, I stayed at the home of my longtime supporter Malcolm Forbes. For years, he had said to me that if I ever wanted to take a vacation I could stay at any one of his homes, if they were not being used. His London residence, a wonderful Christopher Wren house that Malcolm had restored, happened to be available at the time of my visit, so I stayed there.

My traveling party consisted of my friends Bruce and Mary Barron; David and Barbara Margolis; Diane Coffey, my chief of staff; and, because I was still mayor, two New York City police detectives for security. The Barrons and the Margolises stayed at one of those expensive London hotels, and the rest of us stayed in the house. I hate spending money on expensive hotels. Four hundred dollars a night just seems ridiculous to me. I can afford it now, but I never enjoy myself at those prices.

I was grateful for Malcolm's offer. He opened up his home, and made his household staff available to us. We were treated royally. The home was simply magnificent, beautifully restored, with lovely paintings throughout. Opulent, but tasteful. The master bedroom suite is where I stayed, at Malcolm's insistence. In the master bathroom, my host had collected and displayed various Victorian antiques and artifacts, including Queen Victoria's bloomers, gloves, and shirtwaist, which he had laid out very impressively under glass. She was a big lady, Queen Victoria.

The first evening we went out to dinner at a restaurant and, by eleven, I started to feel woozy. I thought it might be from jet lag, so I went outside for some air. Bruce Barron suggested that I go back to my room to rest. Bruce is a gynecological surgeon. He is also my doctor. I know that sounds bizarre, but he is an extraordinary diagnostician and selects my treating doctors. I followed his advice. When I returned to Forbes's home, I became very sick and diarrheic. Then I started to hemorrhage. It was one of the most frightening things I have ever suffered, to have blood gushing out of my rectum. Nothing like this had ever happened to me before. I really thought I was dying. I didn't know what else to think. I was positively terrified.

I was also embarrassed, when I stopped to consider what I was doing to Malcolm Forbes's fancy master bathroom. When I was able, I walked to the door and called weakly down the hall for Eddie Martinez, my security guard, who was nearby.

"What is it, Mayor?" he said, racing into my suite.

"I think I'm dying, Eddie," I said. "I'm hemorrhaging. Call Bruce."

As it happened, there was an ambulance strike on that night, so Malcolm's housekeeper, a wonderfully resourceful lady, drove me to the hospital, where Bruce was waiting for me. From Eddie's frantic description over the phone, he had made a preliminary diagnosis. Just a week prior to this trip, I had had my first colonoscopy, an invasive examination for polyps. (The examination revealed a benign polyp, which was then removed.) Bruce determined that a scab must have formed after the procedure, and had now come off. Since my stroke, I had been taking an aspirin every day, to thin my blood, which meant that when I cut myself I bled freely.

While they were working on me at the hospital, I thought that the incident would find its way into the papers. After all, I was still the mayor of New York City. I asked the English physician in charge if we could keep the event out of the papers.

"Well," he assured me, in his delightful upper-class accent, "we've never had a breach, so I don't think you need to worry. And besides, you may not believe this, but probably no one here knows who you are." He said it without rancor—not necessarily a British put-down: rather, the truth.

Indeed, word of this incident never did make it into the papers, in New York or in London. The hospital had no leaks, unlike American hospitals. Malcolm Forbes and his household staff were discreet and respected my privacy. I was very appreciative. This book marks the first time the episode has ever been made public.

It is customary for a houseguest to bring a gift for his host, but buying something for Malcolm Forbes was not easy. I decided to get him a tie case, because it's not the kind of thing most people think to buy for themselves. I had been given a cheap one and thought it essential now, but of course I could not buy Malcolm a cheap one. The Barrons had arranged for us to have tea with Lord Asprey, the owner of one of London's finest and most expensive shops, which bore his name. He showed us around the store.

"Do you carry tie cases?" I asked.

"Of course," he said, and he dispatched a saleswoman to collect one for my inspection. She returned with a per-

fectly splendid tie case, at the perfectly splendid price of
$330. Now, $330 wasn't exactly what I had planned on
spending, but I had to consider my options. I could not
reject one of Lord Asprey's tie cases because it was too
expensive, not after having tea with him. And, I could
not exactly comparison-shop for someone like Malcolm
Forbes.

So I bought it for him. And he liked it.

After Malcolm's death, I was asked by Malcolm's children to contribute a short reminiscence for a book they
were preparing, as a memorial. I was saddened by his
passing. Malcolm Forbes was a very unusual man—gracious, warm, and clearly beloved by his children and the
public. He had always been very supportive of me. He was
an archconservative, and he certainly didn't agree with me
on many matters, but he was supportive just the same,
both with his personal checks, and as host of various fund-
raisers throughout my years in Congress and in City Hall.
I decided to write the tale of the tie case and suggested
that his family use it to ship Malcolm's ashes to Fiji, where
they were to be interred. As long as he was going, I
thought he would like to travel in style.

Diane Von Furstenberg, whom I had come to know
early on in my term as mayor, had a beautiful apartment
in Paris, which she also made available to me on this trip.
Again, I had the unhappy dilemma of shopping for someone who had everything. What do you buy for Diane Von
Furstenberg? I went to Hermès and picked out a black
cashmere shawl—the most beautiful one in the store.

I returned to New York refreshed and began to plan my
future. First, I had to move out of Gracie Mansion. In
packing, I thought of taking two enormous Ralph Lauren
towels with me. Surely, David Dinkins would be getting
new ones. I thought they would make a marvelous souve-
nir, and I nearly placed them in one of my packing boxes.
On reflection, though, I decided to leave the towels behind, even though I knew they would probably be turned

into cleaning rags once I left. They weren't mine, so they stayed.

I still hadn't really gotten around to planning my professional future. So much was up in the air. It took the involvement of my good friend Allen Schwartz to get me to start thinking seriously in this area. He arranged a partnership for me at a rather large Manhattan law firm. It would have been a very prestigious move for me, just as, I suspect, it would have been good for the firm to have my name on its letterhead. Nevertheless, as Allen and I were ironing out the details of my position, I also entered into conversations with the law firm of Robinson, Silverman, Pearce, Aronsohn & Berman—much smaller, but also highly regarded. That firm, where I am now a partner, had as one of its senior partners an old friend, Jim Gill. He was the one who convinced me to go there. It is probably one of the most important professional decisions I have ever made. I've never been happier. The partners and associates, secretaries and paraprofessionals are among the most competent and nicest people I have ever worked with. I shall be eternally grateful to Jim Gill, who has become one of my close friends, for having asked me to sign on.

Is there life after politics? Well, I was determined to find out. One of my functions as a partner was to bring new business to the firm. It was no trouble to sell the talents of Robinson, Silverman, because it was well known on its own. I didn't pretend to prospective clients that I had reclaimed the legal skills I had when I gave up the practice of law in 1969, or that I would be attending to the technical aspects of their cases, but I did promise them my involvement, my common sense, and my political judgment, as well as the services of my partners, all skilled practitioners. Those, more often than not, they were happy to have.

And I was happy with this firm base from which to explore my various opportunities. In one of my first moves, I signed on with the Harry Walker lecture agency, which also handled Henry Kissinger, Jeane Kirkpatrick, and a host of business and political heavyweights. I quickly became one of their most requested clients. I told a reporter for *The New York Times* that Kissinger charged more for his appearances, but that I was a better value because, with me, everyone would understand all of what I might say. It was a lame attempt at a joke, a cheap shot, and a stupid thing to say, and when I saw the line in print I regretted it immediately.

Kissinger and I are friends, and I wanted to explain away my remarks before he had a chance to be angry, so I called him at his home in Connecticut. "Henry," I began, "I'm embarrassed. I don't know whether you read what I said or not, but I'm very upset with myself." I explained what had happened and said, "I thought it was going to be a little bit flip, but it turned out boorish. I just called to apologize."

"Listen," he said, laughing it off, "if that's the worst you ever say about me, I'm lucky."

In other areas, for speaking engagements or product endorsements (I did ads for the Ultra Slim Fast diet, the *New York Post,* and Coca-Cola, among others), I charged what the market would bear, and accepted my fees quite happily. Despite the sudden and steep rise in my income, the money didn't really mean anything to me; all I wanted was to have enough to provide for my needs, which are modest. I am still careful in making my purchases. When I walked into Balducci's and priced sheep yogurt at $1.69, when at Murray's Cheese Store it was only $1.29, I went back to Murray's.

I have never much cared for material possessions. In the study of my new apartment, for example, I have a coffee table that Diane Coffey found for five dollars at the Salvation Army, back when I was in Congress. I've kept the table for over twenty years for sentimental reasons. I've certainly never lived in high style. I remember when my Washington apartment was burglarized, the cops who arrived to examine the premises couldn't believe a United

States Congressman would live in such Spartan, unpretentious digs.

One of the more prominent long-running jobs of my third career began less than a month after I left office. It lasted a little less than a year, but the end was the most interesting aspect. I had been hired by WCBS-TV, the flagship CBS television station in New York, to cohost a weekly Sunday-morning talk show. Management had problems with me from the very start, but the audience liked me; the same controversies disapproved by station executives were approved by the viewers. I should have known it wouldn't last.

It all came to an end on January 31, 1991, with my very public dismissal from the station, which I will explain here. Over the previous weeks, I had been extremely critical of New York Congressman Charles Rangel for his endorsement of Illinois Congressman Gus Savage, a notorious anti-Semite. Rangel is always treated gingerly by most people, but not by me; most of our white leaders are afraid of criticizing black leaders out of fear of being called racists, but I have never had this problem, even when I was in office. In fact, I have been under attack for speaking the truth on racial matters for nearly twenty years. I must admit that, because I speak extemporaneously, my comments on occasion are too expansive, with too much heat and hyperbole. When I participated in an oral history project at Columbia University in 1974, for example, I observed that most whites dislike blacks, and most blacks dislike whites. I also said that blacks are basically anti-Semitic. When my comments were later made public, I did modify them. I acknowledged that I could not speak about all or most blacks because I had not met all or most blacks, but I maintained that many of the black leaders I knew were anti-Semitic.

I think my comments were close to the truth. White leaders, civic and political, and members of the news media are afraid of being called racist so they refuse to see things as they really are. David Dinkins recently claimed that black politicians are held to a higher standard than white politicians. That's not true, and Dinkins surely knows that. If he doesn't know, he should. After all, he's the one who didn't file income-tax returns for several years and still got elected mayor. I couldn't have done that. Harold Washington, the late mayor of Chicago, had served time in jail and was suspended from the practice of law before he was elected mayor. If that was me or some other white politician, our careers would have been over. Eleanor Holmes Norton was elected as delegate to Congress from the District of Columbia after it was revealed that she and her husband had not filed tax returns for several years. White candidates could never win election to anything with that kind of baggage, and Dinkins knows this best of all. Yes, there is racism at work here, but he and other black leaders in these circumstances are the beneficiaries of it, not the victims. He and other black leaders are held to lower standards, and that is indeed racism, and it is wrong.

My run-in with WCBS-TV management festered in this hold-your-tongue, politically correct environment. My first year on the air had been rocky behind the scenes, but successful on the air. "Sunday Edition," as our program was called, generally beat Gabe Pressman's show, "Newsforum," in the ratings, and often held its own against John McLaughlin and David Brinkley. But despite our strong showing, it seemed that often there would be a dispute between me and Roger Coloff, the vice president and general manager of the station (sadly, he has since passed away, a victim of colon cancer at forty-six), and Paul Sagan, the producer of my show, who ultimately left CBS and is now with Time Warner. I was a loose cannon to them, but I brought them ratings, so they kept me on. Until I fired my last salvo.

On January 20, 1991, I interviewed Charlie Rangel, who was opposed to military action against Iraq. I remarked on this during our interview. After the segment, I also remarked that Rangel was sending mixed signals to the Jewish community. If Rangel was so concerned about Israel, I said, then he should not have endorsed Congressman Gus Savage, who was not only anti-Israel, but anti-Semitic. I never said that Rangel himself was anti-Semitic, or anti-Israel, but that Gus Savage was, and that Rangel had supported Savage. All of which was true.

The following week, in a personal letter sent to me at my law firm, Rangel characterized my remarks as "slanderous . . . at the very least, unfortunate . . . and really quite sad." And in comments obviously directed at WCBS officials (and later incorporated by Rangel's office in a news release), he continued: "How WCBS-TV allows you to slander its guests and offend the audience, under the guise of commentary, without some semblance of balance, at least the opportunity to respond, I just don't understand. I would only hope that WCBS-TV would take the time to review the transcript of the program, including your remarks after I had left, and let me know whether they were within the bounds of decency."

WCBS crumbled almost immediately. Paul Sagan, through my agent, sought to censure me. He asked that I apologize to Rangel, which of course I would not do. It was Rangel's position that was worthy of criticism. I did write to Rangel, but I told him I stood by what I had said and would not withdraw a single word. I also informed my agent that if Sagan and Coloff were looking to end our relationship over this incident, then they were welcome to buy out my contract. This they did, which was not surprising. What was surprising, and particularly galling, was that no political, civic, or religious leader—except for my friend Cardinal O'Connor, and City Council Speaker Peter Vallone—raised any objection to my "firing." Most troubling was that no Jewish organization thought the matter worth pursuing.

I couldn't believe it, but I should have expected it. If I were black, I knew, there would have been demonstrations and organized boycotts against WCBS-TV over my dismissal. If I were a left-winger, the organized left would have protested loudly; I suspect Arthur Miller and Susan Sontag would have organized a committee on my behalf. And, if I were some regular reporter, rather than a mayor-turned-journalist, editorial writers and columnists would have rallied to their beleaguered colleague's defense, whether my politics fell on the right, the left, or somewhere in the middle. But no one objected. I was an outsider for the press, and not worthy of defense.

I have often felt like the lone voice of reason in debating the positions of many of our black leaders—civic, political, and religious. Nobody will say what they really think. Instead, they say what they think they should say, or what is politically correct. The lack of criticism of Jesse Jackson during the 1988 Presidential campaign was a good example of this. I was critical of Jackson, and was denounced by the editorial writers and columnists for my comments. Most troubling of all was the way many of the Jewish leaders gave Jackson a free ride, especially considering his long association with such avowed anti-Semites as Louis Farrakhan.

I am equally appalled by the things that white racists like David Duke say about blacks and Jews, and I denounce him and them in equally harsh terms. I also denounced Rabbi Meier Kahane, before he was murdered, as scum, for his racist views against blacks and Arabs.

A telling illustration of Jesse Jackson at his worst took place in January 1991, just before President Bush's state of the union address. Jackson, who had recently been elected as "shadow senator" for the District of Columbia, complained that he was being seated in the balcony of the House of Representatives, while the district's new mayor, Sharon Pratt Dixon, was seated on the House floor. Now, Dixon held a real public office, unlike Jackson, who could have been elected mayor except that he didn't have the stomach to run for a job where he would have to perform and establish a record that people could judge him on. Jackson's objection didn't get him a seat on the House floor but did get Sharon Pratt Dixon moved into the balcony, which seemed to me somewhat self-defeating.

Let me slip in an anecdote from the 1988 Presidential campaign, before I get too far away from it. As was widely reported, I backed Al Gore in the New York primary. The only real choices at the time were among Gore, Jesse Jackson, and Michael Dukakis. If I were faced with the same choices today, I'd pick Gore again. I have already stated my feelings about Jackson. I will get to my opinion of Dukakis. My feeling about Gore, which I elaborated in my endorsement of him, was that he had the potential to be a great leader, not that he was already great. There's a big difference.

Dukakis was clearly upset that I had chosen Gore over him, but I really got it from Kitty Dukakis. At the time, I was unaware of her addiction problems, but I liked her even less than her husband, and I wasn't all that wild about him. Every time Kitty Dukakis saw me, she would remind me that she too was Jewish. It was as if she pushed the Jew button in her brain. (Governor Hugh Carey's former wife, Engie, used to do a similar thing, although she wasn't Jewish; she was forever finding ways to mention to me all the trees she had planted in Israel and honors she had received from Jewish organizations.)

Just before I announced for Gore, Kitty approached me at some function and said, "You really have no choice," meaning, none but to support her husband. She actually said that to me. I couldn't believe it. Whether I had no choice because Kitty Dukakis was Jewish, or because her husband would win and I would be made to suffer for throwing my support elsewhere, was not made clear. Well, I always had a choice, and Michael Dukakis didn't convince me that I should exercise it on his behalf. I interviewed him at Gracie Mansion, as I did Gore, and found him glib and simplistic.

When I decided to support Gore, I called Dukakis to tell him. A lot of politicians would not have done that, and would have assigned the task to others, but it wasn't like me to shy from the uncomfortable. "Governor," I said. "I want to tell you that I'm supporting Gore, but I also want to tell you that you're going to win the nomination, and when you do I will be a soldier in your army if you want me."

Kitty, I was told, was livid that I was not supporting her husband. It didn't take long for her to let me know directly what she thought of me. At a reception before Dukakis was to make a major foreign-policy address at New York University, I stood on a receiving line to greet the candidate and his wife. Michael Dukakis didn't greet me warmly, but we did shake hands and say hello. He was his usual self—courteous but perfunctory. A Greek friend of mine once joked that only the Democrats could find the one Greek in America without a heart.

Then came Kitty's turn. She kissed everybody ahead of me, about five people or so, but when she got to me she simply held out her hand. It was clear that she was absolutely pissed. That was okay with me. I understood. We shook hands.

A few weeks later, Dukakis made another appearance in the city, at a fund-raiser. Governor Cuomo had introduced him to the audience at NYU, but Cuomo didn't like him either, so he turned to me afterward and said, "You're the mayor. The next time Dukakis comes to New York City, you can introduce him, whether he likes it or not." It wasn't that Cuomo loved me more, but that he loved Dukakis less. So this time, I had to make the opening speech. There was another private reception before the speech, and Dukakis and Kitty walked in again. Kitty, once again, was kissing everybody, but when she came to me, I held out my hand. I didn't want to give her the chance to snub me again. Later, on stage, there was some more kissing and hugging with others.

When Kitty got to me, she said, "Aren't you ever going to forgive me?"

I didn't respond, so she tried again. "Won't you kiss me?" she said.

We were on stage, in front of several thousand people, and we were both concerned about public appearances. So I backed down. "Sure," I said.

And I did.

One thing to Michael Dukakis's credit: He called me about a year later to express his sympathies, after I was defeated in the 1989 mayoral primary. He knew how it felt to get beaten, he said, and he wanted me to know he was thinking of me. It was a very decent thing for him to do, and I appreciated it.

These days, now that I am out of office, my endorsement still seems to carry weight. At least to some people. One of these is Geraldine Ferraro, who as this is written is seeking the Democratic nomination to unseat my friend Al D'Amato from the United States Senate.

Now, I was the one who first recommended to Walter Mondale when he ran for president in 1984 that Ferraro be considered for the vice presidency. I actually recommended two women for consideration: Ferraro, and San Francisco Mayor Diane Feinstein. Ferraro seemed like a natural choice. She and I were friends, at the time. I campaigned for her when she first ran for Congress; she campaigned for me when I ran for mayor. We were helpful to each other, but mostly I was helpful to her, which is why I couldn't understand it when she turned on me after I lost the mayoral election. Here's what happened. Around the time the Democratic National Committee was casting about for a site for its 1992 convention, Ferraro teamed with Mayor Dinkins, and others, to lobby for New York City as the location. There was some travel involved in this undertaking, and she and Dinkins were both on the road together.

I picked up the paper one morning during this period and saw a comment from Ferraro that simply infuriated me. She said that she was happy to be traveling with David Dinkins, and that she'd hate the thought of spending a week with Ed Koch. It was just a gratuitous insult. It wasn't said jocularly, so far as I could detect. I was incensed, but also confused. I couldn't understand it. There had been no falling-out between us, not that I was aware of.

A few months later, as she was launching her run for the Senate, she called me at my law office, seeking my support. She thought an endorsement from me would cancel out David Dinkins's endorsement of State Attorney General Robert Abrams, one of her opponents in the Democratic field.

"Well, Gerry," I said, "it's strange that you should call me, because you are the last person I would support."

"Why do you say that, Ed?" she said. "I thought we were friends."

"I thought so too," I replied. I then reminded her of her remarks from several months back.

"Did I say that?" she said.

"Yes," I said.

"Well, I don't remember ever saying that."

"I have the clipping here at my office," I explained. "I can send you a copy to refresh your memory."

"Well, if I did say it," she allowed, "it must have been taken out of context."

"Did you write a letter to the editor, stating you had been quoted out of context?"

"No."

"Did you call the reporter, or send him a note, seeking a retraction?"

"No."

"Did you call me, to apologize, or offer an explanation?"

"No."

"Then it wasn't out of context," I said.

She was really rather surprised and followed up our conversation with a "personal and off the record" letter on May 23, 1991. (These were her terms, not mine, so read on.) In it, Ferraro claimed she was taken aback by our conversation, and then she inanely listed the various snubs and perceived snubs, from me to her, which she attempted to equate with her "out of context" comment. The short letter read like a long whine. She said she didn't recall me trying to apologize or explain myself when I publicly commented that she had no political future, after the 1984 election. She said she didn't recall me trying to apologize or explain myself when I said on the radio that she wasn't qualified to be Vice President in 1984. She even said that I didn't apologize or explain myself when I challenged her over D'Amato's voting record during our most recent telephone conversation. She closed the letter by calling me and my comments insensitive and thoughtless, while dismissing her own insensitive and thoughtless comments as a tiny misunderstanding. It was one of the silliest letters I have ever received.

I responded a few days later. "Dear Gerry," I wrote, "You misunderstand the differences in our comments. You told me that your comments were either taken out of context, or you never said them, it's not clear to me which, and that you didn't mean them. Under those circumstances, you should have called me, if you decided not to write a letter to the offending reporter. Any comments that I made concerning you I meant and were not taken out of context. If you have a particular comment in mind that you want me to defend, just call. But there would be no reason for me either to send a letter or to call you since there was no error in transmission."

It may not be the most popular opinion, but Dan Quayle, I maintain, was certainly better qualified for the Vice Presidential nod than Ferraro ever was. I like Quayle, and I think he's gotten a bum rap from the press. He's not dumb. Do you think John Warner is a rocket scientist? John Glenn? And what about Ted Kennedy, the great swimmer and moralist? Quayle unseated a very capable Senator in Birch Bayh, and he was only thirty-three at the time. That impressed me.

Ferraro, as long as I'm comparing apples and oranges, was no giant in the House. She didn't even have a well-thought-out philosophy. Quayle has a clear philosophy (too conservative for me), and to his credit, he picks bright people for his staff. Quayle was a much better selection than William Miller, the undistinguished Congressman from Buffalo who was Goldwater's running mate in 1964. He was even better qualified than Nixon, when Eisenhower picked him in 1952. Nixon was just a one-issue guy back then, bashing the communists, and he'd only been in politics for six years. Of course, President Nixon has been rehabilitated with the passage of time, and has emerged as a seminal thinker, particularly on foreign-policy issues, but at the time he was a suspect choice for the national ticket.

At least Quayle does his homework. If Ferraro had done hers on this matter, she would have known that I was on record supporting D'Amato, no matter who the Democrats nominated to oppose him.

Rudolph Giuliani also came calling for my support and my advice, when he was exploring the 1993 race for the mayoralty of New York City. He invited me to lunch to discuss his campaign and his chances. I think he has a good shot, the way things are going for David Dinkins. I will always be extremely grateful to Giuliani for his kindness to me personally during the corruption crisis, although there are some members of my administration who will never forgive him for the damning rhetoric he directed at almost everyone else in the city government at the time of the scandal.

Regrettably, even this personal kindness was tempered by Giuliani's harsh assessment of me as a political opponent. During the 1989 mayoral campaign, he told *The New York Times* that the mayor had responded to the corruption crisis with "his eyes closed, his ears clogged, and his mouth open." On another occasion, he said, "This is a mayor who looks for the divisions between people—religious, racial, ethnic—and he tries to get his support by playing off those divisions."

Nevertheless, I was happy to hear him out and to share

my views on his coming campaign. At the lunch, he asked my evaluation of his chances.

"I have publicly announced that the only person who could cause me to vote for David Dinkins is you," I said.

"Why?" Giuliani wondered.

"Well," I said, "let me explain it to you. You did two things that cause me, whenever I describe you, to refer to you as Inspector Javert. But I want you to know you are very lucky, because every time I refer to you as Inspector Javert, nobody seems to know who he is."

"Who is he?" he asked.

"Have you seen *Les Miserables*? That's Inspector Javert. He's the man for whom the end always justifies the means."

"Oh yes," said Rudy, "I do know of him."

I then related the incidents which caused me to think of him in this way. The first was a case involving the stockbrokers whom Giuliani had arrested at gunpoint and placed in handcuffs at their office in the middle of the day. It was an unnecessary indignity. That the charges were ultimately dropped makes that seem especially true. It was unacceptable to me that two white-collar suspects, who were not dangerous, were humiliated in this way before their guilt or innocence was ever adjudicated, clearly for publicity purposes.

"Oh, but that wasn't me," Giuliani interjected. "I had nothing to do with that. That was the federal marshall's decision."

"If it was, Rudy, you better get that out. The people don't know that."

The other incident involved the Bess Myerson case I described earlier in these pages, in which Giuliani apparently instructed Sukhreet Gabel to tape an alleged incriminating conversation with her mother, Judge Hortense Gabel, on the telephone. That, too, was unacceptable to me. We do not live in a society where it is okay for a prosecutor to use a child to entrap a parent.

"But that's not how it happened," Giuliani jumped in.

"It's not?"

"No. I warned her not to do it."

"Well, the people don't know that either, Rudy, and you better get that out, too."

Maybe he was telling me the truth, and maybe he wasn't. I was telling him he had an image problem, and these were two images contributing to it.

"Rudy," I advised, "what you have to do is convey to people that you're running for mayor, not prosecutor."

I think he understood me. As a matter of fact, I might just vote for Giuliani, David Dinkins is doing such a poor job. But I haven't decided yet.

A footnote: Months later, after I told this story a few times, *Wall Street Journal* reporter Gordon Crovitz asked if he could refer to it in print. I said he could. In print, however, Crovitz only mentioned the part where I told Giuliani that I could never vote for him. Giuliani, upon reading the article, called Crovitz and told him the conversation quoted had never taken place. The reporter then called me for an explanation.

"Gordon," I said, "I didn't make it up. Ask him about the Inspector Javert part."

Crovitz called me back shortly thereafter, with an update: "He remembers that part," he said, "but he also remembers knowing who Inspector Javert was."

I laughed. "This is ridiculous," I said.

"Rudy is incensed," Crovitz continued, "because he thinks your saying you could never vote for him is very damaging."

"That was months ago," I said, "and Dinkins is so bad, I could very well end up voting for Giuliani."

I got off the phone with Crovitz and called Giuliani to explain. "Rudy," I began, "don't be angry. It really happened that way." I thought about saying, "This is really like Rashomon," but I worried he might say, "Who is Rashomon?" Then I explained to him that the way things were going, I could end up voting for him, and that put an end to our little misunderstanding.

I really do think David Dinkins is costing himself his own job. I am truly surprised by his lack of leadership qualities. He is a decent man, but no leader, and New Yorkers desperately need a leader. They need someone to inspire them, someone to root for, and someone to place their confidence in. Dinkins offers none of these qualities, and I think it will cost him his reelection. Few, if any, believe he can lead us across the Red Sea or out of the desert.

When I was mayor, the people knew I'd find a way to pull the city through, whatever the problem. And I did. My critics will point out that I had the good luck of a strong economy, but that wasn't always the case. For my first six years in office, the economy wasn't too terrific. For the second six years, it was. In any case, it is said that luck is for the able, and Dinkins is neither lucky nor able. Only during the Dinkins administration could New York City suffer a drought in the winter.

Racial tensions in New York City, under Dinkins, are at a boiling point. And the surprise here is that they are in no way mitigated by the presence of a black mayor. In fact, I think Dinkins is making the situation worse, although not intentionally. With Dinkins as mayor, there is a kind of "our time has come" mentality within some of the city's black communities, reducing some people's inhibitions.

I had problems, but I never had his. I never had race riots in my administration. I never had pogroms in my administration. I don't blame Dinkins directly, but I think he has unwittingly created a climate in which black-white relations can't help but flare up. Just look at the headlines. In January 1992, there were fifteen separate hate crimes, or bias incidents, committed in the city within fifteen days. If they had happened on my watch with such alarming frequency, there would have been picket lines galore down at City Hall. There would have been delegations of black and white ministers demanding that the mayor do something to stem the tide. They would have blamed me.

But nobody blames David Dinkins, the man who promised to bring racial harmony to New York City.

One of Dinkins's problems is he wants to be nice. He's afraid to anger anyone. But to govern effectively, and to lead, you've got to anger some of the people, some of the time. I believe he will be voted out of office. I didn't always feel this way. During most of the first two years of his administration, I was convinced he would be reelected, despite his problems. I said so publicly on several occasions. I imagined a 1993 Democratic primary run-off with Herman Badillo and Andy Stein. I thought Dinkins would retain the black vote, which is about 35 percent of the primary vote, and draw on the same constituency he used to defeat me in 1989 (the unions, and the "progressives," including a great many very liberal Jews who voted for him the last time) to pull in the 40 percent he'd need to avoid a run-off in a three-way race. In a general election, though, I knew he'd have a tougher time of it. (We now know the size of the progressive Jewish vote. It is 11 percent of the Jewish vote. That is the percentage that Jerry Brown got in the 1992 Presidential primary in New York City after he said he would ask Jesse Jackson to be his Vice President.)

Still, I thought Dinkins would squeak by. I am no longer of this view. The second term was his to lose, and I think he's lost it. I still predict that Dinkins will win the primary, but will lose in the general election to the Republican candidate, presumably Giuliani.

But I'm getting ahead of myself, by just a little. Let me get back to 1990, and my new life. I quickly replaced my television gig at WCBS-TV with another, at WNYW-TV, the local Fox station, where I offered political and general commentary, live, one morning each week, during the station's morning program, "Good Day, New York," and one evening a week on the "10 O'Clock News." My appearances there were successful from the start, and they continue.

Another broadcasting opportunity found me on the radio, doing a morning drive-time program for WNEW-AM. Happily, I had some experience in this area. In the 1970s, as a Congressman, I did a fifteen-minute weekly show for WNYC-AM in New York. I simply sat in a Congressional studio in Washington and talked into a microphone, making a tape for New York. It was very lonely. Generally, I spoke on Congressional subjects. I never knew if anyone was even listening. I never got any mail. One day, I leaned over the microphone and asked plaintively, "Is there anyone out there listening? If there is, please write to me and I will send you my Shrimp Jambalaya recipe." I didn't know what Shrimp Jambalaya was, but it sounded exotic.

I got one card, so I went immediately to a Congressman from New Orleans, and he gave me a Shrimp Jambalaya recipe to send to my lone listener.

This WNEW assignment, fortunately, pulled a much larger audience. It proved to be enormously popular, and a terrific outlet for my spoken opinions. Like many of the turns my career has taken since leaving government, I didn't see this one coming. I was approached one night when I was out at dinner by a man named Michael Kakoyannis. He had a proposition he wanted me to consider: Would I appear on WNEW every morning for five minutes and talk about the issues of the day with two disc jockeys with somewhat opposing points of view? I thought to myself, I could do this easily, and so I accepted. We worked things out so I could do the broadcast from my apartment every morning, by telephone.

I went on the air in the first weeks after I left office. I started out making twenty-five thousand dollars for the first year, which I thought was a nice salary for five minutes of work each day. For the second year, my contract called for seventy-five thousand dollars, which was even nicer. By the next year, I had priced myself out of a job (my contract called for a third option year, at $125,000). WNEW, struggling financially, and laying off many of its people, decided not exercise the option, so I looked to replace the one radio gig with another.

I found one right away. In January 1992, I began an hour-long daily talk show on WABC-AM radio, which I continue to do out of my midtown law office. I usually open the show with note and comment on the news and editorials of the day, but most of the hour is given over to listener call-ins, and I particularly enjoy the give and take with the people of New York, New Jersey, and Connecticut, our audience. It's like being mayor again, only better. Obviously, it takes more preparation to fill an hour of airtime each day, and to make the show provocative and interesting. Early on, after being asked by the station manager to repeat the call letters WABC before each call, I added the following identification: "This is WABC, Ed Koch speaking, your voice of reason."

Wonderfully, just as in Congress and during the mayoralty, when the phrase "How'm I doin'?" became my introduction, now, "the voice of reason," has taken its place.

One of my most satisfying new assignments has been a stint as a weekly columnist for the *New York Post,* in which I was given a rare opportunity to air my views on subjects of my choosing in the most traditional and influential of our public forums. My beat is anything that moves me. I have always made my feelings known, and spoken freely, almost without restraint, even on the most sensitive issues; however, the prospect of setting my views down on paper, in black and white, for the record and for all time, was both daunting and exhilarating.

I have, I think, put the column to good use. I set the tone very early on. One of my favorite subjects, naturally, was Israel. On March 23, 1990, for example, after President George Bush declared that no new Jewish "settlements" be allowed in East Jerusalem, I urged the President to consult his Bible, specifically the 137th Psalm, before he said anything else on the subject of Jerusalem. (The psalm, which I quoted, is translated as follows: "If I forget thee, O Jerusalem, let my right hand lose its cun-

ning, let my tongue cleave to the roof of my mouth.")
"When Russia gives back to Japan and Poland the territory it captured in war," I concluded the column, "when
the United States gives Texas and California back to Mex-
ico, then we can ask Israel to give up the land for which
tens of thousands of its soldiers and citizens have shed
their blood."

I compared the federal bailout of the savings-and-loan
industry to the Teapot Dome scandal of the 1920s; I challenged *The New York Times,* for holding the National En-
dowment for the Arts above criticism, when the NEA had
shown serious errors in judgment and grant procedures; I
proposed a program of universal military and civilian service, to supplant or supplement drug-treatment programs
for convicted drug users; I pressed President Bush to address a national health plan; I was among the first to call
the August 19, 1991, Crown Heights murder of Yankel
Rosenbaum a pogrom, and a lynching, and in the wake of
the tragedy I urged a march against anti-Semitism; I questioned David Dinkins's leadership abilities, his fiscal integrity, and some of his top-level appointments; I castigated
David Duke as a racist, while urging that we take a serious
look at the legitimate issues concerning some of his supporters. I also supported the right of abortion, encouraged
the Bush administration to devote more monies to AIDS
research, and explained the scandal at BCCI, the Bank of
Credit and Commerce International, in terms the average
reader could understand (I hope).

My columns are making a difference, and I'm quite
proud of them. *New York Post* management told me they
sell twelve thousand more papers on Fridays, when my
column appears, than they do on any other day of the
week. People engage me in debate on the street over what
I've written. And, occasionally, an idea put forth in my
column is embraced and examined by those in a position
to act on it. One of the most gratifying examples of this
resulted from my February 1, 1991, column, in which I
urged New York State to consider reducing Medicaid, ed-

ucation, housing, corrections, and welfare expenses to where it would be the fifth most generous state in these areas instead of the first. After all, I argued, if the state is willing to accept being third from the bottom in its bond ratings (now second from the bottom), it should have no trouble being fifth from the top in services. Such a move could save taxpayers more than $4 billion each year for the state and about $2 billion for the city.

I closed the column, in which I referred to both the city and the state as "financial basket cases," by relating a conversation I had with Governor Cuomo, urging him to explore my proposal. He apparently wasn't interested in doing so. I did hear from a public-interest group called the Empire Foundation, which issued a November 1991 report based on the recommendations outlined in my column. "Although there certainly will be a contentious debate over how to cut $4 billion, few people could dispute the reasonableness of the goal suggested by Koch," the foundation concluded in its favorable study. "It is clear that New York State can save billions of dollars annually by adopting the Koch proposal."

Perhaps the most sensational example of the column's reach occurred on March 6, 1992, when I lashed out against President Bush and Secretary of State James Baker for the administration's divisive rhetoric concerning Israel and its loan-guarantee request. "U.S. support of Israel has changed dramatically under Bush and Baker," I wrote. "The latter showed his hostility toward Israel often when he was chief of staff under President Reagan, a friend of Israel—but Reagan always overrode him. Now that Baker has the dominant position in U.S. foreign policy, he is able to act on his hostilities.

"In fact, when Baker was criticized recently at a meeting of high-level White House advisers for his belligerent attitude toward Israel, he responded, 'Fuck 'em. They [the Jews] didn't vote for us.'"

I knew this was hot stuff, as I was writing it, but I had no idea of the firestorm of controversy this column would spark. The fallout was really quite astonishing. Baker's comment, reported by me for the first time, was front-page news throughout the country. Indeed, it made head-lines all over the world. Predictably, Baker denied the comment, as did his spokeswoman, Margaret Tutwiler, and I was pressed by reporters, and by the White House, to disclose my source for this particular piece of information. I would not. No, I was not in the room when the secretary of state chose to dismiss American Jews in just this way, but I have it on good authority from someone who was, and I stand by my story exactly as I reported it. I also stand by my source, and I will take his or her name with me to my grave. If I wasn't entirely sure that the remark was entirely accurate, and that my source was ut-terly unimpeachable, I would not have run with it. And, if I couldn't convince my editors at the *Post* of the same, they wouldn't have either. The editors were so sure the remark was accurate, and incendiary, that they assigned their own reporters to do a regular news story on it, which accompanied my column.

The ensuing controversy didn't die down any time soon. I was denounced on CNN by the *Wall Street Journal*'s Washington bureau chief, Al Hunt, who said, "Eddie Koch is even less credible as a journalist than as a politi-cian." (When I responded to Hunt, in a letter, I called his attention to William Safire's corroborating column, which was far more pejorative than mine. "Do you or will you refer to him as 'Billy' when you comment on his column?" I wondered.)

As I write this, in late April 1992, the controversy is still swirling. It even swirled to President Bush, who wrote me the following note on the very day the column appeared, while he was en route to a Super Tuesday campaign stop in Baton Rouge, Louisiana:

"Dear Ed," he began, "Someone called to my attention that ugly story about Jim Baker in today's *New York Post* by Broderick, Burke, and Goldstein. I don't accept that Jim would say such a thing. He is working relentlessly to find a solution to a difficult problem—one that will benefit Israel and the cause of peace in the Middle East. He would not have had any White House meeting on the subject of loan guarantees except in my presence; and, Ed, I never ever heard such ugliness out of Jim Baker.

"As a matter of principle, I don't think it is fair to have a guy attacked like this by some nameless source. I don't know who allegedly would report to have heard such a statement, but I simply do not believe the allegation. . . .

"Ed, you know I respect you, and I hope you will accept the truth of these statements that come from the heart."

He signed the note with warm regards, and a handwritten kicker: "P.S. In spite of this 'flap' your #1 fan remains BPB [Mrs. Bush]—she sends her best."

I responded two days after receiving it. "Dear Mr. President," I wrote, "Regarding Secretary of State Jim Baker and his alleged remarks, which I reported in my column, you must know that if I did not have total confidence in my source, who was present when the remarks were made, I would not have reported it as such. Believe me, the source is impeccable and is one that even you would find totally credible.

"I have gone out of my way to say I do not perceive Secretary Baker's remarks as anti-Semitic, but rather as crude, political comments, writing off Jewish voters, which I am sure is not what you would want. . . .

"Now that I am no longer a party official but rather, in addition to other things, a journalist, I do not perceive my party affiliation to be my primary political loyalty. It is hard for Democratic officials to understand that I might very well vote for you in November, but despite my Democratic inclination, my mind is open. However, I'm sure you understand that every ethnic and religious community has its priorities. One of my priorities is the security of the State of Israel. I believe the special relationship between the U.S. and Israel, which began with Harry Truman and continued through Ronald Reagan, has been considerably weakened. I hope I'm wrong."

Fortunately, my reporting of Baker's unfortunate comment gave me the President's ear on the subject of Israel, at least for a while. We exchanged several more letters on the matter, and I always used mine to press my positions. "I know how much confidence you have in Jim Baker," I wrote to President Bush on March 26, 1992. "I like him personally and don't doubt his intention to create an ambiance conducive to peace among the Arab states and Israel. What distresses supporters of Israel is that he seems to be directing his pressure exclusively on Israel.

"An example. There is no question that the single most important issue to be resolved is the disposition of the West Bank. There are three positions: (1) The Arabs want it all. (2) Prime Minister Shamir believes that it all belongs to Israel. (3) My position and the position held by most people I know is that the West Bank should be divided, with the Arab population under Arab sovereignty and the Jewish population under Israeli sovereignty. Many supporters of Israel feel that the Arabs should know that their delay in achieving peace ultimately reduces the territory over which they will have sovereignty.

"By demanding a freeze on new settlements, including those that Israel deems necessary for security reasons, Secretary Baker is reducing Israel's bargaining position and enhancing that of the Arab states. Why should the Arabs bargain if the United States has demanded a freeze on new settlements and makes no demand upon the Arabs for a quid pro quo? Along with a freeze of new settlements, shouldn't Secretary Baker require a simultaneous lifting of the economic boycott of Israel by Saudi Arabia and other Arab states? Shouldn't Syria be required to allow the four thousand Jews being held against their will there to emigrate? Shouldn't the Arab population on the West Bank be required to give up the intifada [insurrection] which now costs both Jewish and Arab lives?"

The Baker controversy confirmed for me what I already knew, from a different perspective: the power of the press is enormous. From the other side, where I now sit, I am made to recognize that the responsibility of the press is also enormous. It is a responsibility I take very seriously. I look on my column as a kind of public trust, just as my career in government was a public trust, and I will never betray that trust. I will always honor it.

Understand, I am not above ruffling a few feathers, particularly when they are in need of ruffling, and particularly where it concerns Israel. My number one priority, as an American Jew, is the security of Israel. What's most troubling to me is that the vast majority of American Jews are not as concerned about Israel as they should be. They feel it isn't that important, or worry that they will in some way separate themselves from mainstream society if they make Israel their priority. That's absurd. The organized Irish make the reunification of Ireland their number one issue. The blacks have South Africa and the elimination of apartheid as their number one issue. For many Puerto Ricans, statehood is a key issue. Regrettably, for too many Jews, the number one issue is Save the Whales, or some other environmental concern, or the safeguarding of the right to abortion. These are important issues, and worthy of our support, but for a descendent of the Ten Tribes of Israel, wherever he or she lives, the security of Israel should surely be of uppermost importance.

Israel doesn't always help its own cause. I happen to think that Prime Minister Yitzhak Shamir is the worst spokesman for Israel since Moses the stutterer. Most people don't know it, but Moses was a terrible speaker. He had his brother Aaron speak for him. I've had a few encounters with Shamir, and as far as I'm concerned he has a head of granite. He's smart, but unmovable. The last time I saw him was in December 1990, while I was visiting Jerusalem to encourage tourism. An Arab had struck me in the head with a stone (the wound required nine stitches to close) several hours before my meeting with Prime Minister Shamir. In that meeting, Shamir kept telling me how wonderful relations were between Israel and the United States.

"Mr. Prime Minister," I said, "I love you and I love Israel, but I think relations are terrible. I don't think they have ever been so bad in the history of our two countries. And I'll tell you why. You have to start talking in terms of territorial compromise. That's what people want to hear today. If the Arabs denounce Israel, then you must denounce the use of their countries as sanctuaries for terrorists, and urge them to open their borders to peaceful commerce and say, only then can you begin to discuss territorial compromise in the occupied territories."

With this, Shamir turned to me and said, in his East European Israeli accent, "You t'ink you know better than me." Then he said, "You'll say it your way, and I'll say it my way." Then he waved his hand dismissively and told me he was looking for three American Jews with courage, and had yet to find one. There were about ten other people in the room when he said this. He was partly right—American Jewish leadership is extremely cowardly—but I did not appreciate being lumped in with the rest of them. It was clear that was what he was doing.

Shamir is difficult—I have often joked that he would get along better with President Bush if he took up tennis, or golf—but the Labor Party is even worse. Their leaders are more articulate than Shamir, but they are too soft, which is why the Israeli voters have repudiated them. Shimon Peres is highly intelligent, but he is too glib. His replacement in the Labor Party, Yitzak Rabin, is far tougher in every way and an improvement. I look at Israel today and I sorely miss my late friend Menachem Begin. He was courtly, courageous, and brilliant—a better advocate for Israel then Shamir or Peres could ever hope to be.

On the homefront, I continued to find interesting outlets for my opinions, beyond the *New York Post*, and off the air. As a guest lecturer at New York University, for example, I conducted a series of lectures on "The State of the City," "The State of the State," and "The State of the Nation," held in the autumn of 1991, and I addressed both the financial and emotional health of our local and national communities.

Whenever I traveled the country to make my various speeches, I tried to schedule meetings with important leaders in the host city. The best example of this was in the spring of 1991, when I made a speaking trip to California. I decided to call on President Reagan and his wife while I was in town, and they graciously agreed to meet with me. I went to see them with my friend Victor Botnick, who accompanied me on this trip.

We were to meet them at the President's office, on the top floor of a Century City high-rise. It was quite an impressive office, warm and tastefully appointed. The President and Mrs. Reagan were in the boardroom when we arrived. We could see them behind the clear glass doors, which I thought was a rather strange design touch. What's the point of having a conference room if the people in the reception area can see right into it? They could see us too, so they finished up their business and came outside to greet us.

"Forgive me," the President said, as he made to hurry past. "I have something to do in my office for a moment."

"Of course, Mr. President," I said, and then he left for his office.

When Mrs. Reagan came out, she couldn't figure why we were still being kept waiting. "Why don't we go in?" she said.

"Well," I explained, "the President said he had something to do in his office."

"Oh," she said, "nonsense, come with me." She took me by the hand and led me into the President's office. She was very gracious. We just walked right in. The President was sitting at his desk, looking over some papers, and I sat with Mrs. Reagan and waited for him to look up from his work.

When he did, and we began talking, I got right to what I wanted to say. "Mr. President," I began, "I just want you to know that this country owes you a great debt. I tell people that all the time, wherever I go. I tell them that it's primarily because of you that we are witnessing the dismantling of the Soviet Union, and the downfall of communism throughout Eastern Europe."

"Thank you, Mr. Mayor," he said. He was usually very formal, and almost always called me "Mr. Mayor." Occasionally, when he was feeling colloquial, he called me "Mayor Ed," which I tried to suffer quietly. The only other person who called me "Mayor Ed" was the late Cardinal Terence Cooke, who did it all the time. That, too, I suffered quietly, after some effort and a great deal of practice. I used to feel like a talking horse whenever the cardinal referred to me that way.

"I have so many questions for you, Mr. President," I continued. "When did you know your efforts were succeeding with the Soviets? How did it happen?"

And then he proceeded to tell me a story which he also recounted in his memoirs. "I think the turning point happened in Reykjavik," he said, referring to the Iceland summit with Mikhail Gorbachev. "I planned on taking him back to our house alone, with an interpreter, and talking with him, one on one."

The President then described how he searched for an appropriate break in the proceedings, at which point he asked Gorbachev to join him for a walk. He took him back to his lodge, where he had arranged to have a fire going. The two leaders sat down. Reagan spoke first. "I just want you to know," he said, with friendly emphasis, "that we will never let you have military superiority over us. Whatever it takes, we will spend." The President related the exchange to me and said he could see the air go out of Gorbachev's lungs as he said this.

"I knew then it was over for them," the President confided, "because I knew he understood me."

Then he gave me a copy of his book, *An American Life*, which he inscribed to me, and I gave him a copy of my book, *All the Best*, which I inscribed to him.

Probably the biggest kick of my post-mayoralty career

has come courtesy of my most unexpected career turn. In the summer of 1991, I took a call from Tom Allon, the editor of the *Manhattan Spirit,* a small local weekly. "We know you go to the movies a lot," Tom said, "and we were wondering if you'd like to review movies for us."

The idea was intriguing. "How much do you pay?" I asked.

"Fifty dollars a column," he said.

"I wouldn't cross the street for fifty dollars," I said.

"How much do you want?"

"Two hundred and fifty," I said, thinking this would be fun.

"We can't afford that," he said. "We're a small paper."

"Well," I said, "call me back when you get bigger."

They got bigger the next day. It turned out the *Spirit* was owned by a man named Jerry Finkelstein, father of Andy Stein; he also owned several other local papers. I got my $250, and they got to use my reviews in all of their four papers.

The reviews have been a big hit. They're even being syndicated now, to a few other papers. I try to keep them entertaining, and I write them from the perspective of the average moviegoer. I don't comment on the lighting, or the cinematography, or the sound editing. I care about whether I enjoy the movie, if it makes me think, laugh, or cry. I care if the story is believable, and entertaining. Too often, movie critics get carried away with themselves, filling their reviews with everything technical. If you ask me, people want to know if a reviewer liked the movie or not, that's all, so I include a plus (+) or minus (−) rating with each review: No in-betweens. (For the record, and as an indication of where my moviegoing tastes tend to fall, I recommended *Cape Fear, Frankie and Johnny, JFK,* and *Little Man Tate,* and warned against *Billy Bathgate, For the Boys, My Own Private Idaho,* and *The Last Boy Scout,* which I called "the worst movie I have ever seen.")

In some weeks, if I have extra column inches to fill, I toss in a little something extra to go with the movie reviews. It might be a restaurant review, tips on where to buy men's clothing, or my mother's recipe for the perfect antidote for winter colds and laryngitis, the Glugol Muggle. (Squeeze a grapefruit, an orange, and a lemon into a saucepan. Add one tablespoon of honey, and one or two jiggers of your favorite liquor. Bring to a boil and drink piping hot. If you drink one Glugol Muggle every day, for seven days, your cold will go away.)

With nine jobs, my days are full. And it seems I was given nine lives to go along with my nine jobs. I probably went through a few of them back in the Army without even knowing it, and I went through one more in 1987, when I suffered my stroke. I had to cash in another spare on Wednesday morning, December 18, 1991. I'll explain. When I awoke that morning, at five-thirty, I felt a slight discomfort in my chest, which I attributed to indigestion. I decided to ignore the pain (it was really more of a pressure than a pain) and went about my usual morning routine. I took my pills to control my benign enlarged-prostate condition, aspirin to thin my blood, Zantac for my hiatal hernia, and Landxon for my arrhythmia. I was still doing my radio commentary for WNEW-AM at the time, so I taped my five-minute segment at six-thirty, dressed in my gym clothes, and went to the Sports Training Institute on East Forty-ninth Street to meet my personal trainer at seven o'clock.

By the time I stepped on the treadmill to begin my customary twenty-minute routine, the discomfort in my chest had still not subsided. I started to think that what I was feeling was something other than indigestion, so I got off the machine and asked my trainer, Mark, to take my pulse. It was lower than usual, so I prudently called it quits for the day. Then I showered, dressed, and sat down to read the newspapers until the car arrived to take me to my law office.

The last thing I remember is reaching over for an orange, thinking it would give me some energy. The next thing I remember is waking up, flat on my back, while one of my fellow gym members, a doctor named Hillel Tobias, was taking my blood pressure. I had blacked out for about thirty seconds, I later learned.

"Lie down," the doctor said, when I tried to stand up. "Your pressure is ninety over sixty, and if you stand up you'll pass out again."

So I stayed down. "Please call my doctor," I said. "Bruce Barron, at Columbia Presbyterian.'"

"I know Bruce Barron," Dr. Tobias said. "He can't be your doctor, he's a gynecological surgeon."

"I know," I said, "and it's always embarrassing, but he's a friend of mine, and he always tells all the other doctors who treat me what to do."

By this time, Emergency Medical Service personnel, and several police officers, began to race into the gym. Someone had called 911 when I blacked out. Five police cars and five ambulances came.

I told Dr. Tobias I wanted to be taken to Columbia Presbyterian Hospital, where all my records were kept, and where my regular doctors were on staff.

"They won't do it," he said. "Regulations say they have to take you to the closest hospital." (In this case it was NYU Hospital.)

A burly police officer was standing near enough to over-hear our conversation. "We'll take him wherever he wants to go," he interrupted. I thought to myself, What a nice guy. Thank you, God.

I was carried out of the gym on a stretcher. A large crowd had assembled outside on the street, obviously attracted by the five ambulances and five police cars. As I emerged from the building, the crowd began to applaud. Clearly, they knew who I was, but what was not clear was whether they were applauding because I was alive, or because I was on a stretcher.

FDR Drive was at a morning-rush-hour standstill, so we took to the city streets. I looked through the back window of my ambulance and saw that we were being followed by the other four ambulances, and many police cars. I was later told that each time our procession passed through a new police precinct, we were joined by a new police car.

Television news crews were waiting for us by the time we arrived at the hospital, after nearly twenty minutes. The news that I had collapsed traveled faster than we did. Bruce Barron was already there too, and he directed my stretcher-bearers to a small, private room on the sixth floor of the hospital's new Milstein Building. There were no beds available in intensive care, otherwise I would have been taken there. My room overlooked the Hudson River, with a lovely view of the George Washington Bridge.

My cardiologist is Joe Tenenbaum, who has treated me for arrhythmia, or irregular heartbeat. Arrhythmia can cause insufficient blood to go to the brain, and if the regular heart beat, called sinuous rhythm, doesn't reoccur quickly, it can cause a blackout. Although I had a history of arrhythmia, this was the first time I had blacked out, and Dr. Tenenbaum was therefore concerned, and determined to discover what had caused the episode. I was feeling fine, and determined to leave the hospital as quickly as possible.

Dr. Tenenbaum's team monitored my heart overnight, and they detected several arrhythmic episodes. In the morning, I underwent a stress test, after which the doctor told reporters I performed "like a man twenty-five to thirty years younger." When I had my stroke, doctors said I had the brain of a twenty-eight-year-old, so I later told the pool reporter, Marcia Kramer of WCBS-TV, that I was bringing brain and body into closer alignment.

As the tests took place, the doctors were still unsure what was causing the arrhythmia. With each procedure, I was required to sign a separate written release form, detailing the morbidity statistics and other attendant risks. The forms told me a lot more than I wanted to know; I signed them without really reading them. One of the doctors actually asked me if I wanted to watch on a television monitor while a catheter was inserted into a vein in my right groin area and then through the vein to my heart. "No," I said, "maybe on someone else." Despite my initial aversion, I confess that when the doctors began the procedure I found myself peeking through the spread fingers of the hand I held over my face, which was the same way I watched the movie *Frankenstein* as a child.

I needed a pacemaker, the catheter test revealed, and, after I was assured that its insertion was a routine procedure, I agreed to have it put in right away. Dr. Henry Spotnitz did the operation. He was on standby, waiting to see if the pacemaker was indeed required, and he began the operation a half-hour later. I was conscious throughout, although this time I was unable to follow along on the television, which was just as well. I became too sick to watch, anyway. During the procedure, my blood pressure rose to more than 200/100. My vision became blurred. My speech slurred. I was extremely nauseous. I lay there recalling that these were the same symptoms I had before my stroke four years earlier.

For the first time, I began to think things were not as routine as I had been led to believe, and in my head I began a silent conversation with God. I was doing all the talking. "Listen, God," I said, "if I have to die, I am not afraid, but under no circumstances do I want You to take me piecemeal. I do not want to be paralyzed with a stroke, so either take me all at once, or pull me through altogether."

Apparently, He was listening.

I was in my law office at nine o'clock the following morning, barely forty-eight hours after I reached for that orange back at the gym. I was back to my regular workout routine at the gym by the following week. Physically, it is as if the ordeal never really happened. The pacemaker causes no sensation in my body, and I don't think about it, except as backup protection for me.

Emotionally, though, the incident had a profound impact on me. I will never forget it, because of the way the city responded to it. My hospitalization was carried at the top of every local news program, and was covered by all the local papers. It was even reported overseas.

Five years earlier, my friend Charles Kaiser, a journalist, observed that the city shuddered when I had my stroke. I loved the image, and was flattered by it. I even believed it was true. The city did stop, and hold its breath for the fallen mayor.

This time around, the city reacted in much the same way, which I thought was remarkable because I was no longer in office. There has been, and will always be, a special relationship between me and the people of New York City. It's really quite extraordinary. I cherish this relationship dearly, and at the same time I am humbled by it. It transcends politics. I've devoted my life to the city, and if the response to this brief hospitalization is any indication, the devotion has been returned.

I hope this relationship never changes, although I suspect it will, over time. My plan is to keep it going for as long as I can, because I've only just started on this third career of mine. If it is to be my last act, then I'd like it to be a long one, and a productive one, and I'd like to work up until the last moment. For now, though, I'm still here, and I'm still whole, and I've got a *lot* left to do.

Index